DAVID
the AUTOBIOGRAPHY *of*
BOON

DAVID

the AUTOBIOGRAPHY *of*

BOON

UNDER THE
SOUTHERN CROSS

Harper*Sports*
An imprint of HarperCollins*Publishers*

DAVID BOON'S DEDICATION

I dedicate this book to the person who has been my
Rock of Gibraltar for more years than I can remember.
Without her support, much of what I have
achieved would never have been possible.
Her strength, judgment and friendship will never be surpassed.
Thank you, Pip.

Mark Thomas' Dedication

To Kathryn Mary and Benjamin Maxwell, who are my all.

Harper*Sports*
An imprint of HarperCollins*Publishers*

First published in Australia in 1996
by HarperCollins*Publishers* Pty Limited
ACN 009 913 517
A member of HarperCollins*Publishers* (Australia) Pty Limited Group

Copyright © 1996 David Boon

HarperCollins*Publishers*
25 Ryde Road, Pymble, Sydney NSW 2073, Australia
31 View Road, Glenfield, Auckland 10, New Zealand
77–85 Fulham Palace Road, London W6 8JB, United Kingdom
Hazelton Lanes, 55 Avenue Road, Suite 2900, Toronto, Ontario M5R 3L2
and 1995 Markham Road, Scarborough, Ontario M1B 5M8, Canada
10 East 53rd Street, New York NY 10032, USA

National Library of Australia Cataloguing-in-Publication data:

Boon, David, 1960- .
   Under the Southern Cross:
   the autobiography of David Boon.

   ISBN 0 7322 5728 X.
   1. Boon, David, 1960- . 2. Cricket players – Tasmania – Biography.
   3. Cricket players – Australia – Biography. I. Title
796.358092.

Printed in Australia by Griffin Colour, Australia.

9 8 7 6 5 4 3 2 1
00 99 98 97 96

Foreword

DAVID BOON HAS AN OUTSTANDING RECORD IN AUSTRALIAN CRICKET
AND THIS AUTOBIOGRAPHY WILL BE WELCOMED BY HIS MANY FRIENDS
AND ALSO SUPPORTERS OF THE GAME. IT IS A STORY ONLY BOONIE
COULD WRITE WITH SUCH DIRECTNESS, HONESTY AND
CHARACTERISTIC MODESTY.

He is today one of the most successful and popular Australian players in the history of this remarkable game. What a record it is. Clearly, the greatest cricketer to come from the state of Tasmania, he took part in 107 Tests, batted in 190 innings, was not out in 20 of them and scored 7422 runs to become the second highest run-getter for his country, surpassed only by Allan Border.

David's achievements and his extraordinary popularity present a huge challenge to those who follow in his footsteps. A right-hander, he was the most consistent Australian batsman for almost 12 years and always posed a threat to the English Test side. His determination and toughness at the crease, particularly against England and the West Indies, earned him a place in the hearts of cricket enthusiasts. Few players have enjoyed greater admiration for their bravery, composure and stoicism when under attack from the world's best fast bowlers.

He established himself as an opener, but with the emergence of Mark Taylor to partner Geoff Marsh, reverted to No. 3, arguably his best position, which gave stability to the batting order. As a solid and reliable bat, he was pugnacious, impervious to intimidation, built to cut and hook well, brilliantly neat off the front foot and his toes, and masterful in defence.

He added to this reliability in fielding at silly leg, where, with his somewhat surprising 'cobra-like' reactions, extremely difficult catches became his trademark.

Throughout, his sportsmanship shone in every facet of his game.

His current appearances for his beloved Tasmania say much for his devotion to the game and he continues to support both cricket and many philanthropic organisations within the community. He is a great example to his fellow Australians: modest, successful and always available to assist others.

David has earned himself a special place in the annals of cricket. As Allan Border, has said of him, 'He is a man for all seasons, someone you can depend on in all situations.'

It is therefore not surprising that David Boon has attracted such loyalty and support during his great career from players and public alike. He is a great Australian sportsman who has earned the respect and admiration of all who know him. I'm sure those who read this book will also come to admire him.

General Sir Phillip Bennett, AC, KBE, DSO
(former Chief of the Australian Defence Force
and Governor of Tasmania, 1987–95)

Canberra, July 7, 1996.

Contents

INTRODUCTION

BY A. MARK THOMAS

DAVID BOON HAS ALWAYS BEEN EXTREMELY UNCOMFORTABLE WITH COMPARISONS BETWEEN HIMSELF AND THE GENTLEMEN WHOSE CAREER STATISTICS HE PASSED DURING HIS LIFE IN CRICKET. HOWEVER, HE CANNOT ESCAPE THE FACTS.

Between 1984 and 1996, he played in 107 Test matches, scoring a total of 7422 runs at an average of 43.66. He made 21 centuries and 32 half-centuries. His highest Test score was 200, made against New Zealand at the WACA Ground in Perth in late 1989. Boon's consistency with the bat can also be demonstrated via computer — Tasmanian statistician Ric Finlay's breakdown of the Launceston-born right-hander's career shows that Boon averaged 43.60 in his first Test innings and 43.75 in his second innings.

Boon's performances in Test matches leaves him second on the all-time Australian run-scorers' list — behind his long-time captain and friend, the great Allan Border. Behind Boon on that list are players of the calibre of Greg Chappell, Sir Donald Bradman, Neil Harvey, Doug Walters, Ian Chappell, Bill Lawry, Bob Simpson and Ian Redpath — Australian cricket legends all.

At career's end, Boon was 13th on the list of Test run-scorers — only Border (11,174 runs), Sunil Gavaskar (10,122), Graham Gooch (8900), Javed Miandad (8832), Viv Richards (8540), David Gower (8231), Geoff Boycott (8114), Sir Garfield Sobers (8072), Colin Cowdrey (7624), Gordon Greenidge (7558), Clive Lloyd (7515) and Desmond Haynes (7487) precede him. And he was only the second Australian to play more than 100 Test matches, behind, inevitably, Border, who wore the nigh-mythical baggy green cap an astonishing 156 times. Sometimes statistics cannot lie. Boon's place in cricket's pantheon is secure.

Boon's one-day international career record is no less impressive. He played 181 matches and scored 5964 runs, at an average of 37.04. He made five one-day hundreds and 37 fifties, his top score 122, against Sri Lanka at the Adelaide Oval in 1987–88. Impressive as these figures are, his long-time batting partner Geoff Marsh states later in this book that Boon's record in one-day internationals would have been even better but for a pact they made — David's job was to play shots, Geoff's to rotate the strike.

Opposite: David Boon at Edgbaston during the triumphant 1989 Ashes series in England.

Boon enjoyed a period of major international success between 1987 and 1994, to the point where some critics rated him the best batsman in the world for periods during that time. He was a key figure in Australia's 1987 World Cup success, finishing the tournament as Australia's leading run-scorer, and winning man-of-the-match awards along the way (including in the final, against England in Calcutta). His contribution to his country's 200th birthday celebrations was an unconquered 184 in the Bicentennial Test against England in Sydney. In 1988–89, the first time Australia saw Curtly Ambrose, Boon scored 397 runs against the West Indies. In 1989, on that marvellous Ashes tour of England, Boon's series return was 442 runs.

In 1990–91, another Ashes summer in Australia, Boon scored 530 runs, including a century and three fifties. Then came series aggregates of 266 runs against the West Indies in the Caribbean in 1991, and 556 runs against India at home in 1991–92. Good as these performances were, the best was still to come. In 1992–93, the mighty West Indies returned to Australia, and Boon tallied 490 runs in five Test matches. In England, 1993, another 555 runs went into the bank — including three consecutive centuries, at Lord's (his first-ever in England), Trent Bridge and Headingley. In the summer of 1993–94, Australia played New Zealand, followed by a split series against South Africa — three Tests in Australia, three in South Africa: Boon's total in the nine matches played was 695 runs.

But these are mere statistics, which illustrate that David Boon could bat, against all Test-playing nations, and that he enjoyed excellent longevity and consistency at the highest level. What the figures can never explain is the essence of Boon, the man, or the manner in which he scored those runs . . .

I began my journalistic career in Launceston, the home of David Boon, as a graduate cadet at *The Examiner* newspaper on January 9, 1984. Fifteen days later, Boon made 134 against the West Indies for the Prime Minister's XI in Canberra. I remember enjoying the match with the father of a University of Tasmania friend. As we watched the game unfold, this gentleman reeled off endless anecdotes about the young Boon, who had only just turned 23. Stories from Boon's childhood, of centuries scored, football tales, then more cricket exploits as a junior and a Sheffield Shield batsman. I was discovering very swiftly — in Launceston and the rest of Tasmania — David Boon was everybody's property.

In researching this autobiography, David and I combed the scrapbooks meticulously kept by his late father Clarrie until his death in 1993. We discovered a column in *The Sunday Examiner* by Neil Kearney, the multi-media, national journalist, illustrated with a Graham Dazeley cartoon depicting Boon walking a tightrope strung over the state. David chuckled at Kearney's extrapolation, which suggested that Boon's exploits provided so much pleasure and inspiration for Tasmanians; that his every move was observed. The downside of this was that if the cricketing superstar failed to notice someone in the street, he was arrogant; but if he stopped and talked, he was a big-head.

Kearney, inevitably, was right. However, the other side of that coin — always acknowledged by Boon — is the immense value and pride the sheer amount of support he receives within his home state gives him. Everyone in Tasmania knows David Boon and everyone has an opinion about him: why he retired, if he was 'pushed', what had deserted him (if anything) in his final season.

One aspect of Boon which has always amazed me is his acceptance and understanding of that near-claustrophobic adulation, of having the microscope always focussed upon him. If the stress of having to score Test runs wasn't enough, the pressure of having such concentrated and total Tasmanian support must, at times, have been unbearable. But Boon took it all in his stride.

Not that every other Test cricketer doesn't receive support and 'rock'n'roll star' status in his own hometown. But, in the other states, there are more Test players. In Tasmania, with due respect to Roger Woolley, who preceded Boon into the Test team, to Greg Campbell, who was picked for the Ashes tour of 1989 and to the outrageously gifted Ricky Ponting, who won his first Test cap in Boon's farewell season — for almost his entire career, Boon stood alone as the sole Tasmanian in the national side.

In many ways, he personified the state — David Boon WAS Tasmania.

Boon rarely wavered and never cracked. Don't get me wrong, the man is not perfect. However, the number of times he has declined an autograph, or the chance to say hello or have a chat are almost zero.

His on-field behaviour withstands hard scrutiny, too. Perhaps the one-day international at the Gabba when he walked off the ground swearing with the television cameras zeroed in on his lips was a blemish. Or another one-dayer, in Ahmedabad on the tour of India in 1986, when an opposition player mentioned the word 'cheat' in relation to Geoff Marsh and Boon went ballistic (some reports said that David was physically restrained by his team-mates from confronting the men in white in a fashion more than just verbal). Boon apologised to umpires B.R. Kheshava Murthy and Mukulgopal Mukherjee after that incident.

Boon is a demi-god in Tasmania, and perhaps the rest of Australia, if the reaction at the Test matches in Melbourne and Adelaide in his final season is anything to judge such matters. A market survey commissioned by the Australian Cricket Board, the results of which were made public after the 1995 West Indies tour, showed that Boon was regarded by the public as a 'hero', more so than any of his other team-mates. People between the ages of 18 and 25, from all parts of Australia, had been polled and Boon was most popular with males, while Shane Warne pipped him in the female vote.

Boon had become an 'everyman' figure, to whom most Australians could relate. They appreciate his outward demeanour, which is reserved, and his efforts at the crease for his country, which, at the very least, were determined. Boon's courage, his toughness, became a catchcry. His ability to endure, and triumph against, the physical pressure applied by the West Indies pace battery, in particular, became the stuff of legends. He scored a century in Kingston, Jamaica, in 1991, during which he was hit in the face by Patrick Patterson and was later stitched up — without anaesthetic. Australians respect such courage. In 1992–93, Curtly Ambrose hit him an horrific blow on the left elbow, which saw Boon carom about the field, like a pinball within his own pain machine. The bone was feared broken, but Boon returned the next day, wearing an arm guard . . . and was undefeated when the innings closed. I remember whenever he was hit, how he tried so hard not to show discomfort. He nearly always succeeded. But the spectator in the stands, or sitting at home on the lounge chair, realised that pain had been inflicted and admired Boon's brave show of stoicism.

When Boon sparred and missed — the ball whistling past his blade — again he attempted to show no concern. But it was there. Not fear of failure, but the extreme apprehension that his dismissal would involve not performing to the ultra-high standard he set himself. He would reach within, deep down inside his reserves of resolve, and take block again, his eyes narrowed, until the ball approached, when they would widen suddenly as his next decision was made. Cricket fans recognised his burning desire to play for his country. And to succeed, because in doing so, Australia might profit on the cricket fields of the world.

They saw him struggle in 1986–87 against England, which led to his axing from the Test team. What to do? He came home to Launceston, re-assessed his situation, failed in his next innings against Queensland at the NTCA Ground in Launceston and then scored 172 in the second innings. By well before the conclusion of the '87 World Cup, he had safely re-established his place in the side. They also saw him make the 'bat-pad' fielding position his own, in doing so demonstrating that his build didn't interfere with his astonishing athleticism. People, cricket fans or not, liked that.

Boon reveals in this book the level of self-doubt that plagued him throughout his career. Which may surprise many of his fans. The way he countered this mental disadvantage was by sheer hard work in the nets — in concert with Geoff Marsh, batting more often and longer than his Test team-mates. This was a practice that evolved from his early Tasmanian Sheffield Shield days.

This was an example of what might be Boon's greatest strength — what he calls his 'tunnel vision'. He is an extremely modest man, but one who possessed great ambition. By concentrating solely on his goals, playing Test cricket for his country and making runs — almost to the exclusion of everything else in life —

he succeeded. But he would not have been able to do any of this but for his wife, Pip. I count myself lucky and honoured to call them my friends. They are the equal cornerstones of 'Team Boon'. Pip supports her partner to the ultimate degree, so often cutting through the blarney of a male-dominated sport to offer clear, concise advice.

While David made his mark on world cricket, climbing its mountains, Pip raised their three children — Georgina, Jack and Elizabeth — and provided the home base to which he could repair, recharge his tremendous mental powers and return to the fray again. She is a wonderful woman, true in the sense of a fine blade, intelligent, witty and protective.

David, on the other hand and despite endless tales of his on-camera reticence, is an extremely funny individual, who is one of the most generous people — with his time, his favours and his advice — I have ever met. As a friend, his loyalty is unquestioned. His concern for his chosen comrades is as legendary as his courage. And, as a cricket ambassador, he was second to none in terms of building bridges between Test teams.

Throughout this book, Boon decries the ever-increasing death of interaction between opposing sides. Perhaps this has become the first easy victim of the sport's exponential professionalism. David, though, will continue to do his part in creating cricket friendship.

Just one example (there are hundreds): In the summer of 1995–96, Australia played Pakistan at Bellerive Oval in Hobart; this was Tasmania's third Test match. Australia won and the team, in celebration mode, returned to their hotel, where their opponents were also staying.

With the Australian cricketers on one side of the Grand Chancellor bar, Boon sat with family and friends . . . until a party of Pakistani cricketers arrived and sat in lounges nearby. Boon went to them, and talked for more than an hour with Wasim Akram, Mushtaq Ahmed and other players. He didn't have to, of course, he could have joined his team-mates in toasting another memorable victory, but he chose his own path. And he didn't see his team-mates as failing in their responsibilities; he just believed his way was the right course of action.

When David retired, he rang to tell me of his decision before flying to Adelaide for his final Test. Unfortunately, I couldn't make the trip to South Australia, but the night his retirement was made public, WIN Television in Hobart (where I now work) ran two stories, first and second in the bulletin. One was Shane Warne's piece for the National Nine Network, the latter my own. I finished the story with the line: 'David Boon, Australian hero, Tasmanian legend.'

It still holds true.

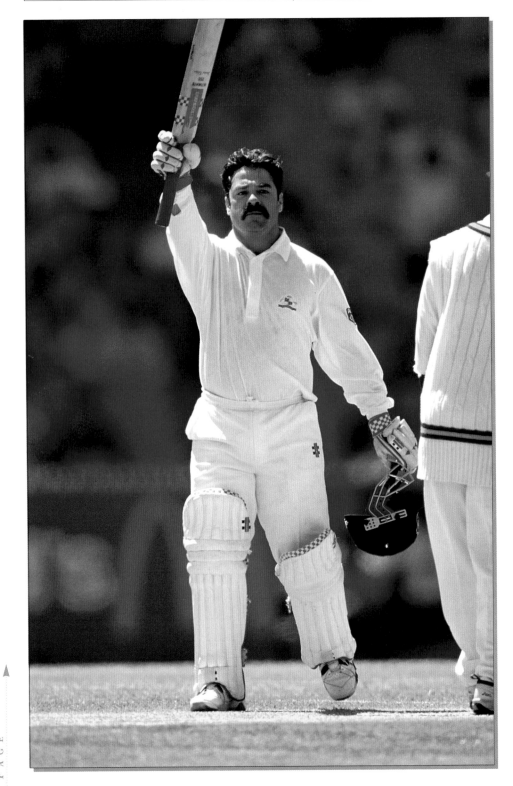

1: The Right Decision

My international cricket career came to an end on January 29, 1996, on the last day of the third Test against Sri Lanka at the Adelaide Oval. Australia won the match and the series, 3–0.

I announced my retirement on the day before the game began, Wednesday, January 25, having informed the Australian management and my team-mates of my decision the evening before. It was perhaps the most difficult episode of my career, which had included being dropped from the Australian team, periods of poor form — and enormous successes almost too numerous to mention — because of the emotion involved.

To fully explain the reasons behind my retirement, it is necessary to backtrack to the beginning of the 1995–96 season.

Australia had returned from winning the Frank Worrell Trophy in the West Indies in May, 1995. I had finished that tour, Australia successful in a Test series against the Caribbean nations for the first time since 1978, somewhat down the order of batting averages and aggregate. In fact, I was fifth on the average table, having scored 152 runs at 25.33 in four Test matches. In terms of aggregate, I was fourth, but apart from Steve and Mark Waugh, all the other major Australian batsmen scored between 128 and 153 runs for the series. I won't make any excuses about my form, but the West Indies tour was one of the only ones in which I have been involved where the bowlers dominated — Steve Waugh, who scored 429 runs at an average of 107.25, with a highest score of 200, was really the only exception.

When the '95–96 summer began, I had no thoughts of retirement. My long-term ambition was to tour England again for the fourth time, in 1997, but that, of course, had been placed on a shelf at the back of my mind as I tried to concentrate on what lay immediately ahead.

In November, in Brisbane, the Australian team met to prepare for the first Test against Pakistan. And, almost from day one, there were rumblings in the media about my position within the side. I realised that as each season passed and my

Opposite: My final Test century, Melbourne, December 1995.

age increased — every Boxing Day Test in Melbourne, another Boon birthday came and went, always embarrassingly highlighted on giant video screens — that logical questions would be raised about my longevity. However, despite only limited success in the West Indies, I felt that I was still hitting the ball well and, significantly, that my one-day form was good, batting at No. 4 behind the openers, Michael Slater and Australian captain Mark Taylor, and Mark Waugh.

In the four (of five) limited-overs internationals in which I played in the West Indies, I had scored 85, 48, 4 and 33. And the reason I missed a match had nothing to do with injury or lack of form. Rather, Greg Blewett and I were rested for the final game, with the series already won by the West Indies, to allow Ricky Ponting and Justin Langer to have a game.

Before that Test against Pakistan at the Gabba, I played two Sheffield Shield matches for Tasmania — against NSW in Sydney and Queensland at Bellerive Oval. I scored 26 and 57 against the Blues, and in the second innings was caught and bowled by Shane Lee. Against the Bulls, I made 88 and 56, and in the first innings was caught and bowled by Craig McDermott.

When I arrived in Brisbane, Australian coach Bob Simpson raised the subject of the two caught-and-bowled dismissals. So, we decided to take advantage of

Dressing-room celebrations after our defeat of Pakistan in the first Test, in Brisbane, in 1995–96. At back, left to right: Simpson, McGrath, M. Waugh, Reiffel, Taylor, Blewett, Warne, S Waugh, McDermott, Julian. At front: Healy, Slater, Boon.

the technology now available. In a split-screen video presentation, we compared my batting in the nets at the Gabba to the same shots I played against English paceman Neil Foster on the Ashes tour of 1993, when I scored three consecutive Test centuries.

Before I watched that video, I had been thinking the worst; perhaps I was losing my edge. Throughout my career, I had suffered from self-doubts and raised question marks about my ability. My solution had always been to work harder in the nets.

When I compared the two slow-motion images, it was clear that my feet and body were not reacting to the ball upon delivery in the same way they had in 1993. This discovery helped me a lot, and calmed some of my inner fears, for it seemed my problems were technical. No matter how long you play, or how good you are, you never stop learning about this great game. And you can never quite conquer it totally.

So it was back to the nets. I concentrated on where my feet were going, my balance, my forward press — the speed of the whole process — and at what point in the bowler's delivery was I making the necessary, crucial decisions about line and length.

Australia batted first at the Gabba and I made 54. I should have converted that score into a century, but chased a wide one from Wasim Akram and was caught by Inzamam-Ul-Haq at slip. Even so, I felt that I had performed to at least something approaching my standard, and that fact helped alleviate the inner pressure even more.

The second game of the series was in Hobart — Tasmania's third Test, following the match against Sri Lanka in 1989 and one against New Zealand in 1993. Before the game, the Tasmanian Cricket Association staged another one of its gala Test match dinners, which was attended by both teams, and by some special guests, the members of the very first Australian team to play Pakistan in a Test. It was a marvellous occasion and I was looking forward to continuing to find form in front of my home crowd. The previous time I'd batted in a Test in Hobart, I'd been lucky enough to score a century.

However, in the first innings, I was run out for 32, following a batting mix-up with 'Tubby' Taylor. In the second dig, after getting tied down by their leg-spinner, Mushtaq Ahmed, I went for a big cover drive, when I should have been patient, and was caught by Waqar Younis for a duck.

Immediately, the 'Boon's place in jeopardy' media campaign was back on. I honestly don't believe that anyone from the press had been given a 'line' by one of the Australian selectors. However, I was definitely struggling to come to terms with the situation. 'Why me?' was my first thought, accompanied by a lot of mental anguish about the turn of events.

Fortunately, my captain was very supportive and said that I'd been dismissed trying to be positive, while Australia went on to win the match comfortably, to take an unbeatable 2–0 lead in the three-Test series.

In between the second and third Test matches, Tasmania played NSW at Bellerive Oval. I scored 6 and 17, which in no way relieved the pressure upon me. From Hobart, I headed to Sydney for the final Test against Pakistan, where, unfortunately, the horror run continued. In the first innings, I was caught behind by Rashid Latif for 16, trying to play a stupid late cut off leg-spinner Mushtaq Ahmed. I was very late in making the decision to play the shot in the first place and that was my undoing. In the second innings, the situation became farcical — I somehow managed to roll the ball down the back of my bat, and was caught at bat-pad on the off-side for 6.

It was one of those moments when time seemed to freeze. I couldn't have knocked the ball away, although there was plenty of opportunity, because to do that would have been obstructing the field.

As I trailed off the Sydney Cricket Ground, I can remember pleading: 'God, you've got to be out there somewhere!'

From this moment, the media pressure became like a furnace. It was true, I was about to turn 35, but I didn't see my age as the solitary factor behind whether I should continue playing or not. Others, it seemed, did not agree, and the situation was not eased by the fact that Australia lost the third Test in Sydney, scoring 257 and 172 to Pakistan's 299 and 204. But we had won the series 2–1.

At this point in time, I had had no discussions with any of the five Australian selectors — chairman Trevor Hohns, Jim Higgs, Steve Bernard, Peter Taylor and my old batting partner, Geoff Marsh. As a senior player, the usual process was to talk about your form with your captain and coach, because they were part of the overall selection process during the domestic season. This I had done.

The next match of the summer was the first Test against Sri Lanka at the WACA Ground in Perth. It was a game which I should have enjoyed, for I was joined in the side for the first time by fellow Tasmanian Ricky Ponting. Ricky, with Queensland's Stuart Law, had come into the side for Steve Waugh, who was injured, and Greg Blewett, who'd been dropped.

However, there were other, more pressing and personal matters on my mind. When I went out to bat, I felt like a kid, perhaps even more nervous than I was in my first Test match against the West Indies, at the Gabba back in 1984. I just froze.

This was my 105th Test match; it was almost a joke.

I remember, before I went out to bat in our first innings, that I was trying to appear relaxed in the dressing-room. I kept chatting to the newcomers, Ponting and Law — talking to others immediately before I batted was something I never

One of the lowpoints of my summer — caught in close, off the back of my bat, during our second innings against Pakistan in Sydney

did, or at least not to the same extent as that day. Normally, I would sit quietly in my place, talk to people only when spoken to, and, when Australia went out to bat, watch our openers, usually Taylor and Michael Slater, go about their business. Looking back, my behaviour on that day in Perth was a huge cover-up for the insecurities I was suffering, as I forlornly tried to quieten the nerves before having to go out to bat.

Ironically, when I did get out into the middle, I was given out caught Hathurusingha, bowled Muttiah Muralitharan for 13 — and I didn't think the decision was correct. As I trudged off the WACA, I knew I was a shot duck. I honestly believed my Test career was over, and that the time where I would be able to select when I would retire from the game had passed.

During the match, which Australia won easily, I received a telephone call from 'Cracker' Hohns, the former Australian leg-spinner with whom I'd toured England on the successful Ashes series of 1989. He told me that I had been omitted from the first one-day squad and that the selectors wanted me to go back to the Sheffield Shield, score some runs and rebuild my confidence. This was the first time I'd received such a call since the 1986–87 season, when I was dropped from the Test side after a run of bad form against England.

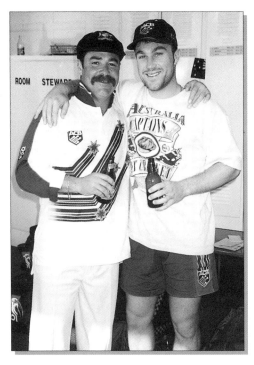

With Michael Slater in Adelaide.

The reality of the situation hit me hard. Before I flew home from Perth, I told a few of the players that I wouldn't be joining them in Adelaide for the first one-day international. At the same time, I handed over the responsibility for singing Australia's victory song — *Under the Southern Cross* — to Michael Slater. But just for the one-dayers.

'You'll be back,' was Slats rejoinder. 'You'll be back.'

I must admit, it was very hard watching the first block of those one-day games, between Australia, Sri Lanka and the West Indies. My son, Jack, watched Australia's first game, against the West Indies in Adelaide, with me.

'Dad. There's Warney and all the others playing for Australia — what are you doing here?' he asked. 'Why aren't you there?'

I had to explain it all to him — at that stage Jack wasn't even five — and it made my predicament even more poignant. But I can honestly say that I wished all my team-mates well; at no stage did I want anyone to fail to open up a spot for me.

It was strange, though, watching Australia play as a cricketer dropped from the team. When you are injured, as I had been on a few occasions in the past, you have no control over the situation. All you can do is get fit again and hope to be re-selected. But in this instance I had missed out because of lack of form. Although I tried to be positive, for much of the time I sat there and wondered: 'Is this the end?'

Back to Shield cricket, where Tasmania played Victoria at the MCG. I made 45 in the first innings, before once again suffering what I honestly believed to be an incorrect decision.

I was given out caught behind, but the ball came off the upper portion of my arm, just before the Australian squad for the second block of one-day games was announced. I couldn't even begin to think about the theory that during a cricketer's career, you receive your fair share of good and bad calls and hopefully they even out in the end. I was batting for my place in the Australian Test side — for my career — and that was all that mattered.

Second innings, well, there was nothing I could have done. The Vics' opening bowler, Damien Fleming, delivered — and so did I. As the ball left my bat, I thought: 'That's four!' However, unfortunately, Ian Harvey in the covers had other ideas and took an absolute blinder. Here was definitely another example of why Harvey has been dubbed 'The Freak' by his Victorian team-mates and in cricket circles around the country. I was out for 6.

As the Boxing Day Test neared, I was asked by numerous media organisations what I wanted for Christmas. To be selected was No. 1 on my wish list, making more than a few runs was No. 2. Fortunately, Santa Claus heard my pleas.

When I arrived back at the MCG for the Test, I was astounded by the reaction of the ground attendants, members of the public, officials . . . everyone.

'Welcome back!' they would say. 'Good to have you back!'

It was heart-warming to have such backing, but also somewhat disturbing. I thought: 'Hang on, here. I haven't been dropped from the Test side and it's only been two weeks since I last played for Australia!' Perhaps this reflects people's perceptions of the modern game, through an Australian summer of virtually wall-to-wall cricket, that if you're gone for a fortnight, you might as well have been gone for the year.

The support continued throughout the Test — walking into practice, going back to the hotel, walking out onto the ground. 'C'mon, Boonie, get a hundred!' was repeated so often. However, I realised the extent of my absence most severely when I first entered the Australian dressing-room. I had been gone for two weeks, but it felt like two years, even though this was through no fault of any of my team-mates.

I just felt different.

I felt as if I'd missed out on so much within the team, which had been *my* team for so long. I sat down exactly where I always sat in the MCG rooms, beside the drink machine, where 'Swampy' Marsh and I used to set up camp. In recent years I've been alongside Slater. Being honest, I didn't feel any big relief at being back within the Australian team environs. Just particularly weird.

At practice, the attention of the media and public on me was very noticeable. Television cameras, photographers and journalists seemed to concentrate on my every move. In interviews, this scrutiny was a two-edged sword. Many of the journalists whom I have known for my entire playing career, or significant portions of it, offered their support — balanced with some extremely pertinent questions about the future. I had no qualms about any of the interrogation, that's what journalism is all about, but to some people in particular, my only comment was that they had short memories.

When Australia batted, on Boxing Day, 1995, I was again nervous, but it was a completely different feeling to the match in Perth. For a start, my family, my wife, Pip, and children, Georgina, Jack and Elizabeth, were in Melbourne with me — and they, like I, had become slightly fatalistic about my position. I knew that I had to accept what happened out in the middle of the 'Gee', where Australia has enjoyed some memorable victories. My first Test century at the ground had come only 12 months before, in the same game in which I caught Devon Malcolm at bat-pad to give Shane Warne his first-ever hat-trick.

Dean Jones, my former Australian team-mate and long-time friend, telephoned before the game to offer his support and advice: 'The wicket's good, but don't drive on the first day, it'll hold up,' he reckoned.

When I entered the MCG, bat in hand, on the first morning, the response was enormous. A huge roar echoed around the stadium, which deafened me and made me feel both humble at the crowd's support . . . and determined to perform.

First ball from the Sri Lankans' opening bowler, Chaminda Vaas, I padded up. And the ball struck my pad . . .

Excellent decision that. Not out nought!

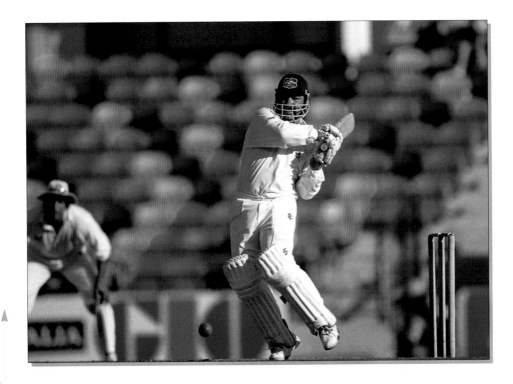

A pull shot against Pakistan during our three-match series in Australia, 1995–96.

With (left to right) ACB media manager Ian McDonald, Shane Warne and Craig McDermott, after we'd gone two-up in the series against Sri Lanka.

What would have happened if the umpire's finger had been raised first ball?

Throughout the innings, I played the way I thought applicable to the situation. I was certainly slow, in terms of balls faced and minutes at the crease, but the effort now rates as one of my best innings, in terms of its character, because of the pressure on me and what succeeding again for my country meant to me. I finished with 110, not dismissed until the second day of the match and Australia declared its first innings at 6–500.

The reception of the Melbourne crowd when I reached three figures was enormous, as was the reaction of my team-mates — irrespective of how, when or why I'd made the hundred, they were as rapt as me. Just as enthusiastic was the response from the team management, media manager Ian McDonald, physiotherapist Errol Alcott and coach Simpson.

Before the innings, I had asked Patrick Keane, the former AAP journalist who is now McDonald's assistant, where the press box was at the MCG. Upon reaching my century, my gesture with my bat in that direction was two-edged — acknowledgement towards those who had supported me and equally 'recognition' for those who had not.

It was the first time that I'd ever felt like that during my career.

Although Sri Lanka were dismissed for 231 and 330, and we won the Test with a day to spare, the pressure was still on concerning my place in the side. Immediately afterwards, the conjecture was almost laughable. How many times in the past had Australia made 500, D.C. Boon a century — as the anchor — and not a word had been said?

There is no doubt that scoring a century was one of the clinchers in my retirement decision-making process. I had first mentioned the idea of finishing to Pip, just as a passing comment. I hadn't been picked for the next block of one-day games, even after scoring a century and I didn't want to even contemplate having to come into the team again as a 'specialist' Test player. I don't believe that as a senior player, you can be one or the other. I've seen too many players regarded solely as limited-overs cricketers. I didn't want to go out the other way.

During this time, I had some conversations with Geoff Marsh, as a friend, not in his role as a selector. I could appreciate the difficulty of the situation for him, but, to be quite honest, at the time I was very annoyed that we couldn't take the discussion as far as I wanted to.

I have since reconciled that predicament with Swamp. I wasn't angry with him, personally, but I was frustrated that because of his job as an Australian selector, my best mate within cricket couldn't really speak to me about something I really needed to speak to him about. In hindsight, I probably wanted him to say to me: 'Babsie, it's going to be okay.'

I wanted to know where I stood. The entire Australian selection panel knew me — I played for Australia with Swamp, Taylor and Hohns and I'd played Shield cricket against both Higgs and Bernard. And I felt they knew me well enough to be honest with me — to have confronted me and said: 'It's time.' Or: 'Your position is in jeopardy.' Instead, what I got, at least initially, was some beating around the bush.

In between the second and final Test matches against Sri Lanka, Tasmania played a Shield game against Victoria at Bellerive Oval, where I scored a hundred. It was during this match that I finally had an extended conversation with Hohns. I promised Trevor then that the specific details of that chat would always remain private, and I see no reason to go back on my word.

However, it would not be breaking confidence to admit that we talked about my form, how I thought I was batting and the future of Australian cricket.

I have always been adamant that Australia should not allow itself to reach the situation which occurred in the early to mid–1980s, when senior players retired en masse and the rebel tours of South Africa occurred. I was a member of the Australian team in 1986 that went on a short tour of New Zealand, followed by a tour of India, where captain Allan Border had almost played more Test cricket than everyone else in the team combined. I could see exactly where the selectors were aiming, and could agree with them 98 per cent. The final two per cent was the bit about D. Boon not wanting to retire, not wanting to give up what had become such an important and satisfying part of his life.

I should stress that, prior to the Test against Sri Lanka in Adelaide, I'd virtually made up my mind to announce my retirement. In contrast, Trevor wasn't convinced about the correctness of such a decision, but would respect it if it occurred.

I would also like to say that every step of my thinking was accompanied by discussion — day in and out — with Pip. When the subject was first raised, by me, her initial reaction was extreme anger. Even she thought, to begin with, that I was being pushed into making such a decision.

But I will state, once again, that I wasn't.

Almost immediately, Pip backed what I was thinking — so, once again, the 'Boon team' went about achieving what we wanted. Before the Adelaide Test, I rang around a number of family and friends to tell them of my decision. I also rang Hohns, as I had promised. The reaction from all of the people involved was similar: confusion as to whether to congratulate me on my retirement or on my career achievements — there's a fine line separating both.

Pip was the one who advised me to announce my retirement before the Test began rather than at its conclusion. Two days before the game, we were scheduled to have our final team meeting; that same day there were also to be meetings at the hotel to discuss the upcoming World Cup. I approached Ian McDonald and asked if I could see the management before the team meeting. Macca was so busy, my request went straight over his head. In fact, he asked me to have lunch with him.

I actually had lunch with Swamp, who I had told of my decision when I went to Perth to play in a benefit match for his testimonial. I suggested we go to a nearby shop which made excellent rolls — he countered with a pie and plenty of sauce.

'It's not going to matter to you any more, mate,' said Marsh, smiling as he looked at my waistline. It was great to have him there.

That afternoon, I sat up in my hotel room and carefully wrote down all the points I wanted to cover with Simpson, Alcott, McDonald and Mark Taylor, and then later with my Australian team-mates. I felt I needed some sort of structure, in case I lost the plot when I made my announcement.

When I told the management, they all just sat there. Stunned. I had at least expected Macca to do some ranting and raving.

Tubby was the first to speak. 'Babs,' he said, 'I would like to congratulate you on what you've done for Australia. It's been magnificent. It's been a great career and this should be a celebration of your career rather than a commiseration.'

Very quietly, Bob asked me whether I was going to retire from all cricket or whether I would keep playing first-class cricket with Tasmania. I told him that I wanted to keep playing for Tasmania, and he was happy with that response. I then asked that I be allowed to tell the players at the team meeting. Macca's reply, his first comment, was that it was going to be very hard to keep my plans from the media. At this point I hadn't really considered any public announcement before the match.

'I totally trust you to do this, Macca, in the way you deem most appropriate,' said I, putting the responsibility for keeping things quiet straight back on him.

The team meeting started as usual, as we discussed the best way to win the Test match. Then I had a minute at the end. Tubby introduced me: 'Boonie's got something to say.' I daresay most of the players thought I was going to make a contribution to team strategy.

I made my announcement, explaining the reasons behind it. To be honest, while it was very difficult telling my team-mates, informing the management had been harder. Simpson, McDonald and Alcott had been with me for almost my entire career — Taylor not far removed from that.

After I told the guys, there was silence.

The press conference where I made public my decision to retire from international cricket.

It seemed like an eternity, but it was probably only 30 seconds at most. It was such an emotional occasion for me, I couldn't tell you who said something first.

I slept well that night, confident that I had made the right decision. The Australian team practised as normal the next day, but half-way through training, everything changed. Macca, in his wisdom, had decided to inform the media before the Test began.

There were two media conferences, one for print, the other for television and radio. But I was quite happy in both, very much aware that the hardest part had been negotiated the night before. Some of the media were shocked, some made reference to my long-term ambition of wanting to tour England in 1997. One person's reaction I will always remember was that of Mike Coward, the long-time cricket correspondent for *The Australian*. Over the years, Coward had written some very complimentary articles about myself, but more importantly, I saw him as an excellent journo, one not afraid to speak his mind or criticise anyone if the situation warranted. Here he made a very nice presentation to me in Adelaide on behalf of the press corps.

I also had two very important extra interviews — one with Shane Warne in his role as a special commentator with the National Nine Network; the other with Australian wicketkeeper Ian Healy, who has the same commitment with the Seven Network. Both were typical of their characters. Heals was pretty controlled, with his questions already in mind. Warney, though, got a bit flustered and kept blowing his questions.

The next day, before the game began, for the very first time in my life, the thought actually passed through my mind — 'It doesn't matter what happens.'

But when Australia won the toss and Tubby decided to bat, and the clock ticked over to 11am, I just wanted to go out and get one last hundred. Walking out onto the Adelaide Oval in the first innings was even more memorable than walking out to the wicket at the MCG, not in terms of the people who were there, or the reception I received, just the emotions which were churning through my mind and body. In Melbourne I really felt that the crowd was urging me on, to regain my lost form; in Adelaide, the intentions of the people were obvious — they knew that this was my final match.

I made 43, bowled by Pushpakumara, in Australia's total of 9–502. We then bowled Sri Lanka out for 317.

In the second innings, with Australia so much in control, my desire to score a farewell hundred was even stronger. Again, I experienced extreme nerves when going out to bat and receiving another ovation. The response of the people in Adelaide was just so tremendous throughout the match. The very first delivery I faced was shortish and down the leg-side. And there is no doubt that the little finger of D. Boon received a faint tickle from the ball on the way through.

However, umpire Lloyd Barker said not out.

When I finally made it up to the other end, Barker asked me if I had made contact. 'No, mate,' was my reply, 'everything's up there together, it flipped my shirt.' It seemed Lloyd agreed with my summary of the situation.

During that last innings, 12th man Tim May came out during a drinks break, fit to burst from laughter. When Michael Slater had been dismissed, he'd stormed into the dressing-room, erupting in profanity, torn off his gear — pads, gloves, the lot — stormed into the toilet and stuffed the lot down into the porcelain, flushing it half a dozen times. By the time Tim came out to the middle, even Slats was having a giggle to himself about his explosion. The only problem was, media manager McDonald wanted to use the facilities, but was refusing to touch any of the equipment that blocked his way. And no-one else was either!

The emotional farewell ... my final walk back to the pavilion after being dismissed in a Test.

I made 35, before being caught behind by Ramesh Kaluwitharana, off the bowling of Chaminda Vaas. Walking off, for the very last time in a Test match, was a truly amazing experience. The ovation from the crowd, the emotions which swept over me, made all the previous times pale almost into insignificance. Afterwards, I was told that the Sri Lankan team stood together as one and applauded me from the ground, which I rate as a very honourable gesture. I still felt my usual disappointment at being dismissed, but there was almost a sense of relief . . . that my journey as a Test batsman was finally over.

For the rest of the day, I sat in the Australian dressing-room, just watching the cricket. And the thought kept reverberating in my mind — that was the last time I was ever going to bat in a Test match. It was almost like being in a dream, but being awake. I suppose it was realisation that the day I had thought would never arrive had come.

Australia declared its second innings at 6–215 and throughout Sri Lanka's final innings, the crowd were calling out for Taylor to give me a bowl.

Tubby kept telling them to shut up, even some of the Australian players started to pump him up. But Mark did the right thing. We were trying to win a Test match for Australia, not write Hans Christian Andersen fairytales.

Mind you, I reckon if I'd taken just one catch — to give me a total of 100 in Test matches — there would have been a riot. But that didn't happen either.

Finally, Australia took the big wickets of Kaluwitharana, Aravinda de Silva and then Sanath Jayasuriya and we ended up winning the match before tea. And that's when the emotion really took off.

I stayed out on the ground for the official presentations, to the winning captain, Mark Taylor, the losing captain, Arjuna Ranatunga, the player of the match, the player of the series and the International Cricketer of the Year, Steve Waugh. Everyone who spoke mentioned me, which was very embarrassing, made even more so by the public pressing close to the presentation area and cheering loudly at every opportunity.

My wife Pip (centre) with her sister Alison (holding baby) and Stephanie Slater, watch me walk off the Adelaide Oval ... for the last time.

It felt like the presentations took forever. Through it all, I stood there, my chin in my hand, not wanting to move. There were no tears, but I felt the moisture welling up continually and I feel no shame in admitting that. Immediately afterwards, while my team-mates drove their cars around the oval, I went straight up the race and sat in the dressing-room.

I had 10 minutes completely on my own — Simpson, McDonald and Alcott in the background — and if 12 years of international cricket, life experience and the rest of it can run through your mind in that brief period, well, that's what happened.

Then the boys came in and the celebrations boiled over. I stood on the dressing-room table to lead the singing of *Under the Southern Cross*, the Australian anthem, one last time.

Normally, we sing it twice through, but this time we sang it three times. There were no TV cameras present, the victory song has been filmed only once to my knowledge, after Australia won back the Ashes in England in 1989. And there was one more major decision to make — to whom was I to pass the enormous responsibility of leading their country in song? My final choice was Ian Healy and he and I led that third rendition together.

Trying to survive the post-Adelaide Test presentations. Shane Warne is on my right, Ian McDonald to my left.

The last time I sang Under the Southern Cross.

When I made the announcement that afternoon — no-one knew who I would choose — Ian was taken aback, at first. But, typically, he embraced the opportunity with open arms. He will lead his country in victory song very, very well. Heals is a wonderful cricketer, secure in his position as wicketkeeper and vice-captain. He is also a fighter, a man who knows how the Australian Test and one-day team should operate. And he's also a senior player. There were, of course, several other options available, but their time will come.

Several of the Sri Lankan players came into our rooms afterwards and, in another meaningful gesture, Arjuna presented me with a Sri Lankan tie and wished me well in retirement. We had our on-field battles with the visiting skipper, but he is a talented cricketer who always fights hard for his country.

We stayed in the rooms until about six o'clock, before returning to the hotel to get ready for a function that evening, which had been organised by Macca. Throughout my final match, I had enjoyed the support of Pip and several family members and close friends in Adelaide. Pip's sister Emma and Emma's husband, Scott, came across from Launceston, as did my long-time friend, Gary Saunders (though Gary's wife Jenny had to stay at home). They all came to the party, as did Dan Johnson, the husband of Pip's younger sister, Alison. The function was held at Tim May's new establishment, The Planet, and was attended by just about everyone and anyone — the commentary team from the Nine Network, all its crew and many of the media who were at the match.

During the night, Mark Taylor got up and spoke, and said some very heartfelt words about the roles our wives and families played in our cricket careers. Mark, as usual, was right on the money, and his words reminded me of the photo from that last Test featuring Pip and Stephanie Slater, Michael's wife, where it appears that the latter is comforting my wife. The truth was the opposite situation.

On this night, though, Pip shed a tear, but not in public.

After Mark came a video presentation of highlights from my career, organised by Nine's Ron Castorina. Then Macca stood up, having performed a feat previously believed impossible. He had conned the match referee and two umpires into letting him have a stump from the game on the third day, had it split and hinged, and attached a gold plaque, which makes reference to the Southern Cross. Ian spoke marvellously, and remains one of my favourite blokes, while the stump now hangs proudly in my study/cricket museum.

Later on that night, and perhaps for the first time in my life, I decided to be sensible. The emotion of the week had exhausted me, not surprisingly, so I made my getaway from the party early, before I fell over!

Before I departed, I went to Pip and said: 'I've got to get out of here.'

'Fine,' she replied, 'but I'm staying.'

Which presented no problem to me. I caught a cab back to the hotel at about midnight, but on the way out she made a bet about the state in which she would find me: on top of our hotel bed — boots and clothes in place. She won the bet.

Mind you, the next morning I discovered (much to my mock horror and absolute amusement) that she had been conned by current and former Australian Test cricketers. It transpired that Philippa Louise Boon had been hoisted onto a table at The Planet, where she proceeded to sing the Australian cricket song!

The only one who was truly horrified was Ian Chappell, who had been indisposed in the toilet at the time and couldn't convince her to repeat her performance.

The next day, Pip and I flew home to Launceston. That was January 30; on February 3, I played for Tasmania against Queensland in a Mercantile Mutual Cup game at Bellerive Oval. My international career had come to a close. I'd be lying, though, if I didn't admit that my mind continually turns to the past, reviewing it, savouring it, even at times despairing at the fact that it is now over. However, the bottom line for me is that I am sure that I made the right decision.

That doesn't mean I'm happy about it, far from it. If you retired from cricket, or the game you play professionally, or whatever you made your career, at the age of 70 — you'd still be unhappy. However, I am content with the decision that I made. I carry the knowledge that no-one made that decision for me. And there is both pride and relief in knowing that.

I will never forget my final Test match in Adelaide and its final night. It was the culmination of a period in my life of which I am very proud and have enjoyed beyond words.

But if there was one thing which did disappoint me throughout my final match, and still niggles at me now, it is that Allan Border missed out on the style of farewell that I received. AB was such a great player, such a mate to me, that I wanted to pass on some of the emotion I felt, and some of the emotion I received from the people of Adelaide and my team-mates and friends. In announcing my retirement, I was lucky in that it had been pretty much cut and dried. It came at the end of an Australian summer, the final Test of the season, as opposed to Allan, who played his last match on the 1994 tour of South Africa and *then* retired, midway through the following off-season.

The thought just won't go away: Everything that I enjoyed would have been increased tenfold in Allan's case. And I think that is a sad situation for someone of the calibre of AB, who gave so much to, and cared so much about, Australian cricket.

Showing Heals how it's done, after handing over the responsibility for leading the singing of the team's victory song.

2: An Exuberant Little Bloke

IF YOU WANT AN INSIGHT INTO A YOUNG DAVID CLARENCE BOON (BORN DECEMBER 29, 1960), WATCH MY SON, JACK, WHO POSSESSES THE SAME FEARLESSNESS, THE SAME NEED TO DO EVERY ACTION AT FULL-TILT. THIS LACK OF CARE FOR MY BODY LED TO ME QUICKLY BECOMING ACQUAINTED WITH THE NURSING STAFF AT THE LAUNCESTON GENERAL HOSPITAL ON A FIRST-NAME BASIS, SO OFTEN WAS I FERRIED THERE FOR STITCHES AND OTHER RUNNING REPAIRS.

I remember trying to fly from the first floor of our home in Charles Street in Launceston and knocking myself senseless. That required a trip to the LGH. When I was two years old, visiting my grandparents, I jumped out of the car and onto the kerb, and split my lip — more minor surgery required. Later that night, I picked the stitches out, a decision for which I have never been forgiven by my mother, and which led to a significant scar which is now hidden safely behind my moustache. These days, whenever I have my hair cut really short, you can see the many scars which tell the story of my younger years. I reckon I was just an exuberant little bloke, but my parents weren't so sure. Often they would tell me that I possessed a very unnatural ability to dismantle new toys, no matter how indestructibly designed they might have been.

I first learned to swim because of a childhood bronchial condition and joined the South Esk Swimming Club when I was still in primary school. Even then, I loved the team aspect of sports. My father, Clarrie, would start work in his newsagency, every morning, at 3.30, and I would be ready to go to the pool at 6am. I wasn't a gun swimmer, but I did enjoy racing and the competition, even if I rarely won any medals. Within the South Esk squad, though, I made some good friends — Stuart and Adrian Wing, Greg and Julie Spence, Deborah and Marie Adams, Gary Wainwright (who died in a car accident in his late teens) — as we travelled around the state competing in carnivals.

My sister Vanessa was born three-and-a-half years after me, which led to a legendary story that my mother loves retelling. Apparently, soon after mother

Opposite: It's hard to believe that this young fella could get into any strife at all.

and daughter came home from hospital, Mum placed my sister in the nearby basinet and went about her business. Moments later, she heard a noise behind her, and spun around to find her son with her daughter in his arms. 'Oh,' she reckons she said, 'That's lovely, to have brought your baby sister into Mummy!' while Vanessa was rescued from me in one swift motion.

I cannot remember the first time I held a cricket bat, but I can hazily recall charging about a hockey field, dribbling a ball with a stick. Mum, who had ended her Australian career in women's hockey after I was born, reckons I was about two, as she was still playing with her old grade club, Penguins.

When I was born, the family lived at Garden Grove in Launceston and Dad worked at the newsagency in Charles Street. Around my sixth birthday, we moved into the house connected to the newsagency, but, later on, we moved back to Garden Grove. My parents ran the newsagency until they moved into a similar business in St John Street, when I was in secondary school.

I first fell for cricket when I was in grade two at Charles Street Primary School. Rather than come home after school finished, I would watch the older boys playing, and stand on the fringes of their practice, fielding balls. The cricket coach at Charles Street was a teacher, Jack Brian, who has now retired to the township of Carrick, outside Launceston, and he became a big influence on my junior cricket and football. By grade three, I was playing cricket with those older boys. At the Charles Street school, most of our matches were played on a huge

Trapped in the play-pen, in the backyard of the family home in Launceston.

With my younger sister Vanessa, in October 1965.

asphalt area, common to most Australian primary schools. In our case, the spring gates between 'big' and 'little' school became the wickets.

I can recall playing a lot of primary school cricket with the Young family — Shane, Ricky and Brett, with whom I went on to play football with at the North Launceston Football Club, where Clarrie had played as a young man. David Smith, later a colleague in the Tasmanian Sheffield Shield team, attended East Launceston Primary School and we played against one another as children, in 13-overs-a-side games. David used to make centuries, I certainly remember that.

I don't remember being exceptionally talented at sport when I was at school. But as a kid, even if you did stand out, you probably wouldn't realise it. It's as you progress through high school years that your ability starts to evolve, and so it was with me — when I was at the Launceston Church Grammar School, things started to happen.

My first formal cricket instruction came from the English fast bowler, Peter Lever, who had a spell as the Northern Tasmanian Cricket Association coach, and sometimes came to Charles Street for clinics. Legend has it that when his stint was completed, Lever returned home to England and told his replacement, fellow Lancastrian Jack Simmons, to 'watch out for a lad named Boon'. Simmons would later become my cricket mentor.

I was similar to most Tasmanian boys of my generation: football in winter, cricket in summer and, where possible, athletics in between. Unfortunately, although I have always been relatively quick over a short distance, I was no athlete.

Certainly, despite what I sometimes read about my past, no-one mentioned D. Boon playing cricket for Australia until I was at least a teenager. From my point of view, it wasn't until after I made the trip to England with an Australian Under-19s team in 1977, and made the Tassie Shield team in 1978–79, that I really thought about reaching the very top. Sure, I watched cricket on television when I was young, but while I was at primary school, I don't know that I ever had any idea of what Test cricket really meant.

Through my early years, Mum and Dad encouraged me at all sports. 'Whatever you want to do, we're happy,' they would say. 'But, whatever you do, try to do the best that you can.'

Perhaps there was a dream there, somewhere in my subconscious. I knew that I really enjoyed cricket, and that I could hold my own in those schoolyard Tests. I now tell school children, perhaps as old as I was when I first started playing, that you start with a dream. You may not know exactly what that dream is, but as you grow up, you gradually work towards it. I don't care what anyone says, most people are born with talent. It's what they do with it afterwards that matters. Most importantly, successful individuals have an innate ability, which

The Australian Under-19s team that journeyed to the UK in 1977. I'm on the extreme right of the front row. Vice-captain Geoff Marsh is third from right, front row, while two other future Australian Test Cricketers — Greg Dyer (front row, second from left), and Wayne Phillips (back row, fourth from right) — were also in the side.

works subconsciously for them, so that they do things slightly differently to others of the same age. Those small differences, things you can't teach, push them to different levels, whether it be sport, music, intelligence, whatever.

After the relative relaxation of primary school, the uniform of blazer, shorts, tie and cap at Grammar were very nerve-racking. Launceston Grammar is one of several Independent schools in Tasmania, and one which possessed two differing cultures — sporting and academic. I was a definite member of the former, and we often used to take extreme physical advantage over the latter.

Yes, I was a jock.

In hindsight, I realise now that our clique was quite cruel to a lot of people whose only failing was that they weren't as proficient at sport as we were. However, I wasn't above retribution. To 'celebrate' my selection in the Under-19s team to tour England in '77, as a 16-year-old in Form 11, I was tied to a chair so that I couldn't move and placed outside the boarding house entrance and Form 12 common room — for two hours — covered in warm water and sugar!

My mates at school were David Bennett, Michael Bennett (the older brother of Richard, who played cricket for Tasmania), Rob Bilson, and Tim Gladman. And a bloke called Peter Faulkner, with whom I would play a lot of Sheffield Shield cricket. Peter, who was once 12th man for an Australian one-day side before choosing to tour South Africa with the 'rebel' tours in 1985 and 1986, is still one of my greatest friends. We had already represented Northern Tasmania in football at primary school — and I still have the photos of those junior teams.

I was in Form 9 when I was selected in the First XVIII, the football team, at Grammar; even younger for the First XI cricket team. Prior to being selected in the senior Tasmanian team, in my final year at school, I played cricket with NTCA club Launceston whenever my commitments with Grammar permitted. As well, I journeyed to Hobart for cricket camps, staying at Christ College, one of the residential colleges at the University of Tasmania, and was coached by Pakistan's Test batsman Sadiq Mohammad, who was having a stint with a Tasmanian club.

The competition between the four Northern independent schools — Grammar, Scotch College, St Patrick's College and Marist College, on the sporting fields of Tasmania's North-West Coast, was enormous. However, the rivalry was all left on the field, as all the lads from all the schools would gather, in the time-old tradition of attempting to find a watering-hole which wasn't overly stringent about under-age drinking. Apart from these illicit visits, one of my treasured memories was winning the state independent schools football premiership, defeating Dominic College from Hobart, whose reputation was such that, earlier in the season, they had been invited to play in a curtain-raiser to a Victorian Football League (now Australian Football League) game. That was also the year, 1977, in which we won the state schools cricket premiership, beating The Hutchins School, a team that boasted players such as Stuart Saunders and Nick Allanby, who both went on to play for Tasmania.

My football at secondary school was similar to my cricket. When not playing for Grammar, I played in the North Launceston thirds. I actually made my senior debut when several North Launceston players were away on state duty and managed to kick three goals as a forward pocket-cum-rover. In my first full game at Windsor Park, playing against opposition Northern Tasmanian Football Association club, Launceston, I took a mark over Wim Vaessen (don't tell anyone, but he was shorter than me!), who went on to become a regular All-Australian amateur player.

Academically, I was a disaster. At school, I was guilty of an extremely poor attitude towards study, which annoys me now. However, to some extent I was coachable — Mrs Mary Hutchins dragged me through hours of extra tutorials in Australian History, even banning me from sports ovals until my work was completed. Unfortunately, though, I never achieved my Higher School Certificate. In Tasmania you had to pass four Level III subjects. I managed three — Australian History, Geography and, believe it or not, English Literature at the first attempt. Looking back, I can see that with an ounce of work, that piece of paper could have been in my filing cabinet.

Basically, my educational achievements are negligible, despite my working knowledge of the Trust Bank's marketing department for the past 12 to 13 years. When I was young, I wanted to be an architect or a draughtsman — I spent hours designing houses and showing them to Mum, rather than studying — but I lacked the mathematical bent for either profession.

My mother and father worked very hard to give Vanessa and I the chance to go to an independent school. Pip and I have done the same, and hopefully it will be within our power to continue to offer the same opportunities to Georgina, Jack and Elizabeth. I would like them to make the most of their education — as their mother did and father did not!

When I left school, I started work at the Launceston Bank for Savings as a trainee teller. The bank has gone through several transformations since then — the LBS Statewide, the Tasmania Bank and now the Trust Bank. I started in the mail room, journeying out in the mail van to deliver internal correspondence to different branches in and around Launceston. We used to count cheques and money — sitting for three hours in a strong room to check the totals — and I never, ever found a mistake.

Before I played cricket for Australia, the bank had always been very generous in its allowing me time to play cricket for Tasmania. However, in 1983, Pip and I very seriously contemplated moving to South Australia, because of a job offer and the added inducement of playing every second Sheffield Shield game on the beautiful batting wickets of the Adelaide Oval. When that move fell though, I was offered a job in the bank's marketing department and have been there ever since, with changing responsibilities and titles.

It was while I was at Grammar that I had first met Pip Wright; I hung around the Wright home so much they finally invited me in. I was in Form 11 at the time, Pip in Form 10, at the all-girls Oakburn College, now the co-educational

With the Rev Bruce Mitchell on our wedding day.

Scotch Oakburn College. We were married six years later — on April 30, 1983 (during the off-season, very much a cricketer's date for a wedding) — at the Grammar Chapel, with about 60 guests attending the ceremony, and the reception, upstairs at the Albert Hall, afterwards. My best man was Peter Milne, with whom I shared a flat in Launceston, and the groomsmen were Peter Faulkner and Greg Wilson, another cricket club team-mate and a Tasmanian paceman. Pip's bridesmaids were her three sisters, Alison, Rebecca and Emma.

After spending our wedding night in Launceston, Pip and I went on a short honeymoon, staying at Bicheno on the East Coast and making our way South, to Port Arthur, the scene of that terrible massacre on April 28, 1996.

I know it's probably inappropriate to refer to that tragedy here, but you must understand how it impacted on me, as a Tasmanian and Australian. I felt a sense of appalled disbelief that something like this could happen in my state, so protected and unblemished as it was in the years that I grew up, and in the years when I was an Australian Test cricketer. How far distant was the carnage of that awful day from the peace, beauty and tranquillity of our honeymoon, 13 years before? I knew people who were at Port Arthur on that dreadful day in 1996. One fellow, Peter Croswell, with whom I have been involved with Camp Quality — which helps children suffering from cancer — was wounded at the Broad Arrow Cafe.

I know that it will take a long time before the people of the Tasman Peninsula recover from this tragedy, if they ever do. A case of innocence lost. I can only hope that people around Tasmania and the rest of Australia continue to visit Port Arthur — it's still a beautiful place and, like so much of the island that has always been my home, remains an important part of Australia's heritage.

3: Jack, Bob and Bacchus

I WAS ONLY 17 WHEN I WAS FIRST SELECTED TO PLAY FOR TASMANIA, IN 1978-79. TASMANIA HAD ONLY BEEN ADMITTED INTO THE SHEFFIELD SHIELD THE PREVIOUS SEASON, AND THEN IT WAS ON A 'PROVISIONAL' BASIS — FIVE MATCHES A YEAR, ONE AGAINST EACH MAINLAND STATE, WHILE THE OTHER STATES PLAYED NINE MATCHES IN ALL. I WAS PICKED FOR THE 'TOUR' OF QUEENSLAND, WHICH INCLUDED A SEMI-FINAL OF THE GILLETTE CUP ONE-DAY COMPETITION, FOLLOWED BY A SHIELD MATCH.

My first state team, the XI for the Cup semi played on December 10, 1978, included 20-year-old Robbie Knight, a batsman with whom I'd played Tasmanian Schoolboys and Colts, and opposed when he played with South Launceston in the NTCA. Robbie's opening partner was Gary Goodman, who like me was making his Tasmanian debut, having moved from Sydney to try to make his mark in the Sheffield Shield. No. 3, Steve Howard, played for Riverside in the NTCA, and he was followed by English professional John Hampshire, then the TCA coach. Jack Simmons was captain, and No. 5, while Gary Cowmeadow, our opening bowler and a lusty hitter, was pushed up the order during our run chase. Roger Woolley was the wicketkeeper, a man who would develop into one of Tasmania's best-ever batsmen and go on to play Test cricket for Australia. All-rounder Tony Benneworth would later become a bank colleague, while long-time friend, Mark Scholes from Hobart, and confirmed No. 11, Gary Whitney, were key parts of the bowling attack.

To be honest, my recollections of the game are somewhat shrouded. However, I can remember that Queensland, a side that boasted Test players in captain John Maclean, Geoff Dymock, Phil Carlson and Gary Cosier, as well as a young leg-spinning all-rounder, Trevor Hohns, set Tasmania a sizeable target, after scoring 6–232 from their 50 six-ball overs. A leading scorer for the Maroons, incidentally,

Opposite: Australian captain Kim Hughes congratulates me on reaching my century for the Prime Minister's XI against the mighty West Indies, January 1984.

was John Buchanan, who made 64. Sixteen seasons later, he would be part of history, as the coach of the first Queensland team to win the Sheffield Shield.

Goodman began brilliantly for his adopted state, scoring 100, and Hampshire reached 63, but then things began to go a little haywire. Jack had intended to bat me at six, but as we kept losing wickets and the pressure mounted, he began pushing me down the order. Eventually, though, he had to put me in, with the score at 7–206, after Goodman, Cowmeadow and then Woolley departed within two runs of each other.

With only two overs left, we still needed 21 runs to win — enter Benneworth, who belted paceman Len Balcam for 14 off four consecutive deliveries. The sequence was: two, four, four and four. But then 'Bennie' departed, caught in the deep trying to hit another boundary. Straightaway, Balcam clean bowled Scholes; Tasmania were 9–226 with one over to go.

Seven runs to win. We all knew that the last man in, Gary Whitney, was not known for his batting prowess, so taking quick singles was not an option. But maybe we wouldn't need to. The first ball of Carlson's over I hit for four to the square-leg boundary, and then, from the third ball, I grabbed two more, to fine leg, to level the scores. Nothing came from ball four, so, with just two balls left, we needed one more run to win, and reach the Gillette Cup final.

At this point, for some reason, Cosier approached Carlson, for a chat. I had met Gary during the senior Australian team's 1977 Ashes tour, when I was also in England, playing with the Australian Schoolboys team, and had memories of a conversation with him about the trouble I was experiencing pulling the ball because the English wickets were so slow. I had this premonition, even though I kept saying in my head: 'Don't anticipate! Don't anticipate!', that Gary was advising Carlson to bowl me a bouncer. Sure enough, down came a short one . . . and I smacked it over wide mid-on for four! Tasmania had won with one ball and one wicket to spare, with D. Boon unconquered on 18.

I don't remember much of the celebrations, but 19 days short of my 18th birthday, *The Australian* newspaper carried a photograph of me having an illegal beer with my captain. Perhaps fortunately, the label on the bottle was conveniently turned away from the camera.

My first Shield appearance came five days later. In my debut innings, on day two of the match, I was obliged to walk into another pressure cooker, coming to the wicket after Queensland paceman Denis Schuller had turned 2–88 into 4–88 by trapping John Hampshire leg before wicket and bowling Roger Woolley around his legs with successive deliveries. Thankfully, I survived a very confident, first ball, bat-pad appeal from acting Queensland captain, David Ogilvie — being the third part of a hat-trick was not quite the way I wanted to begin my first-class career.

Tasmania had bowled Queensland out for 177 on the first day, Jack Simmons the destroyer with 7–59 from 21 superb eight-ball overs (although the one-day matches were being played with six-ball overs, Shield and Test matches in Australia would not revert to the shorter overs until 1979–80). We struggled to 219, my contribution a nervous 22 before I fell, ironically, to the Ogilvie–Schuller combination, and from there the game developed into a rain-interrupted draw — Queensland 6 (declared) for 300, Tasmania 2–105.

Tasmania's next Shield game wasn't scheduled until the last week of January, 1979, but before that we had one of the most important (and, as it turned out, most famous) dates in the state's cricket history — the final of the Gillette Cup, played at the old TCA Ground against Western Australia on January 14.

For much of the day, though, it didn't seem as if we would be covering ourselves in glory. Batting first, we were in absolutely diabolical trouble at 6–84, despite an opening stand of 51 from Gary Goodman and Steve Howard, but then Simmons and Trevor Docking, an extremely good striker of the ball, engineered Tasmania's comeback and we finished with 6–180 from our 50 overs. I made little impact, playing-on to their leggie, Tony Mann, for 8.

In reply, Western Australia's captain John Inverarity and Test opener Graeme Wood put on 39 for the first wicket, before Inverarity became the first of Jack's bag of wickets for the afternoon. Four runs later, he caught and bowled Kim Hughes for one — WA weren't short of a Test player or two. 'Claggy' tried to slog Simmo, but just succeeded in smashing the ball miles into the air.

With the total on 44, Wood was run out; then Mann charged down the wicket to Simmons and missed — 4–58. Ric Charlesworth and Craig Serjeant edged the score into the eighties, but then Bennie took two wickets (Charlesworth and Test off-spinner Bruce Yardley) for no runs in his sixth over, and added a third, Test keeper Kevin Wright, with the score on 89. Unfortunately, Bennie tore shoulder ligaments trying to make a diving save soon after, and had to leave the field, but by then his amazing figures of 3–13 from 8.2 overs had gone a long way to ensuring our victory.

Serjeant, a former Test batsman, and Graeme Porter, a future one-day international player, pushed Western Australia past 120 before Jack returned to the attack. Almost immediately, he had Serjeant, caught by Scholes for 45, to ease our fears, and then Gary Cowmeadow took the final two wickets. Tasmania had won by 47 runs, Western Australia, all out 133!

The actual crowd that day was a bit more than 10,000. As the years have progressed, though, it seems that the entire population of Tasmania was at that match. Whatever, everyone there went, understandably, more than a little berserk. Meanwhile, I was just sitting back, watching it all; it really was just flashing by, all a blur. However, I will never forget Jack standing in the grandstand with the Gillette Cup. As I look back now, it reminded me, in a less dramatic way, of what happened for Australia in England in 1989 and again in 1993. That night we all went down to Wrest Point Casino for our celebrations, before retiring to the Black Buffalo Hotel in North Hobart.

The Gillette Cup final was followed by a one-day game against England at the NTCA Ground in Launceston, in which one Ian Botham top-scored with 61, and was caught by yours truly. It was a catch taken at long-on, in front of a packed home crowd, off the bowling of Greg Wilson, who was playing his first game for Tasmania. And it was a good one to take, seeing as 'Both' had been hitting six after six into the bleachers. Unfortunately, in reply to England's 8–240, Tasmania were somewhat disgraced — all out for 77 — to which I contributed 15, caught Geoffrey Boycott, bowled Phil Edmonds.

Two weeks later, as Gillette Cup champions, we faced the Englishmen again, at the MCG. This time, Tasmania made 6–131 (Boon 8, caught Derek Randall, bowled John Emburey), and England won again, though not as easily, passing Tasmania's total for the loss of seven wickets, with less than five overs to spare.

And that was just about the end of my cricketing contribution to Tasmania's season. I had lost my spot in the starting XI for the Shield match against WA at Devonport to Trevor Docking, but, as 12th man, I had a close-up view of our historic first win in the national competition. I had the same role for our next Shield match, against Victoria in Launceston, but did return for the season finale, in Sydney, where NSW gave us a hiding, and I managed to score 10 and 2.

The photo of 17-year-old David Boon with captain Jack Simmons that appeared in The Australian *after Tasmania's semi-final victory in the 1978–79 Gillette Cup.*

Tasmania's first game of my second Shield season was against South Australia at Devonport Oval — an encounter which saw D.C. Boon meet I.M. Chappell in controversial circumstances on the cricket field. I scored 90 and David Smith, whom I'd played against in primary and secondary school, made 85, and together we put on 158 for the fifth wicket. This broke a partnership record for Tasmania which had stood since 1899–1900, set by George Gatehouse and Ed Windsor.

During our stand, Chappell was reported by umpire Bob Marshall, a policeman of English descent. The incident came about when SA's quick Wayne Prior was bowling to me and the South Australians appealed for leg before wicket. I'd hit the ball, but what I shouldn't have done was turn around and look at the slips cordon. Bad mistake. In true 'Chappelli' fashion, Ian immediately offered some colourful advice along the lines of: 'We'll do the appealing, you worry about your batting.'

Umpire Marshall stepped in and Chappell then rounded on him. Eventually both Ian and I had to front a hearing chaired by the late Bob Ingamells, then president of the Tasmanian Cricket Council. When I was asked by Mr Ingamells to describe the incident, I said that I didn't think there was anything untoward in Ian's attack; to me it was all part of the game.

Another bad mistake. I was quickly and sternly told that I appeared to be backing Chappell and if I didn't keep quiet I'd be suspended as well! Not long after, it was announced that Ian had been suspended for three weeks.

My second summer of first-class cricket also brought about my first meeting with the West Indies, at the NTCA Ground. I had the pleasure of facing Colin Croft, who at that stage was one of the meanest fast bowlers in the world (Andy Roberts and Joel Garner were their other pacemen in this four-day match).

Before the game, Jack Simmons, in all his wisdom, had passed on to a wide-eyed and afterwards quaking 18-year-old the story of Croft playing in England, for Jack's Lancashire, and how he'd knocked Sussex's Ian Gould back through the stumps — Gould swallowed his tongue and there was blood everywhere — during a one-day final. Apparently, Croft's reaction was to appeal for hit wicket! This tale had been countered to some extent, though, by something my mother had told me. She had met a young West Indian paceman in the family's city newsagency before the match began, and explained what a lovely man he was, so quietly-spoken, and how he was missing his family in the Caribbean.

'Who was he, Mum?' I asked.

'Colin Croft,' she replied.

'You've got to be kidding, Mum!'

'David!,' she stated in that special way all mothers possess, 'When he came into the shop he was a lovely man. That's all I can say.'

Croft was very aggressive on the field, but when I met him in the West Indies in 1995, where he was a commentator, I discovered he was an excellent bloke. However, as a player, he had a definite hatred of batsmen; for Colin Croft, cricket was war out in the middle. Croft did tell me that when he bowled to Boycott, he wanted to hurt him before he got him out.

Tasmania was dismissed for 213 on what was described as a 'killer wicket' by our captain, Brian Davison (although Jack was coaching in Tassie, he was no longer playing; because of commitments in England he couldn't devote his full attention to the job). I made 78, batting six, before being stumped by Deryck Murray from off-spinner Derek Parry, while Croft tore us to pieces, with 5–65 from 20 overs!

Before I'd gone out to bat, Jack Simmons advised me that Roberts had two bouncers, one which he held across the seam; if it hit the seam it came off slower. The other one he held seam-down and was much, much faster. Did I listen? Andy bowled me a short ball, I hit it for four, and then I thought: 'I've watched this bloke on television — he's not that quick!' The very next ball, he bounced me again, and I was hit in the chest before I even had my bat up!

The '79–80 season was the first and only Shield season in Tasmania for New Zealand's greatest ever bowler, Richard Hadlee. And he bowled superbly that summer. The only problem was, for most Shield players, he was far too good; there was a lot of playing and missing, and Tasmania's slips cordon wasn't the best, which saw an extraordinary number of catches grassed.

Sadly, Hadlee's time in Tasmania ended in controversy, after he missed the last game of the season against Victoria because of an ankle problem and went

Richard Hadlee, who played for Tasmania in 1979–80, bowling to me in Perth six seasons later.

home. Unfortunately for 'Paddles', his injury recovered very quickly and he was the dominant figure in New Zealand's very next Test match — a performance which saw him cop plenty of stick whenever he returned to Tasmania to play for the Kiwis.

Richard was (and remains) an intense man who set himself specific goals, and when he didn't achieve them he became distraught. Very much a perfectionist. However, his worth to New Zealand's cricket has been devastatingly illustrated since he retired. Even at the end of his career, bowling off his short run, he could dominate a Test batting line-up.

Put simply, Richard Hadlee was a very great bowler, and a bloke who would get me out an awful lot during my career. But you always remember the positives in life. My 143 in the first Test against New Zealand, at the Gabba, in 1987–88, when I made Hadlee bowl to me, rather than the other way around, was technically the best innings I ever played.

My first first-class hundred had come during my third season in Shield cricket, nine days before my 20th birthday in fact, in a game versus Victoria at the old TCA Ground in Hobart — against an attack which included four Test bowlers, Max Walker, Ian Callen, Jim Higgs and Ray Bright.

I scored 114, including 21 boundaries and a six, in a partnership of 174 with Brian Davison, who belted 173 in his inimitable way. However, despite my personal celebrations, Tasmania lost the game. We made 425 in the first innings, Victoria replied with 9 (declared) for 543 and bowled us out for 211 in the second innings (of which I managed 67). The Vics, 4–94 in the end, won by six wickets.

One thing about that innings I can distinctly remember is sweeping Bright and later being told by a selector who was at the game — not the chairman of the Australian selection panel, Phil Ridings, who later spoke positively about my chances of touring England in 1981 — 'The sweep is only a get-off strike shot, son, you only ever get one at the most. You're better off using your feet and hitting the ball through mid-wicket for four.'

For years and years after that, I never swept the ball!

Phil Ridings was not the only person who thought I might be a chance to make the 17-man squad for that '81 Ashes tour. In fact, *Cricketer* magazine polled 17 experts — journalists and ex-players — and I featured in the lists compiled by Percy Beames, Henry Blofeld, Mike Coward, Neil Harvey, Peter McFarline, Ken Piesse and Brian Mossop.

I would like to thank the gentlemen for their suggestion that a 20-year-old, midway through his third season of part-time Sheffield Shield cricket, was that capable, but, realistically, I was too inconsistent and inexperienced to be picked at that stage. The young batsman selected was NSW's Dirk Wellham, who would score a century on debut in the final Test of that tour, and later captain Tasmania.

All the media hype at the time didn't bother me, because I didn't believe I would ever win a spot in the touring party. My only goal at that stage was to try to score runs for Tasmania. However, although I missed the tour party, I did get to go to England in 1981, courtesy of a Tasmanian Government scholarship of $5000, to play with the Netherfield Cricket Club in Lancashire's Northern League. This was a posting arranged by Jack Simmons.

I made some great friends at Netherfield, and my cricket developed. At that point in my career, I was primarily an 'on-side' batsman, but the slow wickets in England forced me to play on the off-side, because there was just no pace to work the ball. During my stay I also played quite a few games for the Lancashire 2nd XI, and generally speaking had a very good time. And I put on a considerable amount of weight.

In fact, there was far too much of the good life and not enough training. NSW's rising left-arm quick, Mike Whitney, was playing in the same league and I caught up with him on more than the odd occasion. Then, in early August, he was plucked from the relative obscurity of that competition to play for Australia in the fifth and sixth Tests, after the touring team suffered a succession of injuries to key bowlers. Ironically, this would be the only time 'Whit' would get to play international cricket in England, despite his excellent record for his country. Peter Devlin, who is now the curator at North Sydney Oval, also played in the Northern League that season, as an amateur.

I lived with the family of Brian and Ruth Otway and their children David and Rachael in Netherfield. David later became something of a Launceston legend in 1984, when he journeyed to Australia and came to stay with us in my home town. During his holiday, Tasmania played a Sheffield Shield game against NSW at the NTCA Ground.

Unfortunately, David had been to the traditional Launceston Cricket Club champagne breakfast on the Saturday morning of the game — I had left him in the far too capable hands of fellow Lions like Tim Coyle (who would later play for Tasmania as a wicketkeeper) and Mick Butler. But they probably shouldn't be blamed for David becoming very tired and emotional through the morning. I was batting reasonably well but, when I reached 98, David thought I'd made a hundred and stormed onto the ground to congratulate me. Understandably, he was apprehended by an officer of the law before he arrived at the wicket, whereupon he pleaded 'tourist'.

'I've travelled 10,000 miles to see my mate make a hundred,' he shouted.

'Well, you'd better wait until he's got two more,' came the not so stern reply.

Fortunately, the police took pity on my Netherfield friend and escorted him back to his new chums at the bar. When I left to play the next day, David was still sound asleep at home!

The Australian Cricket Board granted Tasmania full Sheffield Shield status before the 1982–83 season. It was a decision which finally gave us a secure footing in the national game — previously, playing five Shield fixtures seemed almost like a token gesture by the cricket authorities.

The highlight of our first 'full' season came first-up, a seven-wicket victory over NSW in Sydney, after our bowlers, led by Michael Holding and Peter Clough, the Western Australian who bowled magnificently during his career for his adopted state, knocked over the Blues for 133 in their first innings. Tasmania that year also had the services of Mark Ray, now the chief cricket writer for *The Sunday Age*,

A young Mike Whitney, who went from league to Test cricket in England in 1981.

and my old mate, a New South Welshman himself, Steve 'Jack' Small.

The following season, 1983–84, I made my highest-ever first class score, 227, against Victoria at the MCG. I made runs a lot quicker then, off just 410 balls, against an attack which included Merv Hughes, Simon Davis and Ray Bright. After this performance, the whispers about a possible place in the Test side for D. Boon were stronger than ever. However, whenever I was questioned about this subject, I said what I truly believed at the time: that an Australian cap was still a fair way down the road. As I told one reporter, 'I don't think at this stage I'll get a game for Australia. I'll just have to keep on making runs consistently.' But the dream of wearing the baggy green was very much alive.

In December, 1983, I suffered a chipped bone in my left elbow when I was hit by Pakistan paceman Azeem Hafeez in a four-day match at the old TCA Ground in Hobart. Thankfully, I recovered in time to play for Bob Hawke in his Prime Minister's XI, against the West Indies at Manuka Oval in Canberra in January, 1984. This was a fixture that had been re-introduced by the sports-loving Mr Hawke, who had been elected PM in March 1983. Of course, the original idea had been that of the late Sir Robert Menzies, who, during his long reign in the national capital, had often chosen a side to play against the touring side of the summer.

Once again, I was an extremely nervous new kid on the block. Fellow Tasmanian Roger Woolley was also there, and the team also contained the Australian captain, Kim Hughes, and players of the calibre of Steve Smith, Dean Jones, Greg Matthews, Greg Ritchie and one Gregory Stephen Chappell, as well as bowling legends Dennis Lillee and Jeff Thomson.

I was lucky enough to make 134 from 136 balls, the Prime Minister's XI won easily, and ever since that day, Mr Hawke has laid claim to starting my Test career. Perhaps he's right! I know that I was very chuffed to receive a letter from an Australian Prime Minister, congratulating me on my performance.

Soon after, the Australian squad to tour the West Indies was announced and although I wasn't selected, I was placed on standby, with Graeme Wood, to cover the injured Steve Smith and Greg Ritchie. Both doubtful players were eventually passed fit to tour, but, honestly, missing out again didn't disappoint me. One of my quotes at the time reminds me of my mother, Lesley, and her school of diplomacy: 'You've got to expect these sort of things,' I told a journalist. 'You have to give every selected player a chance of making the side, that's the way it should be.'

Steve Smith's injury, and a World Series Cup final 'tie' between Australia and the West Indies at the MCG, did, though, lead to my first Australian one-day cap. Steve had dislocated his left shoulder and damaged ligaments attempting to field a Richie Richardson cover drive in the second final (best of three) of the one-day international series. The Windies made 5–222 from their 50 overs, Australia dramatically replied with 9–222 and the game was called a tie because no rule was in place to cover these unusual circumstances — the visitors thought they'd won the series, the home side thought they hadn't lost the series, and for a while no-one seemed to know if the third final, scheduled, if required, for the following day, was really going to be needed.

I was actually chosen as Smith's replacement even before the second final was completed. Pip and I were at an antique shop in Longford outside Launceston when I was contacted by my mother-in-law, Pat Wright. 'The Australian Cricket Board just rang,' she yelled, 'You're on a flight at four o'clock this afternoon and the tickets are at the airport. When you get to Melbourne, get a cab to the hotel and go to your room.'

Being an obedient son-in-law, I did exactly as I was told. When I arrived at my room at the Windsor Hotel in Melbourne, I was astounded — it was bigger than our entire flat in Launceston. And I just sat there, maybe on the bed, then the chair, waiting and waiting. I was very nervous and very apprehensive about the whole situation.

Finally, there was a knock on my door and in strode Rodney Marsh, the legendary Australian wicketkeeper, who promptly took me to a party at Ian

'Molly' Meldrum's house in Richmond. We finally made it back to the Windsor about midnight, to learn that the third final was to be played after all. The international cricket career of D.C. Boon was about to begin! The hour might have been late, but I was so hyped up, sleep came in just fits and starts.

I batted at three the next day, a game I will always remember because it was the last game 'Bacchus' Marsh played for his country. I made 39 and didn't hit a four. And Rod kept getting stuck into me all day because my throws from fine leg kept hitting him on the half-volley.

Welcome to the big time!

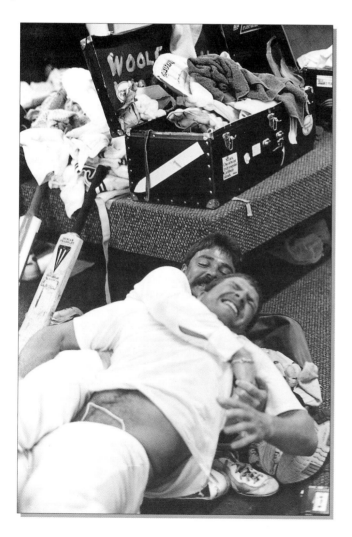

Wrestling with keeper Richard Soule in the Tassie dressing-room, October 1985.

4: The Baggy Green

In July, 1984, I received my first contract from the Australian Cricket Board, but, even so, I missed out on the short tour of India later that year. So, I had to wait until the new Shield season to push my case for a Test berth. A key part of my challenge was one of my best friends, an old taped-up bat I called 'Old Faithful', which had been with me when I made 227 against Victoria the previous summer, helped me score 134 against the West India for the Prime Minister's XI in Canberra and a handy 205 for Launceston in the NTCA grand final. It would last until just before the 1985 Ashes tour, when, sadly, it finally reached its use-by date. But, in a sense, Old Faithful still lives on today, as a proud and highly valued part of my cricket memorabilia collection.

In Tasmania's first match of 1984–85, a draw in Perth, I made just 1 and 2, but then against NSW in Launceston I scored 132 on the second day, before retiring hurt. The Blues fast bowler, David Gilbert, hit me on the right side of the head (this was in the impetuous days of my youth, before I learned the value of a protective helmet) and I had to leave the field with severe pain in my right eye. I did wear a helmet the next day, and made six more runs before Gilbert trapped me leg before wicket.

Straight after that match, Tasmania headed for Melbourne, specifically Princes Park, to play Victoria. Once again, Old Faithful did the job and despite the first three hours of play being lost to a wet wicket, by stumps I was 63 not out with Mark Ray also undefeated on 60, despite the best efforts of Rodney Hogg to end our respective innings, if not our lives, on the green-top. I was very proud of how I batted that day, and went on to make another century, my second in a row, which I hoped was what the Australian selectors were looking for.

After the match, which ended in a first-innings win to the Vics, we headed down to Portland for a game to commemorate Victoria's 150th anniversary and

Opposite: A hook shot during my debut Test, against the West Indies in Brisbane in 1984–85.

it was while we were there that I received the news that I had been named in the Australian team for the second Test against the West Indies, to be played in Brisbane.

Australia had been beaten in three-and-half days in Perth and I was replacing Graham Yallop, who had been injured. I honestly couldn't believe it. I flew back to Launceston that night, saw Mum and Dad briefly, and then went home to Pip to wash the creams. The whole situation was so exciting, but I must admit I was dreading failure — now that the opportunity was finally upon me, I didn't want to blow it. However, I was very aware just who was waiting to bowl to me at the Gabba, so I knew that success was no sure thing. I wasn't overwhelmed, just apprehensive; this was the first time in my life that fear of failure had raised its ugly noggin'. My cricket philosophy had always been to go out and play, do the best you can, and if you do get out, try to discover and then work on your error or weakness.

It probably wasn't until I was sitting on the airplane, bound for Brisbane, that suddenly realised that I was a member of the Australian Test team. When I arrived in Brisbane and headed to the Sheraton Hotel, I remember being enveloped into the team system — and totally shocked by the amount of gear we received! I remember getting my first Australian cap from Ron Steiner, the ACB representative, and going back to my room and just staring at it. I was rooming on my own, so that probably made the build-up even worse.

I tried on the cap and looked at myself in the mirror. I can only describe the feeling as 'special'.

In truth, the unique quality of that moment didn't come home to me until years later, after another Tasmanian, Greg Campbell, played his first Test for Australia, at Leeds on the 1989 tour of England. I told him that he had a baggy green cap, had played for his country and had taken a wicket in the first Test of the series — he could live the rest of his days feeling so proud of what he'd done for Australia — and that no-one could take that away from him. Just getting there is an incredible feeling, all of its own.

Practice was different to what I was used to, and not at all like the system which now exists in the Australian camp. Kim Hughes was captain and he was the boss of the nets; Greg Chappell was a selector, and he hit slips catches to us, while dressed in a collar and tie. With no disrespect to anyone who was in my first Test team, I cannot emphasise just how totally different the atmosphere was within the XII at that time from what prevails today. There was plenty of conversation, but it was a difficult time, especially as the team was coming off a belting in the first Test in Perth.

I was very fortunate in that I sat next to Allan Border in the old dressing rooms at the Gabba, then the visitors' Sheffield Shield rooms. AB's advice was to play my own game . . . and if I opened my mouth, make sure I was 200 per cent correct! In other words, speak when you're spoken to.

On the first morning of the Test, West Indies won the toss and sent Australia in. I was pencilled in at No. 6, and entered the fray, to join Border, after Kim Hughes was dismissed. The score was 4–81. The first ball I faced was from Joel Garner, who tried to bowl a yorker, but which became a shin-high full toss. I hit the ball towards Larry Gomes at mid-on . . . and the single was there.

Unfortunately, my call went somewhat along the lines of: 'Yes! No! Wait! Sorry! Come back for two!' I was almost run out, attempting a second run — my debut might have lasted a solitary ball. At the end of the over, AB came to me and asked, 'How's it looking, mate?'

'I can feel my legs knocking together,' I answered, 'can you see 'em?'

I was out for 11, caught by Richie Richardson at third slip, a very good catch diving to his right, off the bowling of Malcolm Marshall. Australia were all out 175, keeper Wayne Phillips top-scoring with 44, while Joel Garner took four wickets and Courtney Walsh three.

The West Indies replied with 424, of which Richardson scored 130 and Clive Lloyd 114. One thing I will never forget is fielding just in front of square, saving one, when our opening bowler, Geoff Lawson, bounced the great Viv Richards. He pulled it, and I caught it very close to the ground. I was rapt, but after Viv departed, my new team-mates started saying: 'One hand, one bounce, that's not bad, Boonie, especially against the best player in the world . . .

'That's the way to start your career!'

If you think about these things long enough . . . In the end, I was that petrified that it had bounced, as soon as we came off I snuck away to see Ian Chappell in the commentators' box and watch a replay. But I had caught it, they were just stirring me up! I was much relieved.

In Australia's second innings, I was 20 not out at the end of the third day, but Australia were in trouble at 5–134. The next morning, not long after play resumed, I was involved in a discussion with Malcolm Marshall. Or rather, he spoke to me and I listened. I was going along okay, when Marshall trotted down the wicket a few extra steps and called out: 'Boonie, I know this is your first Test match, but are you going to do the right thing and get out or do I have to come around the wicket and kill you?' I think this is what they call a 'rhetorical' question.

I decided to keep going, and was still there when Rodney Hogg came in at No. 10. 'Babs,' he said, 'This is the perfect opportunity to start your career with a not out because I don't think I'm going to hang around too long!'

However, he did hang around and finished with 17 not out, but not before we had another mid-wicket conference. Marshall, by this point, was coming from

My infamous mid-wicket conference with Rodney Hogg at the Gabba.

around the wicket, but I managed to get onto one, hooking it to the boundary. Hogg came storming down the wicket and I thought he was about to play 'pat the debutante on the back'. Instead, he screamed at me: 'What are you trying to do, get us all killed?!'

In the end, I batted a long time, 236 minutes in all, and hit four boundaries for 51, before Malcolm Marshall finally got his man, caught by Michael Holding. I was on such a high after reaching 50 in my first match, but my emotions pitched to the other end of the scale when the West Indies went 2–0 up in the series, by making the mere 26 runs they required in their second innings for victory.

When I was dismissed in our second innings, Kim Hughes, visibly upset, was already in discussion with the Australian team manger Bob Merriman. After the game a media conference was called and Hughes announced his resignation as captain of Australia. At the time, I hardly knew Kim at all. I remember thinking: 'What can I do?' It was so confusing for a player in his first game.

The third Test match, my second, was in Adelaide — AB's first as Australian captain. I was credited with dropping Gordon Greendige in the gully when he was 16 on his way to 95. I beg to differ. I didn't see the thing and it almost broke my leg! The West Indies made 356 and I made 12 in Australia's first innings of 284. West Indies declared their second innings at 7–292 and Australia was all out 173, Boon 9, the match lost by 191 runs; West Indies 3–0 up.

Despite the drubbing Australia were receiving, relations between the teams were quite amicable, with players going into opposing rooms after the end of the day's play. Gradually, though, this part of the sport deteriorated. And that is just about the only major disappointment of my Test career. Obviously, you suffer personal frustration when you fail and when the team loses, but sometimes you have to rise above such feeling; I believe the one thing which could improve this great game is the return of friendly interaction between teams after each day and at the end of a match. The after-game dressing room is a place where you make friends. Maybe I'm old-fashioned, in that I think what happens on the ground should stay on the ground, where you always fight cat and dog to win the game. And, apart from friendship, and the chance to enjoy a beer or a soft drink together, the dressing-room is also a place where you can sit and listen to other players . . . and learn.

It's the same in the Sheffield Shield. The kids today don't get the opportunity to talk to the equivalent of a Greg Chappell, Doug Walters, Rod Marsh, Dennis Lillee or Allan Border. I did. With Tasmania now, my rule as captain is that if it's our turn to visit the opposition, I don't care what they do in return, I want at least 50 per cent of my players in their room. And, at the end of a match, especially if we get beaten, I want my entire complement with me to congratulate the other side.

Back to 1984–85. After the Adelaide loss, we travelled to Melbourne for the Christmas Test, where I was 12th man. The fifth Test, a week later, was in

Sydney, fifth Test, 1984–85 — Australia have just beaten the West Indies by an innings.

Sydney, where Australia batted first, and our South African-born opening bat, Kepler Wessels, made 173 and I scored 49 in our 9 (declared) for 471. We then rock'n'rolled the Windies for 163, with 38-year-old Bob 'Dutchy' Holland taking 6–54 with his leg-spinners.

We ended up winning that Test match, bowling West Indies out again for 253 and I remember especially the performance of one player who was to become a very good friend, NSW left-arm finger spinner Murray Bennett. Murray bowled Viv Richards for 58 with an arm ball in the second innings and we never thought he was going to come back — so excited was 'Maxie' he did a lap of honour of the SCG!

After the World Series Cup matches against the West Indies and Sri Lanka, the season culminated for me in being named Sheffield Shield Player of the Year, the first and only time I have won this prestigious award. The announcement of the team for the Ashes tour of England in 1985 came over ABC Radio soon after, in late March. In situations such as this, if your surname starts with 'B' you don't have to wait that long to discover your fate, and quickly (after captain Allan Border, vice-captain Andrew Hilditch, Terry Alderman and Murray Bennett) I knew that I was 'in'! I was at the LBS Statewide Bank, a large group of us had gathered around the radio, and even before the next name — Bob Holland — was announced, I had been swamped by work-mates and friends.

This was different to being selected for my first Test, because an Ashes tour is the ultimate for an Australian cricketer. It's different to playing England in Australia, this is the longest tour, on the oldest enemy's home turf, and on Test grounds which have been etched into the history books of the game.

This was a time of change. Two veterans, former skipper Kim Hughes and paceman Rodney Hogg had been left out of the original 17-man squad. Then there was turmoil, when it was revealed that at least three players who had been chosen — Alderman, South Australian fast bowler Rod McCurdy and NSW wicketkeeper Steve Rixon — were among a group of Australian first-class players who had signed to take part in a 'rebel' tour of South Africa in 1985–86. That trio were replaced, but two of the three substitutes — pace bowlers Carl Rackemann and John Maguire — were also committed to the rebel trip. So had, it seemed, four other members of the original Ashes squad — Bennett, Wayne Phillips, Dirk Wellham and Graeme Wood, but they had since withdrawn from the team for South Africa.

Before we left for England, the Australian team gathered in Melbourne, where a meeting was held to, in simple terms, okay the places of three of those four players. Bennett's position was different from the other three; he had changed his mind early on, whereas it seemed Phillips, Wellham and Wood had not opted to stay with the establishment until after the Ashes team had been announced.

For me, a first time tourist, the situation was more than a little bizarre. One by one, the players were brought into a room, and captain Allan Border and the rest of the touring party fired questions at them about the rebel tour. At the end of this, we were to vote to decide if we wanted these guys in England with us. I was on my first Australian tour, yet I was being asked to make judgment on these players' eligibility, loyalty and future, even after they'd been picked by Australian selectors and endorsed by the ACB! I looked at all-rounder Simon O'Donnell, another about to go on his first major cricket tour, shrugged my shoulders, and said: 'What are we going to do?'

A square cut at Taunton, during the 1985 tour.

In the end, the guys did tour. Obviously, it was a one-in, all-in situation — one thing that had been established straightaway was that there would be no grudges while on tour. Meanwhile, we learned that, not long after we were to arrive in London, the game's international board of control, now the International Cricket Council, would be meeting to set the bans on the players who would tour South Africa.

I was rooming with Kepler Wessels, who has always denied any involvement with the rebel tours. I can tell you that several telephone conversations, always in Afrikaans, did take place in my presence between the Australian opener and other parties. The morning after the bans had been announced, Wessels obviously knew about their existence and severity before AB told anyone else in the team — and AB had been at the international board meeting until 2am. Perhaps someone had tipped 'Chopper' off, I don't know. But I do recall one night when we all went out for a meal — all except Kepler, who explained he had decided to have an early night — and on the way home we spotted Kepler, deep in discussion with South African cricket chief Ali Bacher.

Now that South Africa has been re-admitted to international cricket, perhaps the ramifications of the rebel tours don't seem so important. But their impact on Australian cricket at the time was considerable. If nothing else, we were below full strength, taking on England without a bowler of the calibre of Terry Alderman, who in 1981 had taken more than 40 Test wickets.

I remember at the time receiving a letter from one of my oldest friends, Peter Faulkner, who was a tremendous all-rounder for Tasmania and is now a State selector. Peter wrote to tell me that he'd been offered a contract to go to South Africa and hoped that our friendship wouldn't be affected by his decision to accept the offer. I rang him back and told him he should go, if that's what he believed to be the right thing to do. Apart from this point we agreed to disagree about our different viewpoints regarding the issue. And, as I recall, we had a pretty healthy argument after he returned from that first tour. But going on that rebel tour did nothing to damage my regard for 'Flossy' as a cricketer, or as a bloke and friend. He eventually served a two-year ban, but came back to play for Tasmania again. And he is also godfather to my first-born, Georgina.

When I compare the 1985 tour to Australia's outstanding successes in '89 and '93, the first time was just basically hard work, even though I had the considerable adrenalin rush of being away for the first time.

The first Test was at Headingley and I was reasonably confident after making a few runs in the preliminary games. But they didn't quite come as easily at the next level. Andrew Hilditch made a hundred in Australia's first innings of 331, to which D. Boon, batting at No. 5, contributed 14 before being dismissed, leg before wicket, to Graham Gooch. England then made 533, with opener Tim Robinson scoring 175.

Australia made 324 in the second innings — Hilditch 80, Wayne Phillips 91 and Boon 22, English off-spinner John Emburey 5-82 — which left England needing 103, which they managed, losing four wickets before Allan Lamb and Ian Botham got them home.

The second Test was at Lord's, and was the beginning of my horror-run — in the first innings I was out for 4, caught off the glove trying to hook Botham, in the second I was bowled by Phil Edmonds for 1. But we won, by four wickets: England 290 and 261 (Holland 5–68), Australia 425 (Border 196, Greg Ritchie 94) and 6–127.

My second-innings dismissal just preceded a break in play — during which the Australian team was introduced to the Queen, Elizabeth II. Because I was in such an angry funk, all I could manage was a quiet, 'Hello' — I hope I didn't seem too rude.

I kept making runs in the county games, but couldn't bat to save myself in the ones that counted. I scored 138 in the second innings of our match against Essex, immediately after the Test at Lord's, but then, in the third Test, at Trent Bridge in Nottingham, I was out for just 15 in our only innings — 539, which included big hundreds to Graeme Wood and Greg Ritchie. Then I made 84 against Minor

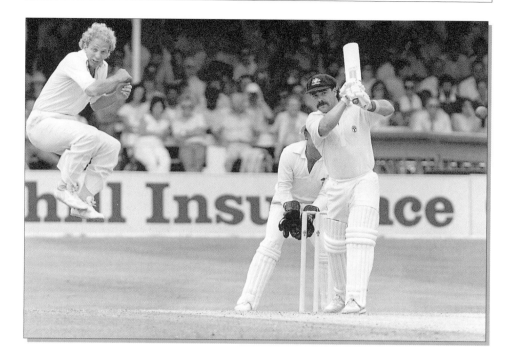

England captain David Gower jumps for his life during the third Test at Trent Bridge.

Counties and 206 in less than a day against Northamptonshire in between the third and fourth Tests.

For the fourth Test, at Old Trafford, I was promoted to No. 3 because Graeme Wood was out injured, after being struck on the face batting against Northants. I felt much more comfortable and made 61, before being caught in gully by Lamb off Botham, in Australia's first innings of 257. But I was back at five in the second dig, where I made only 7, and after that I was relegated to the support staff for the last two Tests, at Edgbaston and The Oval.

In those four Tests I made 124 runs at an average of 17.71 — not overly impressive, especially when compared to my tour aggregate of 838 runs at 55.8.

At the end of the tour, Pip and I had an excellent holiday in the Greek Islands with Murray and Jane Bennett, who remain great friends. I'll never forget our encounter, after a couple of days on one island, with a Greek waiter — whom we had to confront about his abruptness.

To justify his behaviour, he replied simply: 'You bloody Americans!'

So we explained to him that we were Australian. That changed the tenor of the conversation. Did we know his cousin in Melbourne? Could we get his cousin a job?

He became our best mate — and drank all our red wine!

WHISPERING DEATH

When Michael Holding was just about the greatest fast bowler in the world, from the mid '70s to the mid '80s, he was known as 'Whispering Death'.

Nothing could have been truer. For mine, he wasn't just a fast bowler, he was a pure athlete, rumoured to have run an Olympic qualifying time for the 400 metres as the Jamaican track champion.

More importantly, Michael Holding was just a lovely bloke.

I first met him in Tasmania's first full season of Sheffield Shield cricket, 1982–83, when he shared the 'import' role with the West Indian-born Englishman, Roland Butcher. Two things were quickly apparent; besides being a wonderful person, he could bowl bloody quick!

In Tasmania, he was sensational — always professional in his attitude towards young players at the endless coaching clinics to which he was assigned by the then Tasmanian Cricket Council. (This wasn't always the case with some of the imports my state contracted over the years, but that's just different people.) Michael was then one of Test cricket's most respected pacemen, yet he was happy to pass on his knowledge to all those who were willing to listen. As for his presence within the team: the feeling was of rubbing shoulders with greatness. Until I got to know him, and realised that he wasn't just a demi-god, I felt nervous around him. To think that this

marvellous West Indian paceman was actually playing in our team!

And I know now that the whole of Jamaica, his home country, thinks the same way. Everyone there knows him. When we toured the Caribbean, in 1991 and 1995, and stayed in Kingston, I went with Holding for a Chinese meal — his favourite cuisine. The first time I learned, and the second time I was reminded, that to eat with Michael Holding at his choice of restaurant in his home town is to be treated like royalty.

There are very few fast bowlers who have compassion for their fellow cricketers, particularly batsmen. I know this is a broad generalisation, but it is one which would probably stand rigorous investigation. Michael, though, did care about his colleagues, his opponents and the game, even if his main objective was always to get the opposition out as soon as possible.

I remember playing a game for Tasmania against England at the NTCA Ground in Launceston, when the wicket was somewhat difficult.

Michael was bowling superbly, and one delivery just took off a length and cannoned into Derek Randall's face — hitting him between the nose and the top lip. It was a horrible blow, Randall was seriously hurt, there was blood everywhere.

Michael, meanwhile, was mortified. He genuinely hated hitting blokes. There were tears in his eyes because he had hurt someone so badly. He wasn't above hitting batsmen in the body or scaring the living daylights out of them with bouncers, but causing physical damage was another matter altogether.

On this occasion, Michael approached Roger Woolley, the then captain of Tasmania, and said that he would continue bowling, but only off one pace. Which is what he did.

In the Test arena, he was as quick as anyone I ever faced.

I played against him in my first Test match in Brisbane in 1984 and although we were friends, he never spoke to me while we were pitted against one another. However, before the game, he had telephoned my father Clarrie, to offer his congratulations on my selection and also to send a warning that in Test cricket, there would be no favours.

In that very game, Michael struck me one of the worst blows to the groin area I ever received. Allan Border and I were batting together in Australia's second innings, Holding was off his shortened run-up late in the day, and the light at the Gabba was fast waning. AB had a discussion with Mel Johnson about the light situation, but Mel was confident it wasn't dangerous.

So, with that information ringing in his ears, Michael went back to his long run and with his next delivery hit me fair, and square, in the goolies. I felt very sick after that — unsurprisingly — and the day was called for light at the end of the over.

Michael is also a central figure in my favourite Rodney Hogg story. The first Test of that 1984–85 series was held

Michael Holding.

in Perth, a match the West Indies won easily. During the brief Australian first innings of that match, Rodney, while facing Michael, was guilty of an horrific retreat, jumping back from his normal stance towards square leg as the ball was about to be delivered. But Michael saw him go, and followed him, and the ball ricocheted back off Rodney's retreating pads into the stumps.

Rodney stalked off the WACA Ground and into the dressing-room, which had been cracking up until he entered, his face glowering. There was no time to take off his pads; he marched to the phone and rang his wife Denise, who used to video all of his games.

'Denise,' he snarled, 'erase that tape, so that my children cannot see that their father was a coward.'

But I can understand how, with Whispering Death coming at you at that pace, you might not wish to be in line.

5: Testing Times

I WAS APPOINTED CAPTAIN OF TASMANIA FOR THE FIRST TIME WHILE STILL ON THE ASHES TOUR OF ENGLAND (MY PREDECESSOR IN THE ROLE, ROGER WOOLLEY, HAD DECIDED TO STAND DOWN TO CONCENTRATE ON HIS BATTING). AND, THOUGH I MIGHT HAVE MISSED THE FINAL TWO TEST MATCHES IN ENGLAND, I BEGAN THE AUSTRALIAN SUMMER ON A HIGH, SCORING 196 AGAINST NSW AT THE OLD TCA GROUND, IN A GAME IN WHICH TWO GENTLEMEN, BY THE NAMES OF MARK TAYLOR AND MARK WAUGH, MADE THEIR DEBUT FOR THE BLUES.

I was selected for the first Test against New Zealand at the Gabba, batted at No. 3, and made 31 in the first innings (one of Richard Hadlee's nine wickets in the innings) and 1 in the second, as Australia were thrashed by an innings and 41 runs. Then in Sydney, a fortnight later, I was dismissed for a duck, in our first innings, as we struggled to 227 all out, 66 behind the Kiwis' 293. Fortunately, our spin trio of Dutchy Holland, Ray Bright and Greg Matthews brought us back into the Test, and we ended up needing 260 for victory. At the end of day four, I was 6 not out; when I glanced at the papers the next morning, I couldn't help noticing — not for the last time in my career — that people were suggesting that my Test spot was on the line.

Happily, though, I ended up top-scoring with 81, my highest Test score to that point, and we reached our target with six wickets down to level the series. This was an important innings for me — like some critics in the media I was beginning to worry about my inability to deliver at the highest level.

The third Test, in Perth, was another Australian disaster, New Zealand won by six wickets, to take the series, while Hadlee took 11 wickets, to take his tally for the series to a remarkable 33. I fell to this great bowler in both innings, but did manage 50 in the second dig.

There was little time to assess our failings, though, because within two weeks, we were into a three-Test series against India, beginning in Adelaide. I had stayed at first wicket for all three of the New Zealand Tests, but here I was asked to partner Wayne Phillips at the top of the order. This was the debut Test of one Geoffrey Robert Marsh and he batted at three, where he was then batting for Western Australia.

Opposite: Geoff Marsh and I during our 217–run partnership against India at the SCG, 1985–86.

This was an important match in my career for it was here that I scored my first Test century — 123 beautiful runs. I can still recall the excitement and joy of hitting India's off-spinner Shivlal Yadav through the covers to get there, and can also remember meeting Greg Ritchie in mid-pitch and him congratulating me — this, importantly for me, was another major hurdle negotiated in my second summer of Test cricket.

Greg also scored a hundred in Australia's first innings of 381, and then India replied with 520, of which the great Sunil Gavaskar, then the greatest run-scorer in cricket, made 166 and passed 9000 Test runs in his 110th appearance. The game ended in a draw because of rain, but D. Boon and G. Marsh opened together for the first time in the second innings, and added 17 unconquered runs before the end. However, it wasn't until the third Test of the series, in Sydney, that the Boon–Marsh combination became a full-time thing.

The second Test had also been drawn, and in the third India went on something of a run-spree, amassing 4–600, of which Gavaskar got 172, Kris Srikkanth, 116 and Mohinder Armanath, 138. It was that sort of wicket, just the right stage for a new opening partnership to make its fair dinkum debut. At stumps on day three, Boon and Marsh were 0–169, and I had reached my second Test hundred, 100 not out exactly — and so began my love affair with the SCG.

'Swamp' and I ended up putting on 217 runs for the opening stand, breaking a 40-year record for the ground, which had been set by Arthur Morris and Sid Barnes against the Poms back in 1946–47. I finished with 131 and Marsh 92. It was only after this knock that I began to feel as though I belonged in the Australian Test team. Understandably, two centuries had brought about a total change in self-confidence.

That match, and the series, ended in a stalemate, and it was during the latter stages of the season's World Series Cup, that featured Australia, New Zealand and India, that Bob Simpson was invited to take on the coach's role for the upcoming short tour of New Zealand.

I wonder what Bob must have thought when he watched our game in Adelaide against New Zealand, an interesting affair in which they made 7–276 and then bowled us out for 70, in 26.3 overs! One member of the ACB, Des Rundle, was so disgusted with Australia's performance that he wanted the Board to keep our match payments. But, then, in the next game, at the SCG, we bowled New Zealand out for 140, after we had made 7–239. Limited-overs cricket can be like that!

In that day-nighter in Sydney, I had one of my very few run-ins with Allan Border. We were batting easily, and AB told me that I was doing a great job, but with Geoff Marsh out, it was my role to bat through the innings. About an over later, I tried to put Stu Gillespie into the showgrounds and was bowled for 64.

The Adelaide Oval scoreboard tells the story of my first Test hundred.

Allan gave me the 'death look' on the way off and when he was dismissed, run out, I said to the boys in the dressing-room: 'Watch this.' Sure enough, I was summoned to the captain's presence, where he left me in no doubt as to what he thought of my shot. And I couldn't say a word, because he was right.

After the World Series Cup finals, which we won in two straight matches over India, we headed to New Zealand for a three-Test series which began at the Basin Reserve in Wellington. Straightaway, the Boon and Marsh combination continued their form with an opening partnership of 104, on a day when Hadlee took his 300th Test wicket — Border, leg before.

I made 70 — and was almost cleaned up in the process — given out caught behind off my ear from left-armer Gary Troup. Australia made 425, New Zealand 6–379, before the last two days were wiped out by rain.

The second Test in Christchurch was another rain-affected draw, and then, in Auckland, we came a cropper. Batting first, we made 314, in which Geoff Marsh contributed his maiden Test century, 118. New Zealand replied with 258, but then off-spinner John Bracewell took 6–32 and Australia were bowled out for 103. I carried my bat through the debacle for 58 not out, the first Tasmanian and only the eighth Australian to do so. It was not, though, considering the circumstances, a particularly prestigious or satisfying statistic.

It was after this Test and before a series of one-day internationals were due to begin that Allan Border, at an emergency team meeting in Christchurch, threatened to quit as Australian captain. The major problem, as I saw it, was that Allan really only knew me, Wayne Phillips, Greg Ritchie and Craig McDermott at all well — with the remainder of the team there was a real communication problem.

AB was the last survivor of the 'great' Australian teams of the late 1970s and early 1980s. Unlike the rest of us, he'd shared Test wins with the Chappells, the Lillees and the Marshes; that's how he'd learned to succeed in the top grade, by watching and listening to these legends. But some of the blokes in our team found it hard to approach him and he found that terribly frustrating. AB's routine was like mine, a few beers in the rooms and the hotel bar, a meal and a reasonably early night. Some of them thought the only way to speak to him was in the bar after the day's play, which was an environment they weren't used to and maybe didn't enjoy. But all this wasn't really an adequate excuse for Australia's poor performances, and I think AB knew it. Maybe, he thought, someone else had the answer.

It was so frustrating for Allan to be the only consistent performer in a team which had a lot of talent, but was continually being beaten. The bottom line was that AB loved the baggy green as much as anyone. If not more.

When the Australian party for the tour to India in September–October 1986 was announced, AB was, of course, still captain, but one significant name missing was that of keeper/batsman Wayne Phillips. 'Flipper' was a very, very talented player — I can remember batting with him on an Australian Under–25 tour of Zimbabwe, and facing a bloke called Ali Shah. He told me where he was going to hit everything . . . and he did!

'First ball,' Flipper said, 'six over the scoreboard.' Ali Shah pitched the ball a half a metre outside off-stump and over the scoreboard it went.

Wayne had a definite passion for the game and for Australia, although not everyone appreciated his sense of humour, and he played some great innings in one-day internationals and Test cricket. But the South Australian was replaced, by Western Australia's Tim Zoehrer, who was himself to lose his spot a season later to NSW's Greg Dyer, who was a steady gloveman, not spectacular, and a far better batsman than any statistic ever showed.

Bar the captain, the squad to India was desperately inexperienced — Allan Border had played 81 Tests; newly-appointed vice-captain David Boon, 16 Tests, Greg Ritchie, 23, Ray Bright, 22 . . . then look what happened: Simon Davis (1 Test), Greg Dyer (0), Dave Gilbert (7), Dean Jones (2), Craig McDermott (14), Geoff Marsh (6), Greg Matthews (14), Bruce Reid (6), Mike Veletta (0), Steve Waugh (5) and Tim Zoehrer (3) had exactly 58 Tests between them.

The Australian team that travelled to India in 1986, to play in cricket's second tied Test. Back row (left to right): Errol Alcott, Dean Jones, Mike Veletta, Greg Dyer, Tim Zoehrer, Steve Waugh, Greg Matthews, Geoff Marsh, Bob Simpson. Front: Craig McDermott, Greg Ritchie, Ray Bright, Allan Border, Alan Crompton (manager), David Boon, Dave Gilbert, Simon Davis, Bruce Reid.

The vice-captaincy wasn't really a surprise because I had been 'Spotty' Bright's deputy on the one-day tour of Sharjah that took place in between our tour of New Zealand and the Indian adventure. I felt great pride in this appointment, even though, while I had always dreamed of playing cricket for Australia, I had never thought about being vice-captain of my country. I saw my job as providing as much support to AB as possible, marshalling the troops, perhaps offering advice if asked.

India, in fact, the whole sub-continent, is so different — different cultures, different foods, different population density. The first time we drove into Bombay was a definite jolt to the system: the squalor of people's living conditions, watching people relieve themselves at the side of the road . . . but, once I came to terms with that initial shock, I have never, ever had a major problem touring in India. The hotels and accommodation are first-class, so the cricketers are always comfortable; right outside the doors, though, you find a third-world country that takes your breath away. And it's not the sights and smells that create this feeling, it's just the sheer amount of people.

The Indians are very keen on their cricket, extremely keen, and, for some reason, one which to this day I have never fathomed, they are especially keen on yours truly. Perhaps its my physique, or the way they perceive my character. Perhaps it's just the way I play the game. I have received letters from India, simply addressed to 'David Boon, Australia.' which arrive at our home in Launceston. These may be requests for autographs, for themselves or relatives; one man even named his son, who was born on a day when I scored a century, 'David Boon'.

There was one bloke whom I first struck in Bangalore during the opening game of the '86 tour. He had his hair cut like me and told me about catching the train hundreds of kilometres to meet me. No problem. We were staying at a little country motel and there he was — asleep on the mat outside my door. As I went to breakfast, he fell to his knees chanting, 'Boon, you are my god!'

At one level, its funny; on another, it's at least a little disturbing.

India's people have very gentle natures, but are also very proud. If you make a request of them, they don't want to be seen either as not being capable of completing the task or wanting to offend you by admitting they don't understand it. This can lead to interesting situations. For example, you could ask for black coffee and brown toast at breakfast and receive sweet white tea and buttered white toast. And once in Bombay, Marsh and Boon suffered extremely loose bowels and rang reception to ask for more toilet paper — what we received were two bowls of spaghetti and two milkshakes!

In India, the wickets are generally low and slow, but the grounds are very, very quick, suited to one-day cricket and the monumental innings achieved regularly on the sub-continent. I know the wicket on which we played the tied Test in Madras should have just had a white line painted down the middle — it made Bellerive Oval look like a raging seamer!

The first one-day international of the tour, against India at Jaipur, saw Boon and Marsh put on a then world record opening stand of 212 — Swamp made 104 off 103 balls, I finished with 111 from 121 balls. Australia made 3–250 from 47 overs, and we should have scored even more, too. This was in the days before penalties were introduced if you didn't bowl your 50 overs in time; Ravi Shastri was bowling left-arm spinners at one end and fielding at long-on at the other, and walking very, very gently in between. Not that it really mattered, anyway. Their opener, Kris Srikkanth blasted a century, Raman Lamba hit 64 and India finished with 3–251 in 41 overs!

It was on this tour that the value of Bob Simpson's influence and ideas first became apparent. Bob had decided to take on the coaching role full-time, and he introduced extra work for both the bowlers and batsmen — fitness work, burpees, skipping and star jumps, some of it in terrible temperatures. At Baroda, a few of us had completed a fitness test and it was so hot, it wasn't even funny. To cool down, the local fire department — urged on by Australian physiotherapist Errol Alcott — hosed us down. Which was, I guess, a bit over-indulgent in an area where water was in such short supply, but it was very much appreciated.

The first Test match was the game in Madras that became the second-ever tied Test in cricket history. When the match began, the temperature was 46 degrees, with 100 per cent humidity. We reckoned the moisture content stayed constant throughout the match, while the temperature dropped one degree a day, so it was 41 degrees at the end. It was the only place I've played, apart from Sri Lanka, where you could hear your boots squelching with dampness. So oppressive was it, that at the pre-Test team meeting we talked about the tactic of each new batsman looking to take the majority of the strike, so that the man who'd been in longer could have a bit of a rest.

That concept sounded good at the meeting, but it worked differently for different players. I managed to score a century on the opening day, my third in four Tests against India, but I was dismissed, for 122, about 15 minutes before the close of play. For much of the afternoon, I batted with Dean Jones; and at one point, late in the day, he thought that I was starting to look a bit off-colour. With our strategy in mind, he offered to take most of the strike. Then India took the new ball and, obviously, we had to share the load. However, I found that, after not having to concentrate full-on for about 30 minutes, against the new ball I really did begin to get dizzy. I couldn't focus properly.

My theory after that was I would always try to bat as normally as I could, because concentrating helped me. After I was dismissed, I had trouble keeping either food or drink down for any length of time — but that was nothing compared with what Jones had to overcome. Australia was 2–211 overnight, with Ray Bright in as nightwatchman. But the next morning, it was so hot again, that after Spotty fell for 30, he broke down crying, so distressed was he by the heat. And Ray's no sensitive new age guy. Throughout that first day, at the major breaks, I had showered and changed my clothes, always trying to cool down; I was using three or four pairs of gloves a session (again, this was part of Simmo's meticulous preparation; following his advice, I took more than 12 pairs of gloves on tour and several sets of creams). Once Deano was into his second day of batting, at every break we were getting him undressed, showering him, dressing him again and sending him back out to the wicket. Understandably, Dean started to suffer cramps and vomiting, the usual signs of heat exhaustion and dehydration, to the point of incontinence. When you put all that together, his effort in making 210 is even more amazing — he finished up in hospital on a drip to replace his fluid loss.

To this day, I believe that Deano has suffered long-term effects to his health because of that innings. Whenever he gets really tired and loses a lot of fluid, there is a definite change in his facial features. His eyes start to drop in his head, just as he looked at the end of that innings. But his achievement was one of such enormous character — an innings which no-one could or should forget.

AB also scored a hundred and Australia declared their innings closed at 7–574; India made 397 in reply, saved by Kapil Dev's 119, batting at No. 7 (although we thought we had him leg before wicket very early on). We then declared our second innings at 5–170, setting India 348 runs for victory, which at that time was a target no team had made to win a Test on the last day.

But the home team very nearly did. Sunil Gavaskar played just beautifully for 90 and the rest chipped in — Kris Srikkanth 39, Mohinder Armanath 51, Mohammad Azharuddin 42, Chandrakat Pandit 39 and Ravi Shastri 48 not out. The tension through that last day was, understandably, enormous. In the last hour — with the requisite 15 overs to be bowled — AB started to take his time setting fields. One of the umpires complained to Border, accusing him of wasting time. AB fired up and said we had to bowl the overs anyway and there was no problem with the light — so shut up! The umpire then threatened to send AB off.

Allan looked at me and said: 'He can't send me off, can he?'

'Don't know,' I replied, 'I don't think so.' I was just razor-like with my advice!

The excitement at the end, perhaps pandemonium would be a better word, was so extraordinary that I honestly thought Australia had won. The last wicket was that of Maninder Singh, lbw to Greg Matthews, with the second-last ball of the match. India all out 347, Matthews 5–146 from 39.5 overs, Bright 5–94 from 25 overs.

It took a while until the amazing realisation dawned that we had played a tied Test. I thought AB summed it up pretty well afterwards — considering the game was played in Madras, on that wicket, the target was very gettable, and Australia had tried to win the Test match. While it was fantastic to be part of history, it would have been an absolute tragedy if we'd been beaten.

The second Test was in Delhi, but play was impossible because of rain until after tea on the fourth day. Australia made 3–207 from 75 overs and India 3–107 from 26 overs.

The fifth one-day international in Ahmedabad landed me in the headlines after an unsightly, on-field wrangle with the two umpires, B.R. Keshava Murthy and Mukulgopal Mukherjee, both standing in their first games. The controversy arose when Madan Lal hit Dave Gilbert into the deep and Geoff Marsh took what appeared to be an excellent catch at backward square leg. Mukherjee, at square leg, indicated a fair catch, Keshava Murthy, at the bowler's end, gave Madan Lal out, and the batsman headed for the pavilion steps. Swamp thought he'd caught it, but then Ravi Shastri, the non-striker, intervened to tell the umpires that it wasn't a fair catch.

Mukherjee then withdrew his decision and Madan Lal returned. And then Madan Lal headed back to the pavilion when he became convinced we weren't pulling a swiftie. Roger Binny, the next batsman, was by this stage making his way to the wicket, but Keshava Murthy and Shastri decided this wasn't right, and went and brought Madan Lal back to the crease.

When the word 'cheat' was uttered, in relation to G.R. Marsh, I lost it — absolutely and completely — and got into a screaming match with both umpires. India went on to make 193, and during the break between innings, I stopped in at

Mixing in with the locals, Sharjah, 1986.

the umpires' room and apologised to both of them. And then I was dismissed for 5, caught Madan Lal!, as Australia was rolled for 141.

This was to be my only Test tour of India, though, of course, Australia did return for the World Cup in 1987, and leave in triumph. The three-match series in '86 ended in a nil-all draw, with the first game tied. Significantly, Kapil Dev, without doubt one of the world's greatest cricketers, didn't take a wicket through that whole Test series. When a phenomenal statistic like that occurs, maybe the pitches he was bowling on might have been just a little too flat.

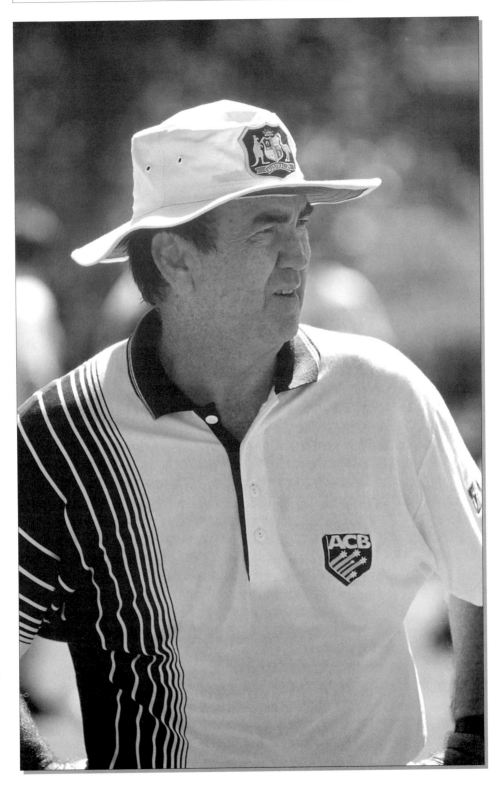

6: Simmo

I THINK I FIRST MET ROBERT BADDELEY SIMPSON IN 1986, WHEN HE WAS APPOINTED COACH OF THE AUSTRALIAN TEAM FOR THE SHORT TOUR OF NEW ZEALAND THAT FOLLOWED OUR DOMESTIC SUMMER. I CAN'T RECALL BEING INTRODUCED TO HIM BEFORE THAT, BUT THAT'S PROBABLY MY WAYWARD MEMORY, BECAUSE HE WAS THE COACH OF THE NSW SHEFFIELD SHIELD TEAM AT THE TIME, AND HAD BEEN SINCE THE START OF THE 1984–85 SEASON.

When I came into the Australian team in 1984, it boasted a manager and the usual support staff. However, after criticism of the team's performances and a degree of media conjecture, the ACB decided to appoint a coach. Today, as I look back on more than 12 seasons of Test cricket, I totally agree with that decision.

First-class cricket teams need coaches for a variety of reasons. In the case of that Australian team in 1986, Bob Simpson's appointment helped relieve the captain of many mundane, organisational duties. And, more importantly, 'Simmo' gave the Australian team a practice routine, one which paid dividends in both the short and long-term.

Simmo introduced a structure into the Australian team's preparations that is the basis of modern sports training — short and sharp sessions, or perhaps longer and softer, with constant variation in all drills.

In cricket, there are three major generalities — someone bowls the ball, someone hits the ball and someone fields, catches or throws the ball. Again, generally speaking, the more times you bowl, hit or catch the ball, the better you get at it — like a golfer hitting thousands of balls or a tennis player practising the same shot for hours. Simmo recognised the worth of this philosophy. He introduced fielding drills, seemingly thousands of them, many of them variations on old exercises. And the players began to look at the idea of practice in a new light. On the Ashes tour of '85, we had done all the work ourselves, directed by captain Allan Border and with help from former Test seamer Geoff Dymock, then the assistant team manager.

Simmo was different. Instead of just standing there and hitting balls into the air to catch, he made the work more specific, and introduced a competitive edge

Opposite: Bob Simpson, coach of the Australian cricket team from 1986 to 1996.

into almost every exercise — you against your team-mates, you against him. I remember a fielding drill in Hamilton, New Zealand, where Bob worked the players from left to right and then back again, covering a specific distance at speed. It suddenly clicked that we could perform a major portion of our fitness training while we were honing our cricket skills — that was a Simpson innovation.

Perhaps the greatest change Simpson implemented was the one of attitude.

On that tour to New Zealand, Bob raised the subject of Australia and its place in the cricket world. He began by saying: 'I think that we can be the best cricket team in the world.' From that point, he drove anyone who was involved with the team for any period of time to complete distraction with that line. But that was his goal. Of course, it was all a psychological ploy, one aimed at making us at least start to believe in ourselves as cricketers and as a team.

But, as the years progressed, so too did the truth of that statement: 'We are the best cricket team in the world.'

After the successes of the Ashes tours in 1989 and '93, the disappointments of the West Indies tour in 1991 and just missing out on winning the Frank Worrell Trophy at home in 1992–93, Australia finally won in the Caribbean in 1995.

Simmo and I shared a ride during the tickertape parade that followed our 1995 Caribbean tour.

It took almost 10 years, but Bob had achieved what he originally set out to do, in helping to make the Australian Test team highly successful again.

Simmo's other great strength was his ability to give many players purpose. It would be ridiculous to believe that his methods worked for everybody, but they did for me. He taught me that I should never, ever be satisfied with my performance. 'You should always think that you can do better, that you can improve, and that you never, ever achieve the ultimate,' he would tell me. The basis of this philosophy was to make sure that all the players kept working. 'If you had a great 12 months in cricket, or a great series, you should still keep working,' was his creed. And he was always on everybody's back about the cardinal sin of complacency, which was especially applicable to one David Clarence Boon.

I have always struggled with my subconscious. After a good summer, in my early years with Bob, I sometimes suffered from thinking: 'I don't need any runs today, I've made heaps in the last six months!' Simmo, however, was a master at recognising such faulty thinking and was forever badgering me about it.

He would talk to the players about their attitudes, whether they thought they were becoming satisfied, whether they thought they could improve in this or that area of their game. Of course, he drove everyone mad with it, but that was his job as coach. Simmo was as aware as anyone that playing Test cricket successfully is 90 per cent based on having the correct mental attitude and 10 per cent on natural ability.

As Australia began to succeed, to win more Test matches, win Test series and take the lead in the one-day game, there can be no doubt that Bob Simpson became an extremely important and influential person in Australian cricket. When he became both coach and selector, his power was enormous.

I'm not breaking anyone's trust in saying that I know that some of the young blokes were scared to talk to him about certain aspects of their game. Some people, within and outside the team, believed that, as soon as Simmo was appointed to that dual role, he became the keystone to the selection process. And he did stamp his authority on Australian cricket, in a lot of ways. However, I never experienced a problem with Simpson as coach and selector and I know of a number of other players who were able to work well within that structure.

It was, though, inevitable that some cricketers — being mistrustful and superstitious at the best of times anyway — saw that if they were struggling and confided in Bob, their self-doubts might actually count against them when it came to picking the team. But I always believed that Bob Simpson was honest and backed his players. If they were struggling, he would defend their performances, arguing that they were working hard, and, while they had been down, would bounce back if confidence was shown in them.

Others, it must be said, did not share my belief, and that was the double-edged sword of the dual role.

Bob Simpson possesses a very strong character. He was, and remains, an ambitious man; most successful people are. Simmo was in the job for Australian cricket, but along the way, he upset a few apple carts. Consequently, there are people who don't share my admiration for him, to the point that Bob could say something was white and his critics would say it was black.

I have a good relationship with Ian and Greg Chappell, like Bob, former Australian captains and legends of the game. But the Chappells and Simpson don't get along. That's life. Everybody's not going to like everybody else all the time. Ian has been a tremendous support to me throughout my career and is a good friend. So too, Greg, who is now my personal manager. But personalities and ideals clash.

Similarly, Simmo had some very public disagreements over the years with various sections of the media. My opinion was that these clashes weren't my business and I didn't see them as bothering the team in any shape or form. No-one likes to see themselves criticised in print and there have been instances where Australia as a team, or as individuals, have investigated whether what's been written has been libellous or not. For mine, any journalist can write what he or she wants so long as it's factually correct and not based on hearsay.

However, it was Bob's nature to take any criticism quite personally and I know that it stung him deeply when people attacked him for what he was trying to do with the team, or attacked the team itself. Again, unfortunately, most of these disagreements were based on personality conflicts. In a sense, I know how he feels. There are particular journalists whom I don't like and won't go out of my way to speak to; I daresay there's one or two who feel the same way about me.

As I see it, Bob's positive attributes definitely outweigh the minuses, but some people have chosen to focus entirely on the negative. He is certainly one of the great survivors. Obviously he was a very, very good player. He made 4869 runs in 62 Test matches at an average of 46.81, scoring 10 centuries and 27 half-centuries — ninth on Australia's all-time list of Australian run-getters.

There are stories that Bob had personality clashes with players in his teams. I'm not comparing the two, but wasn't the same accusation levelled at a man by the name of Sir Donald Bradman? And my long-time skipper and friend, Allan Border, also had trouble, early in his captaincy, communicating with some of the younger players who didn't know him that well. No-one's perfect.

Simmo moulded the Australian team during his time as coach, but in the mid–1990s the role of the coach has changed as the players' attitudes have changed. This is definitely a legacy of what Bob achieved during his time.

Simmo with his right-hand man, physiotherapist Errol Alcott.

The cricketers in the Australian squad now know the amount of work, the quality of work, that is expected at this level. That originated from Bob's approach to the coaching job, and was eventually passed on through Sheffield Shield ranks in all states.

This change in player attitudes was reflected in the way Simmo 'mellowed' as coach. When we defeated the West Indies by 10 wickets in three days in Barbados in 1995, he gave the entire touring party two days off — the time we would have been playing. It was beautiful, sitting on the beach, relaxing. But in situations such as this, we always knew that the next training session would have to be of a very high quality. And, if we played badly, or were beaten, we expected to be worked hard.

7: Rock Bottom

BEFORE THE 1986–87 BATTLE FOR THE ASHES IN AUSTRALIA, THE ENGLISHMEN WERE DESCRIBED BY SOME AS BEING UNABLE TO BAT, BOWL OR FIELD. HOWEVER, THAT CRITICISM, WHICH MAY HAVE LOOKED VALID DURING THE LEAD-UP GAMES TO THE FIRST TEST, IN BRISBANE, PROVED UNFOUNDED WHEN IT CAME TO THE MATCHES THAT MATTERED.

At the Gabba, Mike Gatting's team batted first, and made 456. Ian Botham's contribution was 138, and the faster Merv Hughes tried to bowl to 'Beefy', the further the ball went. I was fielding at mid-off and Merv, as he marched back to his bowling mark, asked me, 'Where am I supposed to bowl to him?'

'I think you've got to try to get it in there tight and full,' I suggested.

'That's what I'm trying to do,' was Merv's exasperated rejoinder. 'Any other smartarse comments?'

Sure enough, the next ball went for six. When we batted, we were dismissed for only 248. Graham Dilley, their opening bowler, took 5–68, while I was dismissed for 10, the start of what was to become one of my most difficult periods in the game, a stressful run of outs which would fully test my character, and the faith I had in my ability to compete at the top level.

Geoff Marsh made 108 in the second innings, his first century in Australia, but we were dismissed for 282 (of which I scored 14) and England went on to win easily, by seven wickets. More disappointments followed in Perth, where I made 2 and 0 in a drawn Test that otherwise featured a lot of runs, including four centuries — to England's Chris Broad, David Gower and Jack Richards, and Australia's Allan Border.

I found some respite in Adelaide, in the third Test, another high-scoring draw, where I managed to score 103 on the first day. I hit them pretty well, too, which made me think that perhaps my bad run was just a passing fad. But I was also in total confusion . . . how can you hit the ball so well when your mindset has you in the middle of a horror stretch? And the second innings only added to my mental turmoil; out, trapped lbw to Phil de Freitas, for another duck.

The fourth Test was at the MCG, and developed into an absolute shocker for Australia. We were dismissed for 141 and 194; in between England scored 349,

Opposite: A rare moment of glory during a disappointing summer . . . a century against England in Adelaide, third Test, 1986–87.

and I scored 7 and 8, my form so out of sorts that I can remember trying to let one go and nicking it anyway, the ball running off the face of the bat into the slips.

We had to go back to Perth for a one-day tournament involving four countries — the two Ashes combatants, plus the West Indies and Pakistan — that was staged to coincide with the America's Cup series being sailed off Fremantle. No more runs were forthcoming, however, and before we left Western Australia, I was told by the chairman of selectors, Lawrie Sawle, that I had been dropped from the team for the fifth Test in Sydney. 'The Colonel', as we call him, was terrific. He said that the selectors wanted me to go back to the Sheffield Shield and score some runs, and he stressed that they believed in me, and that there was definitely a place for me in the upper echelon of the game.

To make things more difficult, rather than being able to slink back to Tasmania and lick my considerable wounds, I, as vice-captain, had to lead the team out for the final dinner in Perth and make a speech, because Allan Border had been called home to Brisbane for personal reasons. Trying to mask my mental anguish was not easy. I had enjoyed almost three years within the Australian team and scored four centuries — now, all of a sudden, I wasn't playing any more.

I think now, looking back, it was purely a confidence problem I suffered from that summer. I was trying too hard, starting to look for technical defects which probably weren't there in the first place. Ian Chappell's advice to me was that I should go home and watch a video of myself playing well; he believed I had reached the stage where I wasn't hitting the ball, that I was 'scared' to hit it.

Despite what Lawrie Sawle had told me, I did start to doubt myself. I knew I had to try very hard to be positive and relax, but, first game back in the Shield, another huge setback occurred, against Queensland at the NTCA Ground in Launceston. Craig McDermott bowled me a ball which bounced irregularly, caught my glove and lobbed to Glenn Trimble in the gully.

Well, didn't I spit it! Made up a million excuses, blamed the world and everybody I could think of, except myself. All afternoon, I prowled the Tasmanian dressing-room and, after the day's play, apart from a chat to Craig, refused to speak to anyone. And it didn't finish there. I went home that night and went out into the backyard and boxed the fence! I took absolutely all of the skin off my knuckles.

Desperate for a solution, I dipped into renowned psychologist Rudi Webster's book, *Winning Ways*, and read some advice from Sir Garfield Sobers — 'All batsmen have rough trots, but it will never, ever finish until he realises that he is at rock bottom.' I had to steel myself to believe that, to say, 'This is it, I cannot play any worse.'

The next day, Tasmania followed on, McDermott bounced me first ball that I faced . . . and I hooked it for four.

It's amazing how quickly things can turn around. I finished the day 99 not out — the last over of the afternoon, 'Billy' bowled me six consecutive short balls with a bat-pad and two back. Obviously a maiden. That night he told me: 'There was no way you were going to get a hundred off my last over!' I was asked by the media how I felt about being 99 not out. 'After what I've been through, it's better than being out for nought,' was my answer.

I went on to make 172 and Tasmania batted out the match for a draw. Then, against Victoria in Melbourne, my form held. I made 69 and 49 at the MCG, and followed that with 80 in a McDonald's Cup game against Western Australia at the WACA. Our victory that day put us into the final of the domestic one-day competition. (Unfortunately, we would lose the final, to South Australia in Hobart. The SACAs hit a massive 6–325 — Glenn Bishop 106, Wayne Phillips 75 — and Tasmania could do no better than 9–239 in reply.)

Despite this flow of runs, my summer of discontent wasn't yet over. The next Shield match saw Tasmania play NSW at the old TCA Ground in Hobart. NSW won outright, and afterwards I was suspended for the next game against Western Australia because of an 'incident' that was alleged to have occurred after the first day's play, when Tasmania had batted and I had made 28.

The team was staying at the Black Buffalo Hotel in North Hobart and that night, Glenn Hughes, the brother of my first Australian captain, Kim, and I went to Tattersall's, a restaurant-bar, for a meal and few beers. I went back to the Black Buffalo and joined a school of blokes in the team who were playing poker. When Hughes came back, he joined in too and sat beside me. Glenn was always the Tasmanian 'clown', the butt of many practical jokes played upon him by myself and Peter Faulkner.

On the fence, playing for Tassie in Launceston, after being dropped from the Test team.

Having enjoyed an ale or two, Glenn kept exposing his cards to me and I was ribbing him, saying, 'There's no use betting on those!' He got excited, calling me a 'cheating so-and-so', and the game progressed; he kept showing his cards and I kept on at him, until he finally said, 'If you look at my cards again, I'm going to deck you.'

Next hand, he showed me his cards and I told him there was no use betting on a pair of threes. He slapped me on the shoulder, we started wrestling, and Glenn squealed like a pig. An ashtray on another table was knocked to the floor and broken.

The next day, Glenn and I were called before the Tasmanian coach Graeme Mansfield and the chairman of the Tasmanian Cricket Council, Jack Bennett. The broken ashtray was mentioned and a charge of excessive noise was laid — plus allegations that a heater had been ripped off the wall and a table broken.

I admitted and apologised for disturbing any other guests through noise and admitted to the broken ashtray, but emphatically denied the rest. Bennett then suspended Glenn and I for one match. I asked whether we would be given a chance to state our side of the story. They listened to us, but Bennett said that the suspension would stand. At the time, it was no secret that my relationship with Mansfield was less than productive.

I didn't need more national headlines after being dropped from the Australian Test team — let alone the double whammy of also being suspended as Tasmanian captain. Rumours ran rife and the affair even ended up on Tasmania's *7.30 Report* on ABC Television. When I got home, Pip said: 'You can't have been suspended for only that — you must have thumped someone!'

This affair was a very black mark on my reputation and I have never forgotten, nor forgiven, the people involved.

The suspension story hit the newspapers on February 24, the day the Australian team to play the one-day tournament in Sharjah was announced. Thankfully, I was included, and I'd like to think I justified the selectors' faith — despite losing all three of our games, to Pakistan, India and England, I was named man of the series after scoring three consecutive half-centuries: 71, 62 and 73. And, I believed, I had booked my place for the World Cup, which was to be played on the Indian sub-continent in October and November. I had only just turned 26 and, with my form returning, now firmly believed that Lawrie Sawle's parting words to me in Perth would bear fruit.

Unfortunately, by the time I departed for the '87 World Cup, I was no longer the Tasmanian captain, and had, in fact, even had discussions with cricket people from Victoria about a possible transfer interstate. This was the second time in my career, I'd contemplated such a move — the other had involved a move to Adelaide four years earlier.

The offer to play cricket for South Australia, complete with a full-time banking position, eventuated after Tasmania's first season of full-time Shield, 1982–83. At the end of that summer, Roger Woolley was selected in the Australian Test squad, after Rod Marsh pulled out of the short trip to Sri Lanka, and Stuart Saunders, Phil Blizzard and I went to Zimbabwe with the Australian Under–25 team, which was captained by Dirk Wellham.

After returning from Zimbabwe, Pip and I were married. That winter, we sold our house in Launceston, in Helen Street. Pip resigned from her nursing position in readiness for the move to Adelaide. A sticking point, though, came in relation to my job; I was supposed to sit a standard banking examination for a financial institution in Adelaide, which shall remain nameless. Yet, even though I was told that there was nothing wrong with my banking skills or experience, it was explained that if I wasn't playing cricket for South Australia, I wouldn't have a job!

That was when I returned home and sought the advice of Mark Atherton, the then general manager of the LBS Statewide Bank. He gave me a wonderful lesson in life. Mr Atherton told me: 'Whichever decision you make, we'll back you up. But whichever way you go, you can't say "what if" later on.'

My innings of 75 won me the man-of-the-match award in the 1987 World Cup final.

This philosophy became one of my cornerstones; being conservative by nature, I decided to stay in Tasmania. Instead of travelling to Adelaide, Pip and I bought a weatherboard house in Everest Place in Launceston, and I began work in the LBS Statewide's marketing department, where I still am, although the institution is now called the Trust Bank, some 13 years on.

Four years after I knocked back that move to South Australia, and while I was still more than a little peeved about that one-match suspension, Jack Bennett telephoned to discuss the captaincy of the Tasmanian team. He told me that some members of the administration were concerned that there was too much responsibility being placed on me as state skipper, at a time when I was trying to also handle my Australian commitments.

I told Mr Bennett that I really enjoyed my role as Tasmanian captain, had the respect of the players, and wanted to continue in the job. Jack said he'd discuss my point of view with the rest of the Board. However, only five minutes later, a friend rang me at the Tasmania Bank (the new, improved version of the LBS) and told me to listen to the next ABC Radio News bulletin.

Which I did, and heard that I had been replaced as captain by Brian Davison, my former skipper. That was at 11 o'clock; at 11.15am, Mr Bennett rang back and said that the board was going to stick by its original decision.

I muttered something like: 'Thanks, Jack, I've already heard the news on the ABC.' Then I hung up, extremely angry.

I stewed for a few days, before being contacted by my Test team-mate Dean Jones. Soon after, Pip and I flew to Melbourne, and I met with Ian Redpath and Ian 'Cocky' Chambers in the offices of the Victorian Cricket Association. The topics of conversation included playing Sheffield Shield cricket for Victoria and joining the Melbourne Cricket Club. Everything seemed so positive. To be honest, if they'd put a contract in front of me right there and then, I'd have signed it!

But it was Redpath, the former great Victorian and Australian batsman, who directed my decision-making process. He talked about the differences in real estate values in Tasmania and Victoria, the difficulties in uprooting family interstate and long-term employment opportunities outside, and after, cricket. He spoke of my being the sole Tasmanian in the Australian Test team and how important that was for me and my state. And slowly the way I was thinking began to change. I will always feel grateful for the way 'Redders' advised me, not as a recruiting officer for the VCA, but as someone looking out for my best interests. As soon as I walked away from that meeting, I knew I would stay in Tasmania.

To this day, I'm still angry about the way I was deposed as captain. In hindsight, perhaps being relieved of the pressures of leading my state, and being able to return to the Shield side and concentrate on my own form may have helped, in the long run, my development as a Test batsman. However, I will never forgive the people involved for the way the matter was handled. As the only Tasmanian playing for Australia, I deserved to be informed of the Tasmanian Cricket Council's decision before the media. If they wanted to speak to me about their reservations — even to dress me down about my captaincy in private — that was their right. But I deserved to be told first.

I was still an angry man when Australia left for the '87 World Cup. Although we were underdogs, we felt extremely comfortable with our preparation. Captain Border, coach Simpson and physiotherapist Alcott worked us hard, and in the process set about readying us for the physical and mental demands of playing top-class cricket in that part of the world.

With the memory of Dean Jones' dehydration during his epic double century 12 months earlier still extremely vivid, we did some testing in a practice game in Madras, prior to our opening game. Each of us was weighed nude before we batted and then again after we'd been dismissed, but before we'd enjoyed a post-innings drink. The results were startling, and proof that batting in Madras' heat and humidity is the easiest diet you could ever experience, especially for someone with a build like mine. I made 40-odd and lost four kilograms — they calculated that I'd had to drink five-and-a-half litres of water to replace the fluid that had poured out of me while I was wearing the pads and gloves in the middle.

There must be something about the concoction of India, Australia and Madras that makes such cricket so dramatic. Who'd have thought, so soon after cricket's second Tied Test, that our opening match of the 1987 World Cup would almost end in a tie as well? Australia made 270, anchored by a Geoff Marsh special of 110 from just 140 deliveries. Swamp and I put on 110 for the first wicket, before I was 'adjudged' lbw to Ravi Shastri for 49 — after the controversy that had occurred in Ahmedabad the previous year, and because I was sure I'd made contact with the ball, a few words were exchanged between Ravi and myself as I departed.

India's run chase got off to an enormous start, the first 100 coming in just 18.5 overs, but they ended up a run short, Steve Waugh bowling Maninder Singh with the fifth ball of the 50th and final scheduled over.

The significance of this win should never be underrated. The value in believing in ourselves, even during periods where the local batsmen were right on top and the home crowd was right behind them, was reinforced by the thrilling end result. There was a buzz in the team ranks, as we celebrated our victory in the dressing-room and later on back at our hotel, that would stay with us all the way to the final.

After comfortably beating Zimbabwe (no sure thing, remember how the Africans had humbled Australia in the 1983 World Cup?), we faced New Zealand in a match that was originally delayed a day because of persistent rain and then reduced to 30 overs per side because the wicket needed extra time to dry. Again, the match came down to the final over, where Steve Waugh was, once again, superb. Three wins from three matches, and I had my first World Cup man-of-the-match award, after hitting 87 from 87 balls, including five fours and two sixes. Those were the days!

We were playing good, confident cricket. The team was extremely tight-knit, individual goals had been shelved, or at least put to the side, in the overall desire for Australia to succeed. And the psychology of being underdogs, almost written off by the critics, was working — we genuinely believed we could win the tournament, if we played as well as we thought we could.

Under the format of the World Cup in 1987, which featured eight teams split for the preliminary games into two groups of four, we played everyone in our group once again. The result this time was two wins and a loss, to India in Delhi, who made 6–289 and bowled us out for 233. Because of an inferior run-rate to our hosts, we finished second in our group, meaning we had to play the winner

The '87 Cup is over . . . victory to Australia.

of the other, Pakistan, while India met England in their semi-final.

For the World Cup organisers, there were a number of possibilities, including the sub-continent's dream of the two host sides opposing one another in the final. Or perhaps even one of the traditional 'establishment' ruining that equation?

Or maybe even both?

Australia played the first semi-final against Pakistan in Lahore, again batting first after Allan Border won the toss. We posted 8–267, of which I top-scored with 65, Mike Veletta providing an important 48 at No. 5 and Steve Waugh slammed 32 off 26 balls — including 18 off the last over.

We bowled Pakistan out for 249, exactly 18 short, with Craig McDermott the star. He finished

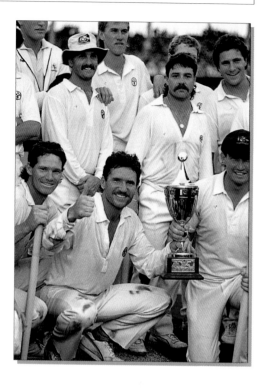

The moments after the Cup final were some of the most exciting of my career.

with 5–44, to take the man-of-the-match award. When the game finished, you could have heard a pin drop in Lahore. So distraught were the Pakistanis that only about three of their players, Abdul Qadir and a couple of young blokes, came out to the official presentation.

The World Cup final was played at Eden Gardens, Calcutta, and AB's luck held as he won yet another toss, to send Australia into bat first, our much-preferred option. We made 5–253, my form holding with 75 from 125 balls, but only after being stifled by Neil Foster's medium pace — his first eight overs yielded a miserly 16 runs. A key innings in this match that has often been forgotten was Veletta's brilliant 45 not out from just 31 deliveries, a major part of which came during a crucial partnership of 73 with his captain.

The key moment in England's reply was the fall of skipper Mike Gatting. Australia were in real trouble until 'Gatt' played what has become one-day cricket's most infamous reverse sweep to Border's first ball. The ball bobbed straight up in the air and was caught by our keeper, Greg Dyer. Gatting, who made 41 from 45 balls, copped a lot of flak for that one. In the end, England needed 75 from the last 10 overs and almost got there. But Steve Waugh took the crucial wicket of Allan Lamb, who'd made 45 from 55 balls, and by the final over, despite some last-minute heroics by Phil de Freitas, the Poms needed 17 to win off the last over. They only got nine of them.

To win the World Cup, after the Australian team had gone through such a lean run in the previous three years, was like a dreamtime for Australian cricket. We, understandably, became extremely fired up and that euphoria was still very apparent when we ventured to the official World Cup dinner that night, where we had a tremendous time. Of course, we were planning even more celebrations afterwards, but when we went back to our hotel we collapsed! We were just so exhausted, emotionally and physically, after such an intense campaign.

The 1987 World Cup proved to be a real turning point in the life of the Australian cricket team. We now knew we could beat the world, albeit only in the limited-overs game at this point, but it was the start. I truly believe that the Ashes successes of 1989 and '93, and even the victory over the West Indies in 1995 can be traced back to the confidence we acquired in 1987.

The massive boost we received was apparent from the very early days of the 1987–88 Australian season. No-one could have compared us to the team of 12 months before. First up, New Zealand came to Australia, and once again the great Richard Hadlee, the man who had taken 33 wickets in just three matches in the summer of 1985–86, was in the touring party. In Brisbane for the first Test, the wicket appeared a classic, juicy Gabba strip, one on which Hadlee would have loved to have first crack. So, Allan Border took the only available option — and won the toss! New Zealand were 9–181 after day one and all out 186 the next morning, with Craig McDermott grabbing that final wicket to take his bag to four, Merv Hughes finishing with three, Bruce Reid two. Then it was our turn.

Geoff Marsh and I put on 65 for the first wicket before 'Swamp' departed. Then I lost Dean Jones, Allan Border and Mike Veletta for not many more, but, in the meantime, I was enjoying technically my best-ever innings — 143 run out, from 255 balls in 342 minutes, including 15 boundaries.

I made Hadlee bowl to me, rather than me trying to bat to him. I felt so comfortable about letting balls go, knowing where I was in relation to my off-stump. Rather than dragging me gradually wider and wider, a tactic of which Hadlee was a past master, I forced him to bowl into my pads, and it was from balls bowled on this line that I scored plenty of runs. Late in the afternoon, Hadlee took the second new ball and my batting partner at the time, Steve Waugh, advised: 'C'mon, let's settle down again and have a look at this.' But it was my day — I hit the first ball through point for four.

I was finally dismissed late in the day, a major disappointment — not so much the fact that I got out (although you're always annoyed when it happens), but *when* I, and Steve, got out, just before stumps. These two setbacks meant we finished the day at 6–219 rather than just four wickets down. In the end, though, it made little difference, as we ended up winning the match by nine wickets, Boon, for 24, being the only wicket to fall in the Australian second innings of 1–97.

The second Test, in Adelaide, belonged to AB, who, in reply to New Zealand's 9 (declared) for 485, made 205 of Australia's total of 496. The game finished in a draw, after the Kiwis batted the final day, one of those stinking hot Adelaide days, out to 5.30pm. And, while our opponents were pushing and prodding their way to stumps, Swamp was driving AB, who'd spent just about the entire game in the middle, mad, by continually repeating, 'I've been living in the desert for a long, long time — but I've never been this effin' hot!' I think Allan was aware how hot it was!

Thus we went to Melbourne needing only a draw to win the series. At this point in my career, I had never been part of an Australian Test team that had won a series. AB had never captained his country to a Test series victory. And, on the final day, we needed 247 to win.

With only 41 runs needed from the final 21 overs, five wickets in hand, we were coasting. Enter Richard Hadlee. He had already dismissed Marsh and

The media, and my captain, look on after the presentations following the Bicentennial Test.

Border, and now he knocked over Peter Sleep, Greg Dyer and Tony Dodemaide. And John Bracewell chipped in, getting Mike Veletta in between Sleep and Dyer.

Which left the mighty batting duo of Craig McDermott and Mike Whitney at the wicket. There were 4.5 overs remaining; thoughts of winning the Test had gone out the window. Not that Billy's not a reasonable striker of the ball, but we all were aware that Michael Roy Whitney wasn't known for his batting classicism. However, we also knew that there are few people who can get more pumped up about their country than 'Big Roy'.

In the end, Whit's statistics say it all — 2 not out, 23 minutes and 18 balls — as he and Billy denied Hadlee one last victory on Australian soil. When he finally got back to the Australian dressing-room, Whit was still punching the air, and I copped one flush on the chin as I moved in to try to congratulate him. But I didn't care, it was such a relief to finally get a series win under the belt. Australia had finished at 9–230, although it should be noted that Hadlee won the man-of-the-match and man-of-the-series awards, after taking 18 wickets in three Tests.

It was turning into a very exciting and rewarding summer for me. After the Tests, Australia defeated New Zealand and Sri Lanka in the World Series Cup, at the end of which I was named the Benson & Hedges International Cricketer of the Year, beating Sri Lanka's Aravinda de Silva by just one point. Strangely, I was only the third Australian to win this prestigious award, which had been running since 1979–80, following in the footsteps of the Western Australia duo of Dennis Lillee and Bruce Yardley.

At the end of January, 1988, Australia and England met at the Sydney Cricket Ground in a Test match that had been scheduled as cricket's contribution to Australia's bicentennial celebrations. From a personal view, this was a very, very important match for me. In 1985, the return from my first tour of England, in terms of Test runs, had been poor. That was followed by a very ordinary season against the Old Enemy in 1986–87, which culminated, of course, in my being dropped from the Australian team.

Since that setback in '86–87, I had done a lot of work on facing spinners, which I had identified as being a significant weakness in my game. I think my success in the World Cup reflected the work I'd put in. I batted in the nets against anyone who would bowl at me, and often resorted to the bowling machine. All the time I was building my confidence, and learning how to use my feet more; no longer would I be allowing myself to get bogged down. The main problem was not that I couldn't play good spin bowlers, but that I struggled to get off strike when I faced them, which gave them more time to work on me.

Opposite: Attacking the English off-spinners, Bicentennial Test, 1988.

Technically, I was okay. I just needed to be more positive and more adaptable.

I practised getting off strike by looking for one around the corner to fine leg, rather than just padding the ball away. I wanted to be the one who was dictating terms, not them.

However, despite all that, and despite the importance of the game to Australia, it was England who seized the upper hand, by scoring 425 in their first innings, with opener Chris Broad, who'd hit three hundreds in a row in 1986–87, making 139. In reply, we could manage only 214, of which I contributed 12, caught behind by Bruce French off Neil Foster.

Following on, we were left with a day and a half to save the match, and by stumps there were signs of a revival. Swamp, on 41, and I (54) were 0–101.

It's history now that Australia batted out the last day and I finished with an unbeaten 184, out of 3–328. This was the longest I have ever stayed at the crease in a Test — 492 minutes of labouring on a classic, last-day Sydney wicket, on a pitch that was turning, but reasonably slowly, against two excellent off-spinners in John Emburey and Eddie Hemmings. One example of the positive attitude I successfully employed during this innings was the way, as often as I could, I hit Emburey over the top of mid-on, until he'd put a fieldsman back. Then I'd push ones into the gap I'd created until the field was brought in. Then I'd go over the top again. Sometimes, though, I might have gone a bit far. At one stage, I charged Hemmings, Eddie but held the ball back and, typically for him with a laugh, threatened to throw the stumps down.

This was a very important day in my cricketing life. Afterwards, I was named man of the match. However, what was much more important for me was the confidence the innings gave me — that meant much more than whatever my final score was, or any trophies I might have picked up. That was why, when the Test was called off, half an hour early, at 5.30pm, I didn't ask for the extra 30 minutes so I could try to reach 200. My task, and Australia's objective, had been completed — we'd saved the Test — at the end of the day nothing else mattered.

However, I couldn't help thinking that just 12 months before, I was at home in Launceston, out of the Test team. In the year since I'd been to Sharjah and been named man of the series, to the World Cup where I'd won the man-of-the-match in the final, played in a winning series against New Zealand, been part of a World Series Cup triumph, been named International Cricketer of the Year, and then scored 184 not out in the Bicentennial Test against England!

The summer continued on, with a 'Bicentennial' one-dayer against England, in which Geoff Marsh was man of the match and Australia won by 22 runs, and then Sri Lanka's first-ever Test match on Australian soil, in Perth. The thing I remember about that game was the recently relaid pitch — there were huge cracks in the strip, so much so that when Merv Hughes bowled to their captain,

Ranjan Madugalle, the ball hit a crack a metre outside leg stump and came back, almost took his head off, and was caught by Steve Waugh in the slips! Australia won the game by a massive innings and 108 runs.

In the Sheffield Shield that summer, Tasmania boasted one D.K. Lillee in their team. Queensland also fielded a big name, Ian Terence Botham, who was playing what would prove to be his only summer of Australian domestic first-class cricket.

Lillee had started his season in spectacular fashion at the Devonport Oval against South Australia, claiming Andrew Hilditch, caught Richard Soule, for a first ball duck. Against Queensland, we batted first and I made 108 in a total of 481. By the end of the second day, Queensland were 5–200, but Lillee had strained his hamstring and was out of the remainder of the match.

The Maroons declared their first innings at 5–383, Glenn Trimble making 138 not out. Tasmania then closed their second innings at 8–290, of which I made 143, to become the first man to score centuries in both innings of a Shield match for Tasmania. And then Tasmania bowled Queensland out for 314, to win by 94 runs.

The hero was a paceman called Claye Young, who took 6–120 from 23.5 overs . . . costly but effective! After 18 overs, Claye had 1–95, but he proceeded to capture 5–25 in an amazing 30-ball period, including the prized wicket of Allan Border for the second time in the match. This, remarkably, was Tasmania's first victory in 45 first-class matches. And we followed it up with another victory over the Maroons, in a McDonald's Cup encounter that followed the Shield game. In that game I scored 73, out of 8–150 (Queensland were all out for 140).

This was a very big weekend, for Tasmania and myself. Twelve months before, I couldn't have dreamed that life could be this good.

8: Mr Reliable

GEOFF MARSH WAS DEFINITELY UNDER-RATED AS AN AUSTRALIAN
PLAYER. HIS FIGURES MIGHT NOT LOOK THAT FLASH — HE AVERAGED 33
AT TEST LEVEL (39 IN THE ONE-DAY GAME) — BUT HIS VALUE WITHIN
THE TEAM WAS NEVER LOST ON HIS GRATEFUL TEAM-MATES. LOOK AT
THE PARTNERSHIPS WHICH EVOLVED AROUND HIM. HE MIGHT HAVE ONLY
SCORED 30, BUT SOMEONE ELSE WAS GETTING 60 OR 70 AT THE OTHER
END. FOR HIM, THE PARTNERSHIP WAS THE ULTIMATE GOAL AND THAT'S
THE WAY HE PLAYED THROUGHOUT HIS ENTIRE CAREER.

He used to get upset by media comment about his one-day batting, but say nothing publicly because this criticism ignored the Australian game-plan and his role in it. We wanted him to bat through the innings, to be the foundation on which a big score was based. And just about every time Geoff batted through an innings, Australia made 250-plus and won.

He was, and remains, very intense about his cricket. When Geoff Marsh and I played Test cricket together, we shared the same objectives. We both wanted to be part of the resurrection of Australian cricket, and do the best we could to help our team realise that goal. We usually roomed together, and on more than one occasion I woke to find Geoffrey Robert, nude but for his bat, gloves and thigh pad, practising strokes in front of a mirror. Maybe this approach was taking attention to detail a bit too far (perhaps it was paranoia), but if it did one thing it showed just how much Swamp wanted to perform for his country.

Geoff was there for me at the end of my career, sharing time with me during the afternoon before I told the Australian management and players of my decision. My only regret is that he missed my farewell party on the last night of the Adelaide Test match — he'd been forced to return to Perth for business. But I know that if he could have been there, he would have.

Never once has he let me down.

Geoff was appointed coach of the Australian cricket team after the World Cup in 1996. I believe he has all the right characteristics to be a good coach. And, because Geoff played so much under his predecessor on the role, Bob Simpson, inevitably many of his concepts will be similar to Bob's — why shouldn't they be

Geoff Marsh, at the Gabba, 1990–91.

when they were successful? But he will also have different ideas from Bob, which, likewise, will not be a bad thing; change can be beneficial to any organisation.

Of course, Bob Simpson's reign extended over a long period — a bit more than 10 years — and, as I've stated earlier, I think his value to Australian cricket was enormous. Nowadays, however, I don't think any coach will be retained for that long, simply because of the sheer amount of cricket which is played today. Geoff may yet prove me wrong, but I see four or five years being the maximum for any individual. Few coaches in the Australian Football League stay at the one club for any great length of time. It's difficult, year after year, to maintain your impact with the same group of players, within the same organisation. And the Australian cricket team can certainly be viewed upon as being one 'club' — perhaps the most exclusive club in the country.

The role of the coach of the Australian cricket team has changed in the past few years. When Simmo accepted the position, Australia was a regular whipping boy for the other Test-playing nations; there was nothing systematic about the team's preparation and they possessed limited ambition. Geoff, on the other hand, has inherited a team at the top of the cricketing world, boasting all the qualities that were once lacking. Because of this, one could be forgiven for saying that Swamp is therefore either going to have a very easy job or be on a hiding to nothing. But they'd be wrong. The guys currently playing for Australia will want to stay at the top and continue to improve.

Geoff's basic philosophy is: 'The captain runs the ship.' Consequently, I expect his relationship with Australian captain, Mark Taylor, to be outstanding. Geoff's a person who will work behind the scenes as coach and, from there, take great satisfaction in the team's achievements. But Swamp has always been a big one for full-on training, so the boys won't find any difference between him and Simmo in that department.

As for setting an example, perhaps even being the disciplinarian when required, Geoff will benefit from having been out of the game at Test level for a few seasons. Of the current team members, Marsh has had extended experience with only Ian Healy, Steve Waugh and Mark Taylor — Australia's three most senior players. All other players will know him, by reputation alone or perhaps in his role as Australian selector in 1995–96, but he has had the necessary period away from the team to come in and take control. However, while there has been a gap between his retirement as a player and appointment as coach, it has not been long enough for him to lose a working knowledge of how the Australian team operates, and what the players' needs are. I'm sure he'll be able to work with the players to alleviate the day-to-day distractions that can interrupt team preparation.

Swamp's attitude to the game of cricket will be of major assistance to the younger players and those coming into the team. He is a pure, hard worker, who takes absolutely nothing for granted. Like me, he wasn't an overly-gifted cricketer, but he played within his own limitations and, for mine, did so superbly. Perhaps his biggest attribute was that the team always came first, over and above any personal ambitions or milestones. That's what he'll be looking for within the Australian team — to create a team environment, rather than a group of individuals.

I was lucky enough to be in Perth when his appointment was announced, and joined him and his family for a short celebration. Typically, he said to me: 'Everyone says Australia is the best cricket team in the world. My perception is that you're the best team in the world when you've controlled world cricket for a decade.' And I can just hear him saying that to the Australian players!

Geoff would be the first to admit, as I would of myself, that he doesn't possess intricate knowledge of every bowling style. However, as Rod Marsh does for the Australian Cricket Academy in Adelaide, he'll be able to call on many former Test players to assist him with their differing skills. I know that if I ever become a coach — and I do harbour that ambition — I would certainly look for such assistance. Sure, I have ideas about most aspects of cricket, but I'd never be too proud to utilise experts in their fields.

For batsmen and the mental approach to cricket, Geoff will be extremely qualified to offer technical advice. Batsmen who lose confidence inevitably try to compensate in some way, and that's when something detrimental to their game creeps in. Conversely, over-confidence can lead to laziness and other problems which can muddle your technique. Swamp, like Simmo, will be very good at recognising such situations.

The night before Geoff's appointment was announced, I spoke at a sporting club function in Western Australia and was asked who I thought would be the next Australian coach. I spoke about various candidates who had been mentioned in the media and then suggested that Geoffrey Robert Marsh (a 'dark horse' at that point) would make a wonderful choice.

Little did I know at the time that he was a dead cert! The people who organised that function rang me the next day and had a genial go at me for leading them on. Swamp, though, had played his cards very, very tight to his chest; he hadn't even let his old mate in on his secret. The ACB should at least be happy with his ability to keep a secret, while everyone involved in the Australian cricket team will take great comfort from the knowledge that if you tell Geoff something that's between you and him — that's the way it'll stay.

And I should add that before I left Perth, I told Swamp to make sure he does a good job — because I want to inherit a good team like he has!

9: Taking a
Stand

DURING HIS ADDRESS TO THE TEAM AT A PRE-TOUR CAMP BEFORE OUR
1988 JOURNEY TO PAKISTAN, THE THEN CHAIRMAN OF THE AUSTRALIAN
CRICKET BOARD, MALCOLM GRAY, SPOKE ABOUT THE FACT THAT
CONDITIONS WOULD BE HARSH, THAT UMPIRING DECISIONS, OR LACK OF
THEM, WOULD BE FRUSTRATING AND IT WAS UP TO US TO ACCEPT THEM.
WHAT HE SAID CONCURRED VERY MUCH WITH HOW I FEEL ABOUT SUCH
THINGS; WHEN TOURING OVERSEAS, YOU'RE REPRESENTING YOUR COUNTRY,
SO YOU HAVE TO BE DIPLOMATIC, SPORTSMANLIKE . . . UP TO A POINT.

No-one, apart from those who were on that 1988 tour and saw and experienced what we did, knew what we went through in the early days of that trip. Twelve months earlier, England's captain Mike Gatting had been involved in a very public on-field clash with an umpire called Shakoor Rana. By the time the first Test, in Karachi, had been completed, we knew how Mike must have felt.

The tour was short, but it was most certainly eventful, especially during, and in the days after, the controversial first Test. There was a stage where it seemed the entire trip was about to be cancelled.

We played two drawn games before Karachi — at Lahore, against a Pakistan Cricket Board's Patron's XI, and at Quetta, against a team known as the Baluchistan Governor's XI. Both matches were played on flat decks which were typical of wickets on the sub-continent. Which was in direct contrast to what awaited us in Karachi — a mosaic jigsaw puzzle of a wicket that was breaking up even before the first ball of the Test was to be bowled.

Imran Khan, Pakistan's great fast-bowling all-rounder and captain, was not playing, in protest at the decision to stage the tour at the hottest time of the Pakistani year. So the home team was relying on their trio of excellent spinners, the brilliant leggie, Abdul Qadir, the offie, Tauseef Ahmed, and the veteran left-armer Iqbal Qasim. Pakistan batted first and declared at 9–469, of which Javed Miandad made 211. Javed batted magnificently, but we believed that he was in

Opposite: Leaving the SCG at stumps on day two of the fourth Test against the Windies, 1988–89.

the right position to be given out leg before wicket at least three or four times. Maybe even more. As one AAP report said, the new Pakistan captain possessed 'remarkable immunity to cricket's most virulent virus on the subcontinent — the lbw'.

Then it was our turn. The Pakistani opening 'attack' of Aamir Malik and opening bat Mudassar Nazar trundled down a few overs, and then the spinners were on. We were out for 165, after being 6–64 at one stage, and Iqbal Qasim, who used the conditions superbly, finished with the outrageous figures of 5–35 from 39 overs, including 24 maidens. After we followed on, Mudassar and Aamir bowled five overs between them, and we crashed to be all out for 116, to lose the match by an innings and plenty.

Javed Miandad, always tough on his own turf.

During the Test, on the third day as our first innings disintegrated, Bob Simpson and Col Egar lodged a protest with the Pakistan Board about the standard of the pitch and the quality of the umpiring. Later in the day, they called a press conference, where again they were highly critical of what was going on. After the game, AB described the pitch as 'the worst he'd ever seen', and revealed that going home was definitely an option being considered. 'It would seem like sour grapes after losing the Test,' he conceded. 'But ultimately somebody has to take a stand.'

It seemed, back in Australia, that people recognised the first part of Allan's statement — the bit about the 'sour grapes' — but didn't care about the second part, which we considered to be very, very, appropriate. The controversy blew up in Australia, fuelled by people who hadn't seen a ball bowled during the Test but were following the cricket via the media. We were told from afar to take it on the chin; what was required was the 'stiff upper lip' approach.

With the players under pressure on tour and from home, the man who filled the breach for us was Col Egar, who was in the unenviable position of being a member of the ACB, and thus responsible for maintaining relations with the

Pakistan Board. He was also, as the Australian team manager, a key figure in ensuring that the team was able to perform to the best of our ability. In such trying circumstances, I thought 'C.Egar' was magnificent. Basically, he put the politics to one side and backed the players. We needed that, to have someone in authority recognise we had a case. He told the Board back home about the situation and what occurred in the first Test, regarding the wicket preparation and umpiring decisions.

What had led to raising the possibility of coming home was pretty straightforward. You don't mind losing a Test fair and square; you may get very annoyed with yourself, but that's cricket. But we believed that there were too many outside influences coming to bear on the Karachi game. To quote Col: 'We were genuine in our goodwill in coming to this country and our guys now want to know when the real cricket starts.'

In the end, the Australian team decided that to protect the reputation of cricket, we would continue the tour, but we wanted a public statement to be made. Which was:

The Australian cricket team is aware of its responsibilities to the game and to future generations of international cricketers. For that reason, we will fulfil our commitments on the tour as agreed by the cricket boards of Australia and Pakistan. We are not alone in our dissatisfaction with the circumstances which surround Test cricket in Pakistan. Other visiting teams have drawn attention to pitches and umpiring decision which are clearly unsatisfactory and contrary to the spirit of the game. The situation is unacceptable and damaging to international cricket, yet nothing seems to be done.

We appeal to the Pakistan Board and the International Cricket Conference to take a long and honest look at the situation confronting visiting teams, for the sake of their own reputations as well as that of the players whose careers are put at risk. We hope the rest of the tour will be completed as a fair contest between international cricketers and we will be doing our utmost to play and win matches in the proper spirit.

In hindsight, perhaps Australia's stand in Pakistan in '88 was another catalyst towards the advent of neutral umpires in Test cricket. I do know that there was a great deal of public condemnation of the Australian team back home, so it was no surprise when reporter Mike Munro and a crew from *60 Minutes* arrived in Pakistan. Journalists have a job to do, sure, and there was certainly a crackerjack story on the boil, but in this situation, I believe things went way too far.

A personal attack was launched against Bob Simpson, while none of us appreciated our hotel doors being knocked on by people looking for provocative comments. I wondered what had happened to loyalty and national pride — and belief in the Australian cricket team. We weren't trying to disgrace the country we represented, but some people tried to give the impression that was our intention.

We hadn't expected the wicket in Karachi to suit Bruce Reid and the rest of the Australian attack, but what we got was a long way from an adequate Test-match track. But that wasn't taken into consideration by countrymen who tried to portray us as whingeing Australians incapable of accepting defeat. Interestingly, we did receive a lot of support from Pakistani cricket fans, who believed we had been dealt a rough hand. That, though, was never reported back home.

The pitches for the final two Tests were in stark contrast to Karachi. Just as we'd expected, they were flat. Both those matches, in Faisalabad and Lahore ended in draws, but we almost won the third Test, two more wickets on the final day (when we were without an injured Bruce Reid) and we would have had an unexpected victory. I took three catches in that third Test, to complete an excellent series for me — although not with the bat, where I made only 117 runs at 19.50. I finished the Tests with 10 catches, four ahead of our new wicketkeeper, a young Queenslander by the name of Ian Healy.

This was also the one and only international tour for the then-Victorian batsman, Jamie Siddons, who is now, of course, the captain of South Australia and still one of the best Sheffield Shield players in the country. In between the second and third Tests, we went to a barbecue in Peshawar and everyone had the same — a few beers and some food. Jamie was in line for a Test spot, but needed a good performance in the three-day game against the North-West Frontier Province Governor's XI, which was due to begin the next morning.

Sadly, by then, Jamie was as sick as I have ever seen anyone in my life. Unfortunately, it was both ends at the same time! Whenever the poor bloke tried to eat or drink anything, the same result. In a few days, he'd lost a phenomenal amount of weight, but still couldn't hold anything down.

By the time we reached Lahore for the third Test, he was just about back on track. The team was staying across the road from the Hilton complex, which contained several top-class restaurants, so, not having eaten for so long, Jamie tried his luck with a huge stack of lasagne. But by the following morning, his internal system was completely shot again. Poor Jamie Siddons did play the last one-day game of the tour, and made 32, but from all reports, it took him some 18 months before he was really fully-fit again.

The only positive of Jamie's ill-health was that he didn't have to face the West Indies latest pace sensation in the Test series played in Australia in 1988–89. Happiness and joy are not the first adjectives which spring to mind when one thinks of facing Curtly Ambrose. The first time I faced the big fella was in the first Test of that series, in Brisbane. It was an encounter with a slightly humorous tale . . . well, humorous if you're prone to be sick and twisted like G.R. Marsh.

You see, the night before the Test match, we had held our usual team meeting during which Swamp made one of his rare, but always heart-felt, speeches.

'We know we're going to get hit,' he told us, 'but when we do, we can't let them know that we're hurt. We've got to tough it out.'

The next morning, facing Ambrose, as I said, for the first time, I discovered that the lanky Antiguan was very adept at bowling into your body. With Gus Logie at bat-pad, Roger Harper at short fine leg, maybe slightly wider than normal, and Jeff Dujon keeping wickets, there were three options — duck if you could, get caught if you nicked it or popped one up ... or get hit. Within minutes, I copped one high on the ribcage, under the left armpit;

A triumphant Dean Jones in Adelaide, scoring 216 against the West Indies.

I wasn't driven back onto my stumps, but it did knock all the air out of my lungs.

I was bent over, gasping for air, trying not to appear 'hurt'. I remembered what my vice-captain and opening partner had told the meeting the previous night. Finally, I looked up to see my great friend coming down the wicket, wearing a rather misplaced grin.

'What?!' I hissed.

'It's all right, Boonie,' Swamp answered, 'you can give it a little rub if you want!'

I was dismissed for 10, lbw to Malcolm Marshall, but it was Ambrose who went on to be man of the match, as the Windies won by nine wickets. In the second Test, in Perth, the barrage continued, and when Swamp and I went into bat on the second day, after our opponents had totalled 449, of which the great Vivian Richards smashed 146, we were hit time and again. At lunch, I went to Allan Border and told him that survival alone wasn't going to work, that my best option was to bat normally. AB said he'd back me, so, while I didn't come out swinging, I did look to hook and cut whenever the ball was there to be hit. I finished with 80, of Australia's 8 (declared) for 395, third top scorer behind

Graeme Wood (111) and Steve Waugh (91, his second consecutive ninety), who put on 200 exactly.

AB's declaration came after Geoff Lawson had his jaw broken by an Ambrose delivery. Understandably, the Australian camp was pretty fired up after seeing 'Henry' felled and badly injured, and when Merv Hughes trapped Gordon Greenidge lbw, first ball of the Windies' second innings, emotions bubbled over. Certainly, Merv's did, because he gave Gordon extremely detailed instructions about where to find the showers.

When play finished, Merv, realising that he had over-reacted, went into the West Indies' dressing-room, where I was already in conversation with Jeff Dujon. As Hughes approached Greenidge, Dujon whispered: 'This will be very interesting.' Merv apologised to Gordon for what he'd said, saying that he'd been pumped up by the situation and offered him a beer. Greenidge replied brusquely: 'You don't mean that.' And then he went and sat in the team bus until the West Indies were ready to return to their hotel.

Although Merv hadn't realised it at the time, Greenidge's wicket was the third part of a very unusual hat-trick. With the last ball of his 36th over in the West Indies first innings, Merv had dismissed Ambrose, caught behind, With the first ball of his 37th over, he had Patrick Patterson caught by Tony Dodemaide at cover point. And then Greenidge, a hat-trick spread over three overs. It was the first Test hat-trick by an Australian in more than 30 years, and only the seventh ever by an Australian in Test cricket. Remarkably, Courtney Walsh had done something similar in Brisbane only two weeks before, taking the last wicket of Australia's first innings, and then wickets with his first two balls of his first spell in our second dig.

Despite Merv's heroics — he finished with 13 wickets for the match and eight in the second innings, a truly magnificent effort with Lawson out of the attack — we lost again, by 169 runs. And the third Test in Melbourne was no better; Ambrose won another man-of-the-match award, to take his tally for the series to 20 wickets, as we crashed to an emphatic 285-runs loss. The problem was . . . well, actually . . . there were four problems: Ambrose, Walsh, Patterson and Malcolm Marshall.

The fourth match of the series was at the SCG and marked my return to the No. 3 batting position for Australia, following the selection of NSW left-hander Mark Taylor for his first Test. Before the game, AB came to me and said of my move in the order: 'It's totally up to you.' Although 'Tubby' had always opened for the Blues, Allan said that if I wanted to continue to open with Geoff, that would be okay.

There was no fuss. Both AB and I knew that I was probably better-suited than Mark to playing at three, having batted there before. And for team balance there was no argument — what was best for the team was my objective. Similarly with Swamp, our whole cricketing philosophy was team-first — and, one must admit now, Mark Taylor has turned out to be a more than useful opener!

West Indies batted first in Sydney and were dismissed for 224 on day one, after reaching 1–144; Terry Alderman and Hughes bowled only 20 overs between them before our spin duo of Peter Taylor and Trevor Hohns were introduced. But the man who did the damage was that bloke, Allan Border, who eventually brought himself on and finished with 7–46 from 26 overs — Richie Richardson, Carl Hooper, Viv Richards (caught Boon), Gus Logie, Jeff Dujon, Roger Harper and Malcolm Marshall in the kitbag! AB always under-rated himself dreadfully as a bowler; he wasn't the world's greatest turner of a ball, but he could definitely land them. Even if there was a lot of ducking and weaving by the bat-pad!

If I had any reservations about the move to No. 3, they were gone by the end of the second day. Australia at stumps were 3–200, and I was 110 not out. I ended up with 149 and Australia made 401 (Border 75 and Steve Waugh 55), after which the Windies were bowled out in their second innings for 256. AB, could you believe it, took another four wickets (he'd bowled exactly two overs in the series before this match!) and we went on to a decisive seven-wicket victory. Of course, Allan was man of the match, for an achievement he takes great delight in recounting ball by ball, every time I see him.

And then to Adelaide, where the first day, and the second, belonged to Dean Jones. He made 131 of 3–283 when the first three sessions were complete and went on to post 216 of a first innings total of 515. Then we bowled the West Indies out for 369, Mike Whitney celebrating figures of 7–89, and, though the match ended in a draw, we enjoyed the experience of declaring our second innings. By this time, the Australian team's psyche was far more positive than it had been in the early Tests, when Ambrose and company had bounced us back onto our heels. In our own minds we were now a confident team, and although not everyone outside the camp had observed this, we knew it, and were eagerly looking forward to travelling to England, to try to get those Ashes back.

THE BEST FAST MAN

It is only since retiring from international cricket that I have really put my mind around who actually was the best fast bowler I have ever faced.

Malcolm Marshall was.

There are a huge number of pacemen who earned my enormous respect; men such as Sir Richard Hadlee, who made you play at nine out of 10 balls, Michael Holding and Curtly Ambrose, the Pakistani duo of Wasim Akram and Waqar Younis, and South Africa's Allan Donald — a group who could work you out or just blast you out, depending on their frame of mind.

But Malcolm Marshall was just that little bit better. He had one of the best brains of any bowler I faced (which he coupled with a wicked sense of humour), and could bowl that quick, and swing it both ways. So, inevitably, you found yourself in trouble more often than not. His bouncer was a 'skidder', rather than one which steepled, so, nine times out of 10, it was on target.

And, to complete the package, he batted as high as No. 6 for the West Indies and was always more than just a late-order batsman with a good eye.

In hindsight, the story from my first Test match, when Malcolm offered to come around the wicket and kill me, was an example of his wit. It was just him taking the mickey out of someone making their debut, But at the time, from where I was quivering, there was nothing even remotely funny in it.

We laugh about it now, and bemoan how serious things have become. Again, the one hobby-horse I cannot get off when I look back over a decade and more of Test cricket: here is another example of the friendships which I was fortunate enough to make with so many players from so many countries. Now, however, the supposed 'professionalism' of the game interferes with the former tradition of both teams getting together — in one or the other dressing-room — for a beer, or a soft drink or just a chat about the greatest game in the world. I look at my friendships with cricketers such as Malcolm, Michael Holding and Jeff Dujon from the West Indies, Allan Lamb and Ian Botham from England — the list is endless — and treasure them all. You might have tried to dismember one another on the pitch, but afterwards was a time for friendship, reflection, and the one thing I think the game's youngsters now miss out on — education.

As I have said, I am somewhat old-fashioned in that I believe that what is said or happens on the field in the heat of the moment should be left there . . . whatever the situation. Because of this, I appreciated that Malcolm was one cricketer who always said 'hello' before and after play. In 1995, I was invited to England to play for a World XI against Warwickshire, in a commemorative game. Malcolm was also playing, for the side I was in, and it was marvellous to catch up again, to recall days gone by. Then he walked out onto the ground and took a wicket with the first ball he bowled. At that stage, Malcolm was playing league cricket in England; his days as a first-class cricketer were behind him.

At his peak, Malcolm was very effective at exerting relentless pressure through an immaculate line and length. It was such a 'contest' to play against him, so I was always very annoyed to be dismissed by him. Mind you, he did that regularly. On one of these occasions, I became Malcolm's 300th Test wicket — leg before wicket at the Melbourne Cricket Ground in 1988–89. It was a very dubious call, and he acknowledged this afterwards, but, as it was already in the scorebook, he didn't knock it back. Of course, I wasn't happy at all, but, looking back, somehow, perhaps very remotely, I am pleased to have been such a significant milestone in the cricket career of such a great bowler.

Malcolm Marshall's 300th Test wicket — Boon, leg before wicket.

10: Allan Border

ALLAN BORDER WAS THE CAPTAIN OF THE AUSTRALIAN CRICKET TEAM FOR 88 OF MY 107 TEST MATCHES. KIM HUGHES, THE WESTERN AUSTRALIAN BATSMAN, WAS MY SKIPPER FOR MY FIRST TEST, IN BRISBANE IN 1984. BUT HUGHES STOOD DOWN AT THE END OF THAT MATCH, ANOTHER LOSS TO THE WEST INDIES, AND BORDER ACCEPTED THE MANTLE.
AB CAPTAINED AUSTRALIA UNTIL THE CONCLUSION OF OUR TOUR OF SOUTH AFRICA IN EARLY 1994; MARK TAYLOR THEN TOOK OVER THE ROLE FOR THE TOUR OF PAKISTAN LATER THAT SAME YEAR . . .

Allan Border is a good friend, and a man with an extremely strong character and a great love for his country and the baggy green cap. He had an unprecedented commitment to the Australian cricket team — to its members and its cause. I saw it time and again. I remember the day Geoff Marsh was dropped from the Test side for the last match of the 1991–92 series against India. AB refused to leave Adelaide for Perth for a day or two, so incensed was he that his vice-captain, his right-hand man, the cricketer who supported him loyally through thick and thin, had been sacked.

It was there again when Australia won the Frank Worrell Trophy in the West Indies in 1995, in the season after his retirement. He entered the dressing-room in Jamaica, after we'd won the series, with a look in his eyes that was just so special. The pride Allan has for his country shone through. A part of him was in that victory; that day he was as moved as any of us.

As I have stated before, it is one of the disappointments of my career that Allan was unable, as a player, to experience that excitement and exhilaration of beating the West Indies. We didn't talk about it on the night of our triumph in Jamaica, because I knew he wouldn't have wanted to. His attitude was brilliant, without a public tinge of regret that he was not directly involved: Australia has done it and I am Australian, and a former Australian captain. I'll enjoy the achievement.

I will always remember the night of what proved to be his final Test, in Durban in 1994. Although AB had not said anything, I sensed, as did most of the Australian players, that South Africa would be his last tour.

Opposite: AB in Sydney in 1993–94, the day he scored his 10,000th run in Test cricket.

That night, the two old fellows, AB and I, sat at the bar of our Durban hotel, while the rest of the team departed for the Hard Rock Cafe.

We spoke about many things and he seemed half-peeved that the boys had gone out, as though we had won the series. Eventually, having built up sufficient courage, I said to him: 'I thought you were thinking about finishing.'

'Yes,' he replied, 'But when it actually came down to the crunch, I just couldn't do it. I just don't know whether I really want to retire or whether I don't.'

AB was like anyone approaching the end of something that has been an enormous part of their life . . . extremely apprehensive. He said he wanted to go home to Queensland, to talk about the whole situation with his wife Jane. He'd make his mind up over the winter.

As he had not made any announcement during the tour, I thought that was a wise move. But when he returned to Australia, things did not go as planned, and he was angry and disappointed by the way some appeared to try to pre-empt his

AB with the Ashes after the fourth Test of the 1993 series.

decision. In the end he made known his intention to retire in May, before, it seems, he was ready to do so.

Deep down, I think AB is an emotional person, but most of the time he is an absolute master at hiding his true feelings. In the early days of his captaincy, he was dubbed, I think unfairly, as 'Captain Grumpy'. He had been handed the leadership role, one which he didn't actively seek, in a Test team which was constantly getting its backside kicked. He had always retained a personal pride in his performance and in the performance of his country. And the media's questions were always the same: 'Why are things so bad, and when are they going to get better?'

It was inevitable that, as captain, he was occasionally going to show just how disappointed he was at losing. Younger players in the squad were still learning about how much it should hurt to lose, and still discovering that there are sacrifices to be made if you want to be successful in international cricket.

There is a school of thought that AB mellowed after Australia's Ashes successes in 1989 and '93. I'm not so sure. The team was playing much better by then, so the pressures from the public and the media were entirely different. However, he would be the first to admit that he had matured in the role.

Back in that Durban bar, AB had a heart-to-heart with me. 'When I've finished, I'll need you to do one thing,' he said. 'We've been doing it for a while, but now it'll be up to you to never, ever let these younger blokes know what it's like to get their backsides kicked week-in, week-out.'

So, when AB retired, we used to relate stories to the new players. 'You guys have never been beaten. You don't know what it's like to lose — and you don't want to know either.'

The message was to keep working hard, to keep the positive nature and direction of Australian cricket going, because no-one would ever want to return to the days of 1983 to '86. This message is AB's legacy to the Australian team.

When AB had his testimonial game in Brisbane in December 1994, all those who played received a leather-bound copy of his autobiography, *Beyond Ten Thousand*. I didn't open mine until I returned home to Launceston. Inside the cover-page, he had written a brief message:

'To Babs, My Rock of Gibraltar. Best wishes, Allan Border.'

From a man of very few words, it meant everything to me. And that was enough.

THE ICEMAN

Stephen Rodger Waugh has climbed to the point where he is now regarded, rightfully, as one of the best players in the world. In fact, his performances, and the job he has done between 1993 and 1996, have been just about unbelievable.

I am not a big statistics man, but for Steve to increase his average from the high thirties to 50-plus in three years from 1993, having already played so much Test cricket in the seven years before, is just phenomenal. The role he has performed has forever silenced any critic he has ever had, especially those who questioned his ability to play short, fast bowling.

In my opinion, Stephen's technique hasn't changed noticeably in the last decade. However, he has matured as a batsman, and has learned, not to nullify, but to curtail some of his natural tendencies. Put simply, he has learned to play within his ability (which is enormous, anyway).

In defending short-pitched deliveries, he is one of those players who likes to play the ball. There's nothing wrong with that. Sure, he does, occasionally, take his eye off the ball, but everyone does that at one time or another. He has learned how to cope with the short stuff, and has become the consummate player, great for Australian cricket in the balance he provides for the team.

Steve is exceptional at batting with the tail, and has taken over from Allan Border, who used to do the same. The lower-order batsmen, as they did with AB, produce runs consistently batting with 'Tugga', because he knows how to protect them, to nurse them through difficult times and to encourage them.

He has been a mate of mine for a long time. I can recall having dinner in Lygon Street in Melbourne with his father, Rodger, and Stephen before his first Test match, against India in December, 1985. He was nervous that night, not overawed but perhaps dumbfounded at the Australian cricket 'system' at that level — a totally different situation to being in a Sheffield Shield team. Fortunately, things don't operate that way any more.

Stephen has had to work for his achievements, having experienced the turmoil which accompanies being dropped as well as carrying injuries to play for his country. Through all the personal crises, S.R. Waugh has remained what he was first dubbed during the World Cup campaign of 1987 — 'The Iceman'. He has matured into a very good, aggressive player, one whom I have never seen take a backward step. Stephen is one man I would take with me into the trenches.

We have become even better mates through the friendship of my wife, Pip, with Lynette, Stephen's wife. Pip was Lynette's matron of honour when the Waughs were married and the Boon troop — Georgina was the flower girl at the ceremony — went to Sydney several days before the big event. As per usual in the Waugh household, there were a number of quite important matters which had to be arranged at the last moment. I reckon I made six or seven trips to Bankstown to pick up items for the wedding. I organised the bus for his buck's night and even drove the family car.

There I was, looking forward to letting the hair down at one of my good mate's weddings. Result: D. Boon, two light beers, look after our three-month-old son, Jack, and then drive everyone home! Pip was very amused.

Without a doubt, Tugga is one of the untidiest cricketers in the world. His gear is always everywhere in the dressing-room.

To watch him pack his coffin at the end of a Test is remarkable, with team-mates called upon to stand on it to ensure its closure. I have never actually roomed with him on tour, thank goodness, but I have seen the state, make that carnage, of his hotel room. He's never, ever really late, but it's all down to the last minute. Not perfectly planned, more living on the edge of potential disaster.

Australia plays a lot of cricket, that's the modern game, and I'm not against such a tough and difficult schedule. Stephen, though, is a victim of the endless itinerary now facing international players. In the winter of 1996, after the World Cup, he had operations on his legs for shin problems, and on his groin.

He's hoping now that the continual discomfort he's endured and played with will be over.

His injuries sometimes meant that he was unable to contribute with the ball. For his batting alone, Steve Waugh will always make the Australian team. But when he's not bowling, the Test side's balance is affected.

To illustrate his value, one has to look no further than the 1995 series in the Caribbean, when Stephen was named player of the series after scoring 429 runs at an average of 107.25.

However, he doubled his input and influence with his bowling and the important wickets he took. He actually finished top of the Test bowling averages as well in that series, with eight wickets at 12.50.

The Waugh twins are different people. Mark is far more confident on the surface — his nickname is 'Junior', but he also answers to 'Golden Bollocks', because of his ability to take a wicket when one has not been forthcoming for hours.

When Mark scored a century on his Test debut, he walked back into the dressing-room and wondered aloud what everyone had been complaining about — Test cricket wasn't that hard! Mark would say that, in jest (or maybe even seriously, so seriously talented is the younger Waugh), but Steve wouldn't.

Stephen, though, has a dry sense of humour and a wickedly vivid imagination when it comes to playing practical jokes on his team-mates.

The bottom line between us is that I know I could count on him if the crunch ever came. I hope he feels the same way about me.

11: The Time of our Lives

I REGARD AUSTRALIA'S PERFORMANCE IN ENGLAND IN 1989, WHEN WE REGAINED THE ASHES AND WON THE SERIES 4–NIL, AS THE BEST TEAM PERFORMANCE BY AN AUSTRALIAN SIDE THAT I WAS A PART OF. I KNOW THAT MY RATING THIS TOUR AHEAD OF OUR DEFEAT OF THE WEST INDIES TO WIN THE FRANK WORRELL TROPHY IN 1995 COULD MAKE FOR LONG AND INVOLVED DEBATE. HOWEVER, I BELIEVE, BECAUSE THE AUSTRALIAN TEAM HAD BEEN GETTING THEIR BACKSIDE KICKED FOR SO LONG IN ENGLAND, AND IN A NUMBER OF OTHER PLACES AS WELL PRIOR TO THE '89 TOUR, THAT WINNING AS DECISIVELY AS WE DID WAS THE SLIGHTLY SUPERIOR ACHIEVEMENT. AND ONE SHOULDN'T FORGET THAT, BUT FOR RAIN INTERVENTION AT EDGBASTON AND THE OVAL, THERE IS A DISTINCT POSSIBILITY AUSTRALIA WOULD HAVE WON 6–0.

The Ashes adventure of '89 began, as every major tour seems to, with the drama of the announcement of the Australian party. On this occasion there was huge disappointment for quicks Mike Whitney and Craig McDermott, and huge excitement for my Tasmanian team-mate Greg Campbell, the young pace bowler selected with an eye to the future. For Whit, non-selection was a cruel blow, after his enormous final Test match against the West Indies in Adelaide, and after finishing the 1988–89 season as Australia's leading wicket-taker in first-class cricket. I know he was desperately hurt by his omission, and that he was desperately unlucky.

The selectors' decisions did, though, mean that I was now no longer the sole Tasmanian in the Australian party, which meant, among other things, that 'Cam' would also be the butt of all those 'two-headed' jokes! However, his career would encompass only two Test matches — the first in England at Headingley, and Tasmania's first Test, which was played the following summer, against Sri Lanka at Bellerive Oval in Hobart. I believe that, initially, he was seen as the long-term replacement for Terry Alderman, but, in the end, 'Cam' suffered a form slump, coupled with a run of injuries. When he lost his outswinger he was

Opposite: Batting at The Oval, sixth Ashes Test, 1989.

without his main weapon, and didn't play Test cricket again. But he did have huge potential — it's such a pity it was never realised.

We returned to England this time with three bowlers from the South African rebel team — Alderman, Trevor Hohns and Carl Rackemann — who had all served their cricket bans.

My first match on tour was the one-dayer against the Duchess of Norfolk's XI at Arundel, where I retired hurt with a leg niggle after scoring 114. Arundel is a beautiful little ground, with a castle overlooking it, and is the traditional site of the tour opener. In such genteel surroundings, you would expect the gentlemen to protect their womenfolk whenever possible, but here, on this day, it was not to be . . .

Allan Border hit a six into the crowd, where hidden among the masses was a lady, fast asleep on her deck chair. Instead of attempting to catch the ball, the men in the vicinity let it fall to earth — but instead of hitting the turf it smashed into the poor lady's face. AB, needless to say, felt terrible (no-one told us how the blokes who ran away from the 'catch' were feeling), and that night went to visit her in hospital, to find she was recovering from shock and a broken nose!

During our next game, at Lord's against the MCC when I teamed with Geoff Marsh at the top of the order to put on 277 (Boon 166 off 165 balls, Swamp 102), I hit off-spinner Vic Marks for six and then consecutive fours — the last of which was a reverse sweep which scooted to the boundary through third man. My first thought after I played that shot was this: I hope Bob Simpson is doing something other than watching the action. But Simmo rarely misses a ball, and his comment afterwards ran along the lines of: 'Well, I hope I don't see you do that in an important game!' Such is his affection for the reverse sweep.

Meeting the Queen at Lord's.

In the last game before the one-day internationals (which always precede the Test series on Ashes tours), a three-dayer against Yorkshire, my form held as I belted 172

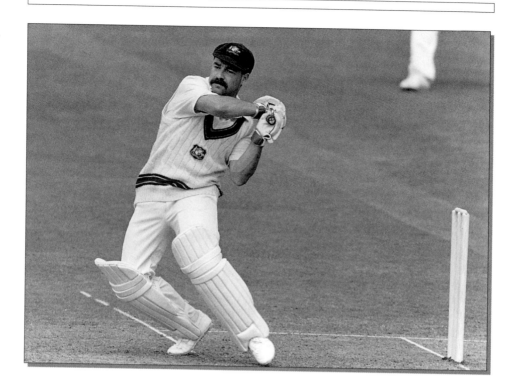

A shot from my century against the MCC.

out of 3–297. And, you wouldn't believe it, I managed to do exactly what AB had done at Arundel — hit a spectator. My 'victim' was an elderly gent who was concentrating on something other than the play at the time. Fortunately, he wasn't seriously hurt, just shaken up, and after receiving treatment returned to his seat, where, later on in my innings, I hit him again!

The first Test was at Headingley and although England won the toss and sent us in, I believe the decisive moment came as the captains were walking back to the pavilion, after the toss, when Allan Border told England captain David Gower he would have batted anyway — Gower was dumb-founded. Traditionally, no-one bats first at Leeds, because of the assistance it inevitably offers to seamers and swing bowlers. AB, however, wanted to be really positive and we had looked at the wicket and didn't think that it had that much in it — although, to be truthful, at Headingley you can never tell.

Ironically, the wicket did seam, but the Englishmen bowled far too short; Bob Simpson took our pacemen out after the first innings and told them if we bowled fuller than they had done, we would take wickets. But before that Australia had started the Test series by declaring their first innings at 7–601. Mark Taylor became the 16th Australian to score a century on debut against England, with

136, AB hit a quickfire 66, Dean Jones scored 79, Steve Waugh 177 not out and Merv Hughes a Test-high 71.

AB was carrying some pretty disturbing mental baggage from previous tours of England — things had sometimes gone wrong when least expected — but with 601 in the bank, Australia could afford to go for broke. However, England's 430 was not to be sniffed at.

An interesting thing happened in Australia's second innings. I made 43, adjudged lbw to Phil de Freitas by umpire John Holder. I was somewhat reluctant to leave the wicket and stared for a considerable time at the ump before I left, and as I was walking off. It certainly seemed to me to be an ordinary call. Afterwards, I was called into the umpires' room. I thought that I had been done for dissent, but Holder was really upset and quickly apologised for making a terrible decision. He'd seen the event replayed on television, and realised he'd made a mistake.

Whether you believe umpires should or shouldn't talk to players about particular decisions, it still took a lot of courage to admit to me that he'd made an error, and I respected him greatly for doing so.

On the final day, England had to make over 400 to win, or bat for 83 overs to achieve a draw, But we were too good for them. Terry Alderman finished the match with 10 wickets (5–107 and 5–44) to pip Steve Waugh and Mark Taylor for the man-of-the-match award, while Merv Hughes and Geoff Lawson also bowled extremely well.

Celebrations after the Test were, needless to say, long and exuberant, but we had a problem. A match against Lancashire at Old Trafford was scheduled to begin the following morning. AB was okay, he'd given himself the game off, so Australia were captained by Marsh, who promptly lost the toss, which wasn't very clever. Australia were in the field.

Early on, Greg Campbell was bowling to Lancashire's Nick Speak, who hit the ball crisply off

Celebrations at Headingley. In the background are Geoff Marsh (centre) and Greg Campbell (right).

his pads. But I stopped the shot at bat-pad. Now, I, like the rest of my team-mates, had vigorously celebrated our first Test win, and the fact that I made contact with the ball was a miracle, but I made sure all the blokes knew that some of us had it, whatever the circumstances.

A couple of deliveries later, Speak fended Campbell off his glove and the ball ballooned up — I looked up, tried to take a step forward and fell over, face first! I didn't even touch the ball, which fell in front of my nose. Everyone on the field, with the exception of Campbell, was in hysterics. Poor Swamp had tears in his eyes at first slip and in the next three overs we dropped about five catches. Speak made 26, we dropped him four times, yet we still won the game.

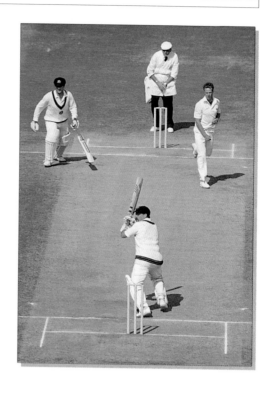

Batting with Steve Waugh on the final day of the second Test, at Lord's.

Despite Greg's excellent effort, we brought in Hohns, a leggie, to replace him for the second Test, at Lord's. Amazingly, the XI that played there was the same combination that appeared throughout the rest of the series. In contrast, England, who were beset by injuries and players losing form, used 29 players in total during the rubber.

At Lord's, England won the toss and batted, making 286, Alderman taking 3–60 and Hughes 4–71. Australia's reply was highlighted by Steve Waugh backing up his 177 not out at Headingley with 152 not out (in the second innings he would remain undefeated on 21 — three knocks, 350 runs, no average, not bad!). D. Boon, idiot, was out for 94. I will never forget how it happened . . .

Graham Dilley was bowling with a relatively newish ball, with only one slip, or rather, Gooch at slip and a half. I tried to guide a delivery down through third man, but instead managed to give Gooch catching practice, as if we were warming up before the game. It went straight to him. An absolutely stupid shot and I had denied myself a century at the home of cricket (at that stage, I knew

Australia have taken a 2–nil lead in the series.

nothing of what awaited me on the 1993 tour).

By the time Steve Waugh had run out of partners, Australia had reached 528 and we then bowled England out for 359. Alderman this time took 6–128 from 38 overs, to leave us with the relatively simple target of 119 for victory.

'Test match' Terry, as he had become known — outside the Tests, Alderman played only five first-class games on tour — was, at this time, a great bowler in superb form. He was also a very, very good impressionist, who had developed a 'deadly' reputation as a swing bowler. Because he bowled so close to the stumps, with the seam upright, he gave the impression the ball was swinging even if it wasn't really swinging. If you watch replays of his performances in England, with a lot of the wickets he took, the ball didn't swing that far, if at all — but the English batsmen had convinced themselves that it had. Terry's other weapon was the one that came back the other way off the wicket. That delivery won him countless lbw decisions.

Despite the modest target, we managed to give ourselves a minor (or is that major) scare, when our score tumbled to 4–67 — Marsh out for 1, Taylor, 27, Border, 1 and Jones, 0. This was the afternoon Border had five showers and three shaves, because the players wouldn't let him back into the dressing-room proper until we won — AB had earlier committed the cardinal error of reminding us of Headingley in 1981, when Australia were all out for 111 when chasing 130 for victory. AB didn't want to come back anyway. He was following Australian cricket's tradition that when things are going well, no-one moves from where they are positioned.

Whether that helped, I'm not sure, but it certainly didn't do any harm. I finished with 58 not out, having added an unconquered 52 with Stephen, and Australia won the Test by six wickets. My late father, Clarrie, always rated that effort as one of my best innings, because it dug Australia out of a potential hole. I value that rating.

I remember the third Test, at Edgbaston, which ended in a rain-interrupted draw, primarily for two reasons. So brutal was the rainstorm that flooded the ground at the end of day one, the water was knee-high at the back of the dressing-room. It was quite extraordinary, and a prelude to two frustrating days of sitting around doing very little. At stumps on the first day we were 4–232; at the same time two days later we were 7–391. We finally were all out for 424, and once England managed to get past the follow-on target, the match had to be a draw.

On that opening day I was out for 38, after a solid, 96-run partnership with Dean Jones which ended when Deano smashed the ball back down the pitch, only for the bowler, Yorkshire's Paul Jarvis, to get a fingertip to it before it hit the stumps, with me out of my ground. Dean went on to 157, while, in a major shock, Steve Waugh was finally dismissed, for 43, which left him with a batting average for the series of seven less than 400.

At this point, after three Tests, I want to make mention of the 'support staff', the members of the Australian squad who watched their team win the Ashes, but, rather than sulk about not being able to play, had a huge input into our performances.

I had a hint of what it was like to be in the backroom in 1985, when I was omitted for the final two Tests. It's tough not playing, especially for batsmen, but when you are hitting them nicely, you want to keep playing, so many of the Test batsmen played the majority of the county games as well, which, inevitably, limited the opportunities for guys such as Tom Moody and Mike Veletta. But those two, and Carl Rackemann, Tim May, Greg Campbell and Tim Zoehrer, kept themselves 'up' from the start of the tour all the way until the final day of the final Test. They were all very much part of Australia's Ashes success, despite Campbell being the only one to play in even one of the six Test matches.

At Hampshire in 1985, I had scored a pair, and people remembered that, in particular the County captain Mark Nicholas, who didn't miss the opportunity to remind me as I took guard. However, I erased that memory in our game there in '89, played between the third and fourth Tests, with 103, while Steve Waugh continued his run-feast, making 112 and 67.

At Old Trafford, the goal was simple. If Australia won, we would win back the Ashes in England, the first side to do so since Bill Woodfull's team — which also included players such as Don Bradman, Stan McCabe, Bill O'Reilly, Bill Ponsford and Clarrie Grimmett — did so in 1934, 55 years previously.

England again won the toss and batted first, making 260, of which 143 runs belonged to Robin Smith. Amazingly, Alderman was wicketless, sending down 25 overs for the loss of 49 runs; the destroyer this time was Geoff Lawson, who took 6–72 from 33 overs. We then made 447 — Taylor 85, Marsh 47, Border 80,

I've just hit the Ashes-winning runs . . .

Jones 69, Waugh 92 — before Alderman recovered his composure in the second innings, taking 5–66. For a while, it seemed we would win by an innings — Jack Russell proved an enormous headache by compiling 128 not out, batting for 350 very stubborn minutes — but eventually England reached 264.

Through the final day, first Russell and then weather threatened to prevent an Australian victory. But, once the final English wicket had fallen, we were always going to get the 78 runs we needed. So, when we were getting close, and with Marsh and Taylor still at the wicket, I said to Allan Border: 'Look, you deserve to get out there and get these runs, why don't you get out there and do it.'

No way, he said. I'd been waiting almost as long as he had for this moment (which wasn't exactly true) and I was the No, 3, so my backside was due in the middle if required. Sure enough, Swamp was dismissed and I went out for 15 minutes, to score 10 not out, including the winning shot, a sweep to the boundary off Cook. I'll never forget that moment.

The dressing-room was absolute pandemonium. But we waited more than an hour to sing the Australian victory anthem, because AB was in talking to Gower, who was understandably dejected after being beaten 3–0 in four Tests. Of course, Allan was able to tell him he knew almost exactly how he felt, because Australia had lost in 1985.

The next morning, Australia was required to play Nottingham at Trent Bridge. The bus duly arrived and Marsh made his way out to the middle to toss the coin. Marsh lost. The Notts captain, Tim Robinson, was of the opinion that he and his team would bat; Marsh disagreed.

'But I won the toss, I get to choose,' was Robinson's not unreasonable argument.

'You may have won the toss, but I've got no bowlers — they're all asleep — you couldn't bat if you wanted to,' Swamp explained, a little sheepishly.

And on the balcony, my team-mates are beginning to party.

The Notts captain deferred; mind you, the Australian batsmen weren't impressed. But, somehow Australia made 284 in its first innings, and I contributed 76 — must have been on memory alone!

The fifth Test at Trent Bridge became 'The Big Wait' for one D. Boon, courtesy of my friends, the opening partnership of G.R. Marsh and M.A. Taylor. They batted all the first day, after AB had won the toss, for 301. And then they batted some more — until not long before lunch on the second day. And all the while I sat, in my pads, for 426 minutes in total. I learned later that I was only the third No. 3 in cricket history to sit with his pads on throughout the opening day of a Test.

As that first day progressed, my other team-mates couldn't resist lending a quiet word. 'You know what happens after a long partnership, Babsie?' they'd chuckle, 'Someone misses out!'

After Swamp was finally dismissed, for 138, after the highest opening partnership in Ashes history, 329, there were suddenly hand grenades in the wicket! To make matters worse, I was nought not out at lunch — all through the break I was still copping it.

Gower provided a moment of levity through that particular lunch. There sat the England captain, calmly sipping a glass of champagne. 'I'm having a toast,'

Life in the baggy green had never been this good.

he announced, 'to the first English wicket for a day and a half.'

I was very pleased to get off the mark, and went on to post 73 in Australia's 6 (declared) for 602. Tubby had been the second wicket to fall, for 219, after a second-wicket stand of 101.

Australia then bowled out England for 255 (Smith 101, Alderman 5–69). Forced to follow-on, England collapsed again, all out 167, and we were 4–0 up, by an innings and 180 runs.

In our game against Essex, that followed the fifth Test, something unusual occurred. Mark Waugh, the county's overseas import, scored 100 not out in his side's first innings. Then, in our second innings, Steve Waugh did exactly the same thing . . . 100 not out. Never before had twins scored hundreds in the same first-class match for opposing teams.

A few days later at The Oval, Stephen kept his batting average for the series above 100, just one of several notable statistical achievements in a match that was eventually drawn. Tubby took his series aggregate to 839. Terry Alderman, who was named man of the series, finished with 41 wickets, the second time he'd taken more than 40 wickets in a Test series in England (the other was in 1981). Dean Jones scored his second hundred of the rubber. For a record-breaking eighth Test in a row Australia posted more than 400 in the first innings of a Test match.

I finished equal fourth on the batting aggregate, with 442 at 55.25, and fifth on the averages, but those above me made my tour return look almost ordinary!

My only bugbear from the entire tour was the 'ban' on wives and girlfriends. Allan's reasoning was that, keeping the team isolated within the team hotel would bring the players together. This hadn't been the case in 1985 and the team was thrashed. But, while I disagreed with this line of thinking, which AB well knew, the bottom line was that I was only one part of the team, so I abided by the decision.

The only time this rule caused me to 'lose it' occurred outside The Westbury Hotel, our base in London. We had a couple of days off, so Pip, Georgina and I were looking around London with Steve and his then fiancee, Lynette. In keeping with the tour rule, I was obliged to make the girls stand on the sidewalk, while I went up to my room to fetch something. However, in the short period I was gone, one of the other player's wives leaned out a fourth floor window and yelled to Pip: 'Why don't you come up. It's great!'

Upon returning downstairs, the look I copped from Pip was nigh-lethal. I don't get angry too often, but I did that day and vented my spleen with the team manager, Lawrie Sawle. I just couldn't stand the fact that the rule was being flaunted, while I, who disagreed with it completely, was toeing the team line.

My view is that if sharing your life with a wife or girlfriend doesn't affect your performance when playing cricket in Australia, I don't see how that lifestyle will hurt your performance on tour. The only sticking point to having extra people on tour is, obviously, small children, particularly babies, who don't understand that waking at 3am will severely hinder their father's ability to bat or bowl the next day in a Test match. When everyone is living under the same hotel-room roof, that can cause problems.

This ban on wives and girlfriends was relaxed after the first two months of the tour, but only during county matches or when a player had a game off. In such instances, you could spend time with your wife or girlfriend in her hotel, but not the team hotel, which remained off-limits for them until the final two weeks of the tour. For some reason, this rule was never applied to any other tour, just England, but when we returned in '93 it still stood.

Returning home was also an unforgettable experience, primarily because of the spectacular tickertape parade we enjoyed in Sydney. Mind you, for a while it didn't seem as though this was going to be such a rewarding event. We had gathered in a room at the Regent Hotel at the northern end of George Street, and when we looked out the window to the streets below we could not see a soul. The jokes were flying and the general consensus was that this was going to be a very, very embarrassing occasion.

However, the people did come out, in large numbers, so that when we drove up George Street in open-topped cars, it was as though Sydney had stopped — thousands and thousands of people had lined the streets. We ended up at Darling Harbour, amid huge crowds, for a presentation and further congratulations.

To be recognised in such a manner — as a team and individually — was an enormous thrill.

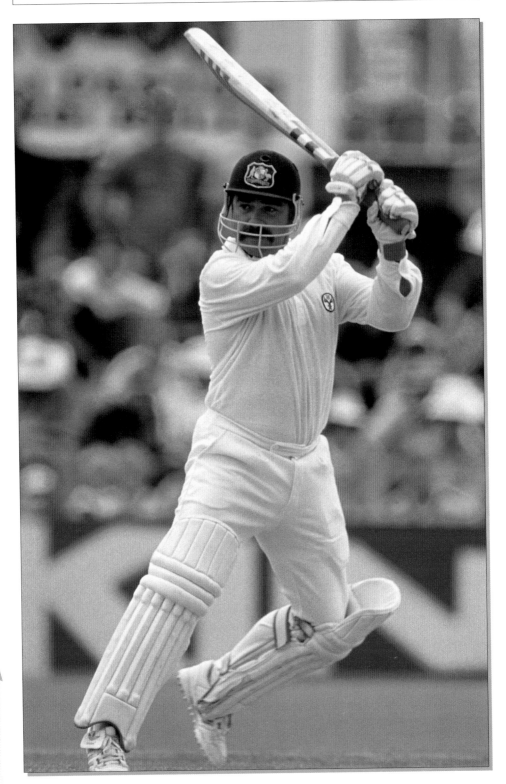

12: The Homecoming

AS A TASMANIAN, ONE OF THE HIGHLIGHTS OF THE 1989–90 SEASON WAS ALWAYS GOING TO BE THE STATE'S FIRST TEST — THE SECOND TEST AGAINST SRI LANKA, AT BELLERIVE OVAL FROM DECEMBER 16 TO 20, 1989. I HAD ALREADY PLAYED 42 TESTS BY THE TIME TEST CRICKET CAME TO MY HOME STATE, AND ENJOYED THE TREMENDOUS SUCCESS OF THE ASHES TOUR IN ENGLAND EARLIER IN THE YEAR. BUT THIS, TASMANIA'S FIRST TEST MATCH, WAS ALSO SOMETHING SPECIAL.

There had been good crowds at one-day internationals and Australian XI games that had been staged in Hobart in the past, and I knew that the people of Tasmania would support this major event. We were, in a sense, very much on trial, in a position where we had to prove ourselves worthy of the responsibility of staging a Test. Today, in the mid-'90s, Hobart appears to have established itself as the 'sixth' Test-match venue in the country, but, back in late 1989, there was no guarantee this would be the case.

Before we were put to the test, though, Australia headed for Perth for a one-off Test against New Zealand. Two days before the match, we lost vice-captain Geoff Marsh, whose left toe was broken by a Carl Rackemann yorker in the nets. Typically, after training Geoff still rode his bicycle back to the family home at Jandakot, but it was a severe break. A doctor insisted a pin be inserted in his toe — but Swamp still wanted to play!

Tom Moody replaced Geoff, and I moved back to the top of the order, where I was quickly involved, after New Zealand sent us in. However, the Kiwis' decision backfired because, after losing Mark Taylor early, Tom and I put on 149 for the second wicket. At stumps, Australia was 2–296, and I was 169 not out. The next day, I finished with exactly 200, becoming the first Tasmanian to score a double century in a Test and the first batsman to do so at the WACA Ground.

When I came into the dressing-room, after being dismissed, I could only hope that Bob Simpson was taking the mickey when he said: 'What are you doing

Opposite: A square cut during my century against England in Adelaide, 1990–91.

getting out? I would have gone on and got 300.' I've never worked out whether he was serious or not (mind you, I never asked him, either).

The match ended in a draw, courtesy of a courageous innings by Kiwi left-hander and man of the match, Mark Greatbatch. He made 146 not out in 655 minutes to save the match for his country, and batted throughout the final day, during which I injured my knee, a setback which was to plague me throughout the summer.

I had first hurt my left knee playing for Tasmania against Western Australia in a day-night limited-overs game at the WACA Ground earlier in November — trying to stop a Tom Moody cover-drive. I started to dive for the ball, but my spikes stuck in the turf and the knee was severely wrenched — I couldn't get off the ground and was trying to crawl after the ball, which must have looked hilarious from a spectator's perspective.

From then on, whenever the joint copped a knock, it blew up like a balloon. I missed Tasmania's Shield game against Victoria in Launceston and went to Brisbane for the first of Australia's two Test matches against Sri Lanka. Swamp was still absent. We batted first, but the pendulum had reversed and I was out for a duck (cricket, as everybody knows, is such a leveller), while Moody scored his maiden Test century in only his second game, in Australia's first innings of 367.

Sri Lanka replied with 418, of which Aravinda de Silva made 167. The situation, though, might have been a great deal different if Merv Hughes hadn't dropped a relatively easy caught-and-bowled chance, early in Aravinda's innings. At one point in the afternoon, as Aravinda thrashed the Australian bowlers around the Gabba, Merv was feeling the pinch and asked Allan Border for a brief respite.

'No,' snarled AB, 'You dropped him, you bowl to him!'

The match petered out into a high-scoring draw, with Mark Taylor making 164 on the final day. Then it was to Hobart, where the crowds were large and vibrant, the Test-match atmosphere outstanding, the Bellerive Oval wicket superb and Australia won the Test match on the last day. This was the start of what, at the beginning of the 1996–97 season, was a perfect record for Australia at the ground — three Tests, three wins, over Sri Lanka, New Zealand and Pakistan.

I had the honour of walking out with Mark Taylor at the start of the game, facing the first ball, and scoring the first Test run on the ground.

Sri Lanka made us work for our victory. We were all out on the opening day for 224 (Boon, caught Mahanama, bowled Ratnayake, 41), but fought back to have the visitors 3–27 at stumps. On the second day, we dismissed Sri Lanka for 216, but I had injured my knee during fielding practice in the morning — there were lumps and bumps all over it! — and had to sit out the entire innings.

When we had to bat again, Ian Healy accompanied me as a runner. Allan Border had given me the option of batting down the order, but I told him my job was as an opener in this Test and Heals would do all the work anyway.

I saw the first ball I faced like an absolute football. Reports later said that I mishit that first ball from Graeme Labrooy. Wrong. I cannot hit the ball harder than I smashed that one. Unfortunately, though, the ball cannoned into Ratnayake's chest in the gully before he'd even moved — and then popped straight up for an easy second take! I just couldn't believe it. Out first ball. I was so disappointed, it took me ages to leave the dressing-room and go upstairs to join my team-mates in the viewing area.

Australia won the match in the last session of the final day, Greg Campbell, trapping Ratnayake leg before wicket. So Tasmania's first Test match ended with a local batsman facing the first ball, and ended with a local bowler taking the final wicket.

In between the Hobart Test and the first Test of a three-match series with Pakistan, in Melbourne immediately after Christmas, Tasmania played Sri Lanka in a three-day match at Devonport Oval. By tea on the opening day, Tasmania's first innings was over — our captain Dirk Wellham had declared, after we had reached 1–210. My contribution, batting at No. 3, was 133 not out, including 101 between lunch and tea, the only time in my first-class career I scored a hundred in a session. I wish those days came more regularly!

At the MCG, Geoff Marsh returned to open with Taylor, and to take a match-winning catch on the final day to dismiss Pakistan's century maker, Ijaz Ahmed. I reckon Geoff still dreams about that one, just as I jump out of bed and catch Brian Lara every night. Taylor, on the other hand, was involved in a less enjoyable incident in our second innings, although no blame should have been put on him. We had a terrible mix-up in our second innings, and television replays later showed that we had crossed by less than a metre, after I called for a single off Tauseef Ahmed. Because we'd crossed, Tubby should have been leaving the middle, and some commentators were absolutely screaming, but I thought I was out and the umpire thought I was out, so I exited (Mark, who went on to get a hundred, still owes me for that one!).

In Adelaide, I again injured my knee, this time on the second day of the Test. Off the ground again, I met with team management — chairman of selectors Lawrie Sawle, physiotherapist Errol Alcott and Simmo — and we agreed that, while I could go on, the knee would keep blowing up. I made the decision to have surgery, because I was letting the team down, so Errol rang orthopaedic surgeon Ian Henderson in Melbourne.

The day after the Test finished in a draw, I flew into Tullamarine and one day later the knee was repaired.

Bellerive Oval, Hobart, scene of the first Test match played in Tasmania, in December 1989.

I was out for the remainder of the Australian season, but was fit to take my place on the short trip to New Zealand at season's end. We won the one-day triangular series, against New Zealand and India, by defeating the Kiwis in the final at Eden Park, which would prove to be Richard Hadlee's farewell limited-overs appearance against Australia.

However, the one-off Test was a different story. I don't recall Australia feeling a misplaced sense of security when we journeyed to Wellington for the game — but, despite the fact we hadn't lost any of our previous 14 Tests, things went horribly wrong.

The game was an absolute disaster. Australia, all out 110 in the first innings, as Hadlee, in his final Test against Australia, took 5–39 — Steve Waugh, Peter Taylor, Greg Campbell and Terry Alderman the victims. Oh, yeah, and the Australian No. 3, D. Boon, leg before wicket for a duck! Two days of torrential rain had meant that both sides practised indoors for the match, but that was no excuse, we were just rock'n'rolled.

New Zealand were dismissed for 202, but the final target we set them, 178, was never going to be enough. Kiwi captain John Wright made 117 not out, as the home side won back the Trans-Tasman Trophy, by nine wickets.

After touring Sharjah and the United States, I had more surgery on my troublesome knee in June, 1990. Following on from the previous arthroscopy, this time Ian Henderson did a complete job — removing a cyst the size of a golf ball from behind my left knee, excising blood clots and re-designing the medial ligament. I hate hospitals at the best of times — sitting in bed doing nothing isn't my 'thing' — and in this case I wanted to get home as soon as possible, as there was a party in Launceston on the Friday. My operation had taken place on the Monday.

Dr Henderson explained that I'd have to be under observation for a week, but on the Thursday morning said that if could go up and down the stairs on crutches and spend a night without painkillers, he would let me travel home. So I sat up all night, sweating, aching and drugless — and learning that there are some terrible movies on national television at 3am.

The doc came in again the next morning and asked me how I was: 'I'm fine,' I told him, 'I went up and down the stairs and had no drugs whatsoever last night.'

He looked at me and laughed: 'It's true, all the stories about you are right — you are an idiot! You could have had some Panadol Forte for the pain! You can give them to yourself. What I meant was you're not allowed to give yourself an injection.'

But I did get to go to the party!

AB with Geoff Marsh and me after the second Ashes Test of 1990–91.

'You and I are going to get these runs. If you get out, I'm going to kill you!'

The words of Geoff Marsh, spoken in the middle of the Melbourne Cricket Ground, on the final day of the second Test of the 1990–91 Ashes series.

To put this quote in context, this is where the game stood. A David Gower century had been the spearhead of England's first innings total of 352 (Bruce Reid 6–97, the first time he'd taken five wickets in a Test innings), to which we had replied with 306. Australia, or more accurately, Reid (7–51), had then bowled England out for 150, an extraordinary scoreline when you consider that the Poms had been 4–147 at tea. That night, Tubby Taylor and Healy, as nightwatchman, were both caught by Mike Atherton, but Marsh and I made it through to 2–28 at stumps.

The media summaries that night spoke of an expected tight finish; for just about the first time since the Bicentennial Test in 1988, England were in with a real chance of defeating Australia in a Test match.

That, though, is not how things worked out. Instead, I finished with 94 not out and Swamp was 79 not out; Australia, 2–197, and owners of a 2–0 lead in the series. But it was far from easy, and especially early on, with the pitch playing low and England's excellent seamer, Angus Fraser, giving nothing away (Fraser had already shown his liking for the MCG wicket by taking 6–82 in the first innings), the pressure was right on us. That was when Swamp approached me in mid-pitch, and uttered his famous words.

At tea, with the Test just about won, we sat together in the dressing-room as usual, and forgot about the rest of the world. It wasn't until later that we realised that we hadn't spoken to anyone else in all the time we were in there. During the post-game celebrations, the boys told us we were just two pairs of dazed eyes.

Towards the end, when Australia were on the verge of victory, Atherton was bowling his leg-spinners — which are about as threatening as my offies — and Robin Smith was trying to pump me up to hit him for six to finish the match. But I let Swamp hit the winning runs instead. The walk off the ground with Geoff was one of the proudest moments of my career — we'd not only won the Test, but also achieved our target for the day.

And I was still alive.

My international summer had begun at the Bellerive Oval, where I captained an Australian XI against the Englishmen, and hit some form, scoring 67 and 108. In the first Test, in Brisbane, which began four days after that match in Hobart, the opening two days were full of drama — England all out 194, Australia dismissed for 152, and England 3–56. And Allan Border had dropped Allan Lamb just before stumps, which made him almost unapproachable in the rooms.

In the end, though, it didn't matter. On day three, we bowled England out for just 114, with Terry Alderman reminding the Poms of the '89 Ashes tour by taking 6–47, the best innings return of his Test career. And then, on a pitch where 30 wickets had fallen for 460 runs in 14 hours, Geoff Marsh and Mark Taylor scored the 157 runs needed without loss, in a bit more than three hours, to complete an Australian victory in less than three days.

In this Test, and in the second that followed in Melbourne, Australia showed what a good side we had become; one able to recover from a first-innings deficit and win. That wouldn't have happened in my early days in the Test team.

The third Test was in Sydney, where we batted first and I followed my Melbourne 94 not out with a 97 out, dismissed, going for glory, in most un-Boon-like fashion.

On 85, I struck Gooch for three fours in four balls — a square cut, an off-drive and an on-drive. The next ball was a short long-hop . . . 'My eyes were full of dollar signs!' was my comment afterwards . . . and I hit it to Atherton at point, who took a very good catch low down. Didn't my chewing gum cop a huge smack on the way off the SCG!

We finished with 518, which, for a team needing no more than a draw to retain the Ashes, was a fabulous result. England got within 49 of our score before declaring, and though there were a few anxious moments on the final day (No. 10, Carl Rackemann, batted for 107 minutes for nine runs as we battled to give our opponents an impossible run-chase), the match eventually ended without an English victory. So, the Ashes stayed in Australia.

The fourth Test, in Adelaide, was notable for the Test debut of Mark Waugh and the return of Craig McDermott to the Australian team. On the first day, Mark, who replaced his twin brother, Stephen, made 116 (he finished with 138), while in our second innings, I made 121, which was a pleasant change after two consecutive 90s. But the match ended in another draw, despite the best efforts of McDermott, who finished his comeback Test with seven wickets, including five in the first innings.

In the fifth Test, however, there was no stopping Billy, who destroyed the Poms by taking 8–97 in the Englishmen's first effort, and 11 wickets for the match. I scored 64 in our first dig, and was 30 not out and in partnership with Geoff Marsh, who finished unbeaten on 63, when we won the Test by nine wickets. Those runs left me with a total for the series of 530, top of the averages and aggregates for both sides, not bad for a bloke whose right to a spot in the Australian side had been questioned before the series began.

A Classic Silent Type

When I watch Curtly Ambrose bowl, he reminds me so much of his predecessor in the West Indies team, Joel Garner. Not in terms of build, because Joel was a giant of a bowler; while Curtly is physically impressive, he possesses a more wiry frame.

Curtly was one of the very best bowlers I faced during my career, and one of the most imposing. If he bowled you a good ball and you played a good shot, he would occasionally smile down the wicket at you. But this wasn't a sarcastic grin, or even a provocative one. It was more enigmatic, for Curtly is the classic 'silent type', complete with body language which always makes you think: 'This bloke's got something up his sleeve.'

I only saw Curtly lose his cool twice on the cricket field. Once was the famous occasion when he and Stephen Waugh stood toe-to-toe in Trinidad, during the third Test of the 1995 series. The other occurred years earlier, in less obvious or controversial circumstances, and I was heavily involved.

The incident in question occurred on a night in Sydney, during a limited-overs international, when Curtly became angry not with the batsmen — who happened to be Geoff Marsh and me — but with himself. In fact, this is a double story, involving another superb West Indian fast bowler, Malcolm Marshall, as well as Curtly.

To say Australia was struggling at the time would be an understatement;

after eight-odd overs, we had eight, maybe nine, runs on the board. Things weren't easy: Malcolm was bowling from one end, Curtly from the other, and, if that wasn't enough, Gus Logie was fielding on one side of the wicket and Roger Harper on the other — two of the world's best-ever fieldsmen cutting off singles before you even thought about them. Every ball was chest-high, just below no-ball height, and the crowd was becoming restless.

Swamp walked that walk of his down the wicket. 'What,' he asked, 'are we going to do?'

'What can we do?' replied I.

'Look,' my batting partner told me, 'I've got no idea what I'm going to do, but you'd better do something really quick.' And then he wandered back to where he'd come from.

Like magic, next ball, I picked Marshall up off my toes beautifully. Six! The fact that we were batting on the far eastern side of the SCG and I had hit the shot over the shortest boundary on the ground was irrelevant. A six, after all, is a six.

For a brief moment I was satisfied ... until I heard that long-time stirrer, Desmond Haynes, pipe up from mid-on: 'Hey, Boonie! Isn't is great when you hit these fast bowlers who think they're quick for six?!'

Thanks Dessie. The next delivery from Malcolm almost sawed me in half.

But Geoff and I were rolling and, after about 15 overs, the total had reached 70-odd and the mood had changed. Curtly charged in again, and I pulled him to the long-on boundary, where the ball crashed into the fence on the full. By this stage, the West Indies captain, the great Vivian Richards, had become somewhat riled, and sought from his bowler an explanation.

But before he could say anything, Curtly started muttering: 'He has no right to do this to me. No right.' So frustrated was he that he wouldn't go back to bowl the next delivery. In fact, as I remember things, I had to advise him to return to his mark and bowl again. The crowd, I suggested, was waiting.

Interestingly, he bowled a lot better after that. Curtly, I think, learned a valuable lesson, one for which the rest of the world's batting fraternity should curse me. Since then, I have noticed that on the rare occasions he bowls a bad ball in one-day cricket, while he still gets annoyed, what he does is go straight back to bowling nigh-perfect line and length.

Curtly Ambrose is actually a very shy man. To be totally honest, I have only ever spoken once at length with him, at the end of the 1992–93 series, when he was named International Cricketer of the Year. That was the summer when Australia had a real chance to win the Frank Worrell Trophy, after years of Windies domination. But we lost the fourth Test in Adelaide by one lousy run, which levelled the series, and then flew to Perth for the final Test, where a greentop wicket greeted us and the

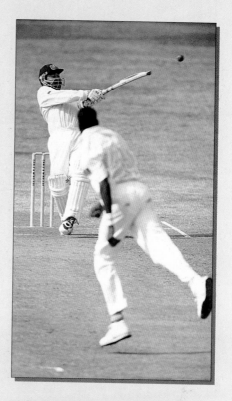

Taking the battle to big Curtly during the second Test of 1995, in Antigua.

West Indies, or, more particularly, Curtly, went through Australia in less than three days. Afterwards, I went into the West Indian dressing-room and sat beside Curtly, and we had a long, interesting, but private conversation.

I always enjoyed playing against him, because it was always a challenge, always an excellent competition. Sometimes he won, sometimes painfully so, by cracking you in the ribcage or sending your stumps cartwheeling. But sometimes I won . . . these were days to be treasured.

One way or the other, you always knew you were in a contest.

13: The Good Life?

THE WEST INDIES ARE AN AMAZING GROUP OF COUNTRIES, VIRTUALLY EVERY ISLAND A DIFFERENT NATION WITH, BARRING ONE OR TWO EXCEPTIONS, ITS OWN CURRENCY. THE PLACE IS BILLED, AT LEAST IN AMERICA AND ENGLAND, AS A SERIES OF PARADISE DESTINATIONS, BUT, AS FAR AS I'M CONCERNED, APART FROM ONE OR TWO ISLANDS, IT'S NOT SOMEWHERE I'D CHOOSE FOR A HOLIDAY — THERE ARE AS GOOD, IF NOT BETTER PLACES AT HOME IN AUSTRALIA.

West Indians certainly have a fervour for life. By the end of a cricket tour to the Caribbean, and I've now been on two, you are absolutely sick to death of the steel drums, which are there to greet you at every airport and every hotel lobby. The other major bugbear for a touring cricket team is the travel, which can test your patience to the limit. With every island a different country, you have to negotiate the respective customs departments at each end of the journey. It's quite common for a one-and-a-half hour flight between countries to consume seven to eight hours, from one hotel door to the other.

My favourite place is the tiny island of St Vincent. Perhaps I'm getting old and conservative, but I found St Vincent to be less touched by commercialism and very relaxed, the ideal setting for a boat trip, fishing or snorkelling.

Kingston, the capital of Jamaica, on the other hand, where in 1991 we played the first one-day international and the first Test, was a very strange city. Here we were advised to stick together and not take risks after dark. I took that to heart, going out once to a Chinese restaurant with Michael Holding and another time for a few beers to an English-style tavern with the rest of the Australian players. But nowhere else.

Neville Oliver, the ABC Radio commentator and one of my oldest friends, had an interesting experience in Kingston, after being introduced to a good friend of Michael Holding's by the great fast bowler. The pair, Neville and his new-found friend, went into a downtown pub for a beer, and the very white Australian

Opposite: I came to the Windies to face the fast men and had my foot cracked . . . by Mark Waugh.

commentator was soon getting plenty of unpleasant eyeball contact from the locals. However, when it was pointed out that Neville was, in fact, a mate of Michael Holding's, everybody wanted to buy him a beer!

The Australian team spent two weeks in Kingston, staying at the Pegasus Hotel and training at the main cricket oval, Sabina Park. We would catch the bus to the ground, but, after practice, would often run back to the hotel, straight past the city's high-security jail, which, we were told, has one of the biggest death rows, per capita of Jamaica's population, in the world. The jail inmates would hang out through the bars, shouting out what the West Indies would do to us. 'Licks! Licks!' they kept yelling, meaning we were going to get hit with bouncers. Thanks guys!

Jamaica was actually the second port of call for us on this trip. Our first game had been in St Kitts, against a President's XI, and on the second day we were introduced to the most popular technique in the West Indies for eliminating water from the wicket square. A huge tropical storm had flooded the area around the batting creases, but not the wicket itself. Rather than use sawdust or a 'Super-Sopper', as we do in Australia, the curator simply poured petrol onto the affected areas . . . and lit it! The water was literally burnt out of the ground.

It was in Jamaica, however, that we first met a 'typical' West Indies crowd, and they continually screamed and yelled for bouncers to be bowled. When Craig McDermott was struck by Courtney Walsh in the tour match — Billy had to have nine stitches inserted in his right eye — the people in the 'cages' just erupted. We thought, naturally, that here was the customary local reaction to the opposition being struck. But then, in the Test, Gus Logie was hit by McDermott — and exactly the same reaction ensued. It didn't matter who got hurt, they just wanted batsmen to get bounced and either hit or be hit; they'd go wild whenever a flashing hook and cut shot was played, and it didn't matter who played them.

And if the wind was right, there was no opportunity to say that you'd tried marijuana and hadn't inhaled.

The Test in Jamaica followed straight after the opening one-day international, which we'd won comfortably, 4–244 (Dean Jones, 88 not out) to 209. Craig McDermott, in his 'comeback' match after copping that awful blow from Courtney Walsh, showed his mettle in that game by taking 4–34. In the Test, he grabbed another five wickets as we bowled the Windies out for 264, after they'd been struggling big-time at 6–75. Gus Logie was their saviour this time, unbeaten at the end of the innings on 77, an incredible display of courage when you consider that, after Billy hit him, he had to go to hospital to have seven stitches inserted around his right eye. But he still returned to do the job for his country. And this was after poor Gus had learned, before the match started, that his mother had died.

Taylor and Geoff Marsh put on 139 for the first wicket, withstanding a pretty fiery start, and after two days, Australia were 4–296; I was not out, on 71. Early the next morning, I lost one from Patrick Patterson and copped it in the chin. I was wearing a beard at the time, so the blow didn't split my skin too much, but the West Indian doctor who stitched me afterwards — all right, without any anaesthetic — made a big fuss about it. In the end, I finished unconquered on 109, out of Australia's total of 371. It was very satisfying to score a century against the West Indies on their

My century in Jamaica was one of the most rewarding of my career.

turf, and especially so in Jamaica, the Caribbean wicket with the most pace and bounce.

In the years leading up to the series, the Australian tail had not performed very effectively against the West Indies, so we had decided to adopt a strategy where the recognised batsman would pay extra attention to protecting the bowlers when they ventured to the batting crease. In Jamaica, our last man in was the prince of No. 11s, Mike Whitney, but when he came out, after Billy and Merv had been dismissed off successive balls, he was extremely pumped up (how surprising!).

Not long after he'd arrived, Whit hit the last ball of an over to fine leg, and took off. None of this protecting the last man, Whit wanted every Test run he could muster. I had to run, because, before I knew it, Big Roy was standing right next to me.

Sure enough, second ball of the next over, Patrick Patterson knocked him over. End of the innings. But Whit's heart was in the right place. It always was.

We lost the entire fourth day of the Test, because rain leaked under the covers, and from that time the match was always going to be drawn, which was disappointing after our tremendous start. Still, we rated the Test as a moral victory, especially as, although we had played well, we felt we could play better.

As further consolation, I shared the man-of-the-match award with Gus Logie, which I regarded as an honour.

The remaining four matches in the one-day series were played between the first and second Tests. Australia won the second international, in Port-of-Spain, Trinidad, but a day later, the West Indies won the third, a rain-affected contest, that we might have won had both teams had to face their full complement of overs. But, in game four, in Bridgetown, Barbados, we wrapped up the series with an emphatic 37-runs victory which featured a superb century by Geoff Marsh, and some excellent bowling by Mark and Steve Waugh. This was the first time the West Indies had ever lost a one-day series at home.

It was just before this game, at training, that Mark Waugh kindly hit me in the big toe, breaking it, 11 days before the second Test. I missed our victory, instead going to the local hospital for an X-ray which, surprisingly, gave me the all clear. With that okay, I led the team in a rain-ruined three-day match in Trinidad, and a limited-overs contest that was staged on the scheduled final day instead, but it didn't feel too good, and I ended up struggling through the rest of the tour, limping for most of it. Further X-rays in Australia, after the tour, revealed, not surprisingly, that there was a crack in the bone.

From Trinidad, we flew to Georgetown, Guyana, for the final one-day international and the second Test. We won the shorter game, with Marsh scoring another hundred, his ninth in one-day internationals, but the Test match was another matter altogether. It was played on one of the flattest wickets I have ever struck, another which made Bellerive look like a seaming minefield. In such an environment, this West Indies team was just so good, so professional. If they didn't get wickets, they'd drop back a cog and bowl beautiful line and length. Their strategy revolved around frustrating the batsmen out, and a key component of this part of their bowling plan was sending down as few overs as possible. But when they did break through, they'd automatically go full-on; the first 20 minutes after a wicket fell were invariably highly dangerous.

On day one of the second Test, in almost seven hours of play (412 minutes), the West Indies sent down only 83 overs and Australia ended the day at 6–249, of which Marsh scored 94. I made 9, controversially given out caught behind off my pad from a Malcolm Marshall delivery — my leg was outside off-stump and my bat and gloves were well away from the ball (in the second innings, I made two, same method of dismissal, Marshall to Dujon . . . but I did hit that one).

This match marked the start of my downhill slide; having started with a hundred, I was to finish the Test series averaging less than 35. At the end of the tour, Bob Simpson and I would sit down and talk about the subconscious and getting into what he called 'satisfaction mode'. Many successful sports persons keep training hard, but, subconsciously, their intensity slackens. Maybe only a fraction, but that is soon revealed by a coincidental drop in performance. This was the first time that I truly realised, after seven years in the Australian team, that even after scoring a century, you must keep working. You can always improve.

We finished with 348, and the West Indies replied with 569, of which Richie Richardson scored 182. We posted a gully very square, a deep point and third man — but, in the mood he was in, five metres either side of a fieldsman at Guyana and you had no hope of cutting off the ball. It was a superlative innings. And then we were bowled out for just 248, Ian Healy top-scoring with 47; soon after we were bemoaning a 10-wicket loss, while the jubilant home supporters celebrated their important 1–0 series lead.

An infamous feature of our second innings was the controversial Dean Jones dismissal, when umpire Clyde Cumberbatch adjudged him run out after Deano had been bowled by a no ball, and walked away towards the dressing rooms, beyond cover. Dean hadn't heard the no-ball call, and was oblivious to Carl Hooper running in, picking up the ball, and uprooting a stump. There was no doubt that Deano should have been recalled, because you can only be run out if you're attempting a run, not leaving the ground believing that you're out.

Simmo was furious. He found reporter Patrick Keane, who was covering the tour for AAP and always carried a copy of *Wisden*, and checked a rule he already knew. Afterwards, Bob made sure everyone else knew, too. However, Dean Jones was still out in the scorebook. The umpire later admitted that he'd made a mistake under pressure, but that was no consolation for Deano or Australia.

The third Test was played at the Queens Park Oval in Port-of-Spain, but was destined for a draw after the first two days were just about washed away. Only 31 overs were bowled before the start of day three! It rained so hard that water splashed about your ankles out on the ground, and, for a while, visibility was less than 10 metres. During this time, Tubby and I played probably our longest innings — both of us not out in the 20s for two days!

The fourth Test, in Barbados, was another disappointment for Australia, especially after we bowled the West Indies out for 149 in just four-and-a-half hours on the first day. The bowlers were sensational — McDermott took 4–49, Hughes 4–44 and Bruce Reid the other two. But, unfortunately, the batsmen didn't back them up; Australia all out for 134.

The wicket might have been slightly up and down, but the West Indies then came out and made 9 (declared) for 536, of which Gordon Greenidge scored a double century — and just smacked the living daylights out of everyone. Mind you, we thought we had him pretty plumb lbw early on in his innings. But don't you always? And, unfortunately, Merv dropped him at fine leg. But we've all done that. And then, in our second innings, Swamp was given out lbw for

Under the Southern Cross *is sung in Barbados after winning the one-day series.*

nought — my opinion was that the ball would have struggled to hit a second set of stumps. It was one of the worst decisions I've ever seen, and one that Marsh, and Australia, didn't need. But, despite all this, we, quite simply, were outplayed by a better team.

Mark Taylor made 76 and I scored 57, but we crashed and burned again. All out 208, to lose by 343 runs, and the West Indies had taken an unbeatable 2–0 series lead.

It was after this match that West Indies captain Viv Richards made a bitter personal attack on Bob Simpson, describing the Australian coach as 'a moaner and a bad loser'. And that Simmo wasn't his 'cup of tea'. When I heard about it later, I sat back and thought: 'Viv, why bother? You've just won a series 2–0. What's the point?'

Although we won the final Test in Antigua (where Mark Waugh scored a brave and brilliant hundred, which was especially outstanding because the West Indies believed Junior struggled against pure pace and as a consequence attacked his body at every opportunity), the 1991 tour was a major disappointment, both personally and team-wise. We'd played so well in Jamaica in the opening Test, even if we did let the West Indies off the hook in the first innings. And then rain intervened. The worst section of the tour was the Guyana Test, and then they over-ran us, in typical West Indian fashion, in Barbados. If this had been the 'World Championship of Cricket', as many critics tagged it before it began, the West Indies had definitely retained their crown.

While I would never say that we should have beaten them, we should've done much better. But, as I've said too many times, 'What if?' is a useless question in cricket. 'What if Gordon Greenidge had been given out lbw in Barbados?' He wasn't, he made 200 and we lost. However, I think we showed twice, in Jamaica and Antigua, that we were good enough to beat them. And at least in Antigua we'd showed that we really could defeat the West Indies on their home soil. But, as we reflected on the series in the months afterwards, as has happened so many times in so many other series, at home and away, so close is still a very long way away from beating the West Indies.

Tubby and I in Trinidad, where, because of the torrential rain our first-innings partnership extended over the first three days of the Test.

Under the Southern Cross

14: MY BEST
MATES

I WAS VERY FORTUNATE TO BE PRESENT AT THE BIRTHS OF MY FIRST TWO CHILDREN. NOT EVERY FIRST-CLASS CRICKETER IS SO LUCKY. GEORGINA, OUR ELDEST, WAS BORN ON APRIL 7, 1988; OUR SON JACK CAME INTO THE WORLD ON JUNE 12, 1991 AND ELIZABETH, OUR THIRD CHILD, BLESSED US WITH HER PRESENCE ON FEBRUARY 3, 1995, THE SECOND DAY OF THE FINAL TEST OF THAT SEASON'S ASHES SERIES, IN PERTH.

I cannot describe fully, just what it meant emotionally for me to be with my wife, Pip, when Georgina and Jack were born. Besides the unbelievable joy I felt in each case, immediately following the birth, the experience gave me, as a man, so much more admiration, understanding and respect for my wife. Sure, such feelings exist when you choose to marry someone, but I can confirm they are certainly enhanced by an absolutely, exhilarating experience such as childbirth.

Immediately after the 1995–96 season, Georgina and I spent the evening together, a night on our own in Hobart. I was to play in a charity basketball game with Tasmania's Women's National Basketball League club, the Tassie Islanders, and she came along to give me some support. On the drive down from Launceston to Hobart, Georgina tried to talk to me non-stop, but I advised her that, with a long night ahead, she should perhaps have a nap.

'No,' said she, 'you've just come from Adelaide and I have to talk to you on the way so that you don't fall asleep!'

She had obviously been speaking to Pip.

Georgina was eight at the time. Because of all the time I had been away, playing cricket all over the world, I had not thought of her as being *that* old, as being capable of looking after her Dad. Many were the times that I felt the stress of the enormous passages of time, when I was unable to be with my family because of cricket — it is remarkable how quickly children grow up and how much of their life experiences you can miss during those years. In such a situation, all you can hope is that you've chosen your own life path correctly and

Opposite: My daughter Georgina (left), son Jack (right) and Santa, Christmas 1994.

that when you've been absent, you have been able to bridge the gap, at least in part, in telephone conversations, postcards and letters.

Now that I have come back into Georgina's life, I have discovered that she understands exactly what I was doing when I was away, and why I was doing it. It wasn't always so. I can remember very vividly two occasions when it was as if she didn't know me.

The first was when she was a baby, about six months old, so it was understandable — still awfully unforgettable, though. There was a rare break in the domestic Australian season, so I was able to come home. Georgina started crying, having woken up in the middle of the night, and I went to her. As I hit the nursery door, the unmistakable aroma of a dirty nappy assailed the nostrils, but she didn't seem too upset. Until I picked her up . . .

Absolute pandemonium!!!

In a dimmed room, all Georgina sensed and saw was a strange man picking her up. It was obvious that she didn't have the slightest clue who I was. That, despite Pip's reassurances, was very hard to come to terms with.

Something similar occurred when Pip and Georgina journeyed to England during the 1989 Ashes tour. They arrived at Lord's the day I was dismissed for 94, six runs short of a treasured century at the home of cricket, an event which

This photo was taken by a **Launceston** **Examiner** *photographer on the day I returned from the Perth Test in 1994–95 — the first time I'd ever seen Elizabeth.*

hadn't put me in the best frame of mind. But after sulking for the requisite time, I went down to the Q Stand to meet my family. Pip and Georgina were sitting with the rest of the Australian players' wives, children and girlfriends. But even though she was older this time, Georgina again seemed extremely apprehensive, almost scared of me. She just wanted to cling to her mother. I didn't know where to look; my own daughter didn't recognise me. Fortunately, Pip sprang to the rescue, by cajoling Georgie into going with me to the dressing-room for some juice and a biscuit. We went to the back of the Long Room, and all the while I was leading Georgina by the hand. But we had made a bad mistake — my 15-month-old baby was wearing a pinafore, which identified her as a member of the opposite sex. The attendant at the dressing-room nabbed us.

'Mr Boon,' he pronounced, 'Women are not allowed to enter here.'

'I beg your pardon?' said I. 'Are you referring to my 15-month-old daughter?'

'That is correct, Mr Boon.' He was halfway between snooty and sorry. 'I know what you must be thinking, but they are the rules. You cannot go up to your dressing-room with a woman.'

'You're kidding, aren't you?'

I know that cricket in England is steeped in history and can be quite old-fashioned in its protection of the philosophies of the 'gentleman's game'. But this one had me stumped.

As our Georgina grows up, I am able to see the similarities between her character and that of her mother. They are both strong-willed, and unafraid to voice their opinions. Consequently, they can sometimes clash. Which is where I come in. Pip reckons I'm soft with our children, which I can't deny, but for some reason, I am able to calm Georgina where others cannot. However, when Jack becomes upset, only his mother can quell the savage beast.

It's marvellous to watch your children develop, to see them start reading and writing, using computers and expressing ideas and logic far beyond anything of which I was capable of at their age. When Jack was younger, he became fascinated with me when I came back from a run, perspiring heavily.

'What's that, Dad?' he asked.

'That's sweat, Jack.' I replied.

'What's sweat, Dad?'

And his sister answered: 'Basically, Jack, Dad's getting older and as you get older and you want to keep playing cricket, you have to work a lot harder. And when you work hard, water appears on your skin — and that is sweat.'

So there!

I can remember sitting in the Australian dressing-room with Allan Border one day, when his eldest son, Dene, came in and asked: 'Dad, can you introduce me to some of these famous players?' I just thought to have your son ask you to do that would be a wonderful moment for a father. And it is. A few seasons later, Jack came out with the same request when Australia played a one-day game at Bellerive Oval.

I remember another occasion in Brisbane, after my father Clarrie died, when the former rugby league international, Peter Jackson, asked AB and I if we could visit his father, who was sick with cancer. I jumped into AB's car, and Dene travelled with us, but when we arrived at the hospital, I couldn't go in. Too many memories of Clarrie dying came back to me. Somehow, Dene sensed things weren't right. He turned to me and said: 'Your Dad died of cancer, didn't he?'

'Yes, he did,' I replied.

'I'll sit here and talk to you, then. It must be hard when you don't want to go in there.'

I was flabbergasted by the little bloke's compassion. But immensely touched.

Hopefully, as my children become older still, they will come to understand more about Test cricket and what I achieved in the game. But I will never pressure any of my children to play this or that sport, or take up this or that pastime. We have already overcome one hurdle, when Georgina decided to play tennis and then wanted to play the piano instead. She's still playing the piano and we told her she can make her own mind up about tennis — if she wants lessons again in a year or two, that's great. If not, that's great, too.

Meanwhile, Jack is at an age where he just loves kicking the footy, playing cricket, playing basketball, skateboarding, running around and terrorising humanity.

I also hope that when they do grow up, they don't find the pressure of having a father who was recognised in one sporting pursuit as being too great a burden. I think they were young enough to miss most of the negative comments that came my way whenever I was failing in Test cricket!

All I want my children to do is to enjoy themselves, and try to make a success of what they do with their lives.

When Elizabeth was born, if Pip and I thought that our first two children had been on this earth before, our third had definitely come back again. Elizabeth is just a beautiful, happy little person — extremely affectionate, with, already, an enormously developed, dry sense of humour.

But, while our first two children missed out on their father at different stages of their important early lives — Georgina more so than Jack — Elizabeth has seen so much more of me, and will continue to do so.

As Pip keeps saying: 'Father's daughter!' The affection I receive from my little girl is amazing.

Our wedding occurred five years before Georgina was born and Pip and I really got to know one another during that time; in a sense we learned to live

In August 1991, Georgina was a flower girl at the wedding of Steve and Lynette Waugh.

with one another. When we were married, we certainly didn't know what lay ahead in terms of my cricket career, even though I would make my Test debut at the end of the following year.

Our first major decision, one of many over the years where the 'Boon team' has been in action, was whether we should move to Adelaide in 1983. I've never taken anything for granted, and I've never had a lot of confidence in my own ability. So we opted to stay in Tasmania, where I had the stability of regular work with the Trust Bank. And we've never looked back and said: 'What if?'

After all, the quality of life we've enjoyed in Launceston and Tasmania has been marvellous.

Throughout my life, I've been an extremely lucky man because of the amount of support I've received. From my earliest days, my late father Clarrie and my mother Lesley did everything for me, in terms of making sure I was able to enjoy my swimming, football and cricket to the best of my ability. For them, providing such opportunity was the essence of 'family', and the responsibility you accepted when you decided to raise children.

As I progressed in cricket, my mother's experience of playing hockey for Australia was invaluable — she had gone through so many of the things I had to learn and achieve. And I couldn't have asked for a prouder father. The time they contributed to my development, to making sure I was all over the State for swimming carnivals, football matches and cricket clinics, was extraordinary. It is only now, sitting back retired, that I can fully appreciate their sacrifice and hope that I will manage to show the same commitment and unquestioning love for my children.

Before and after our marriage, I received a different kind of support from Pip's family. They were in Launceston, never complaining, to assist Pip when I was away playing cricket. For so long, I was the only Tasmanian in the Test team. In contrast, there might have been four or five players in the side from another state, and that sort of situation can lead to a 'network of people' being established for those left at home, where they can get together and talk about their shared circumstances. Pip, though, was at home, on her own.

Yet, she was always able to give me so much support while I was away. The time, patience and years of understanding Pip has shown me, while she was bringing up one, two and then three children as a quasi-single mother, is something I will always appreciate. Throughout my career, Pip was there advising, encouraging and criticising me. She is a very strong person, very passionate and never afraid to speak her mind. She's always been very wary of the media, though, and has been even more reticent about being photographed or interviewed in relation to our lives in cricket.

During my final Test match, against Sri Lanka in Adelaide, it took the Nine Network team, in particular their producer, Ron Castorina, about four days to talk her into doing a short interview with Ian Chappell. Pip has always hated that side of the cricket — the public focus and spotlight — even though I have always felt she does an excellent job in front of a microphone. When Allan Border retired as Australian captain, at the same moment AB's wife, Jane, 'retired' as Australian cricket's 'senior lady'. Not long after, several of the other wives approached Pip and asked her how she felt about accepting that mantle, to become the new 'leader of the clan'. Such is the respect they have for her.

In Tasmania, Pip continues to fight what appears to finally be a successful battle to have the facilities for the families of players at Bellerive Oval improved. As Melbourne, Sydney and Adelaide have adapted to modern-day standards in accommodating women and children at Test venues, so should the other states. When I'm playing, why shouldn't my family be able to watch a Test match or Sheffield Shield game in relative comfort?

Vince Lombardi, he of the Green Bay Packers fame and 'Winning isn't everything, it's the only thing!' quote, once remarked that if the player and his family are happy, then that player is able to give 100 per cent and more to the game, without having to worry about what's happening outside the playing field. At the start of the summer of 1994–95, I was in the mental horrors, doubting whether I was going to be able to achieve the standards I had set for myself. Pip was the one who helped me through that period, as she has done throughout every negative moment of my career. I went and saw sports psychologist Graham Winter in Adelaide, told him of my doubts and related what Pip's advice had been.

'What do you need me for?' was his amused reply.

'Instead of trying to remember all she has told you, write it down, put it in your kit and read it whenever you want to. She has answered all your questions.'

During my career, I received a lot of help from a lot of people, from sports psychologists, team-mates, coaches; even 'Joe Bloggs' in the street was always willing to offer his or her advice. But there has always been one person who has all the right answers for me, who cuts through the blarney to get to the basics. And that is Pip.

My wife has helped me through all the tough times, and as a result we've enjoyed some incredible experiences together. She is a woman with great conviction. It's very, very rare that her judgment about situations or people is wrong. And it is only right now, with my career over, that I fully appreciate her input. This woman is not only my wife and the mother of my children, she is my strength, the one who has helped shape my decisions, and stood by them. And Pip's my best mate. She absolutely hates that Australianism, but there's no doubt that is what she is to me.

With Jack in the nets at the MCG before the Test against Sri Lanka, December 1995.

THE LITTLE MAESTRO

I rate Sachin Tendulkar as one of the three best batsmen in world cricket. At the end of the 1995–96 season, (in no particular order) Tendulkar, Steve Waugh and Brian Lara were my choices for the top three.

Of the trio, technically, Tendulkar stands out, because of his ability to increase the pace at will — to play an inspiring shot, which can quickly wrest the advantage from the bowler. He has the necessary confidence to go over the top, to break a bowler who may have been concentrating on line and length. And, crucially, he is the equal to anyone else in the world in terms of his defensive game.

Comparing the three is almost impossible, because they are each very different players. And, as the cliche says: 'Every dog has his day.' What else can be said about Lara's 375, Test cricket's biggest score? I feel the same way about Waugh's 200 in the final Test of Australia's tour of the West Indies in 1995, when Curtly Ambrose and Courtney Walsh, with a little help from their friends, belted Stephen black and blue. And I will never forget Sachin Tendulkar, as an 18-year-old, making 148 not out against Australia in the third Test, in Sydney, in 1991–92, and backing up with another hundred in the fifth Test, in Perth.

Tendulkar was so full of confidence in both innings. His batting flowed and he refused to be dictated to by a bowler or field setting. In Sydney, as India moved towards a huge total, Australia had players in the deep, but he just kept hitting the ball into the gaps. Even at that stage of his career he was viewed as a prize wicket by all Test opposition. And at home in India, where the wickets are flatter and slower, Tendulkar is simply awesome.

I truly believe that it's a crying shame for the cricket lovers of this country not to have the opportunity to watch more of Tendulkar. However, I know that the Australian Cricket Board has major contracts with England, the West Indies and now South Africa, so scheduling visits by the other Test nations is becoming increasingly difficult. This means, unfortunately, that with the exception of that 1991–92 series and the World Cup in Australia in '92, our appreciation of him has been limited to television highlights packages and the coverage of his performances in the World Cup of 1996.

For such a young man, Tendulkar is aggressive in the right manner. This is particularly evident if he's bowling, when he's willing to try different tactics to get a batsman out. When he bats, he doesn't say much, but put a ball in his hands and he'll have a small dash at you.

Sachin Tendulkar was also the architect behind what was perhaps my most embarrassing moment in Test cricket. I had made a century in Adelaide in that 1991–92 series, and tried to hit him out of the park, but only managed to dribble the ball onto the on-side. There was an easy one there, or so I thought, but I was run out by literally metres, jogging through as the keeper raced around, picked the ball up and threw the stumps down at the bowler's end!

My favourite Tendulkar recollection occurred when Tim May, Dean Jones and I went to India to play some charity games for Kapil Dev. After the last game in Delhi, which was played at their major sports stadium, with the cricket field situated inside a running track, Tendulkar approached me for a chat.

He made me feel both humble and honoured. This young man — for all the talent with which he has been blessed — was seeking my advice.

'We have a series coming up against the West Indies. I would like to talk to you about batting against the West Indies,' he said.

'YOU want to talk to ME?' I said with some disbelief.

'Yes, because your record against the West Indies is very good. I want to talk to you about when to hook and when to cut.'

So Boon and Tendulkar sat down and talked through my theories, about the need to be positive, to decide whether to hook or not and to stick by that.

'You're a good enough player to make that decision while the ball is coming down at you,' was one comment I made. Not many players are.

Despite all the adulation he receives around the world and in his own

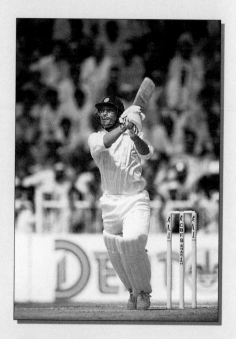

Sachin Tendulkar.

country — which is unbelievable, surpassing anything your average millionaire rock star could even imagine — his obvious love for the game and desire to keep learning is very impressive.

So I like him.

When you consider the pressure that must be on him, because of the religious qualities the Indians invest in their cricket team and their players . . . it must be unbearable. But he manages to keep a lid on all that and himself.

Mind you, I can't imagine him doing the grocery shopping. When Tim May and I tried that in India, we were mobbed by cricket fans, eager for an autograph, within 20 metres of our hotel. Given his status, Sachin wouldn't have made it past the revolving door!

15: Keeping Things Going

AUSTRALIA'S SECOND MATCH OF THE 1991–92 WORLD SERIES ONE-DAY TOURNAMENT (FEATURING AUSTRALIA, INDIA AND THE WEST INDIES) WAS PLAYED AT BELLERIVE OVAL IN HOBART, AGAINST THE INDIANS. IT BECAME A VERY IMPORTANT GAME IN MY CAREER, THE SCENE OF MY FIRST INTERNATIONAL CENTURY IN TASMANIA.

We were chasing 176 for victory, after Craig McDermott and Bruce Reid had dominated the entire Indian batting order, with the exception of Sachin Tendulkar and Sanjay Manjrekar. I opened with Marsh (Mark Taylor was still not a regular member of the Australian one-day team) and together we put on 45 for the first wicket, until he was out for 8, after which it was my turn to play the sheet anchor role.

Dean Jones would end up making 48, 25 of them singles — not the most impressive innings when you think of Deano and his dominance of the one-day game. However, on this December afternoon Dean's performance was selfless; he devoted himself to giving me as much of the strike as possible, so I could achieve my hundred.

I finished with 102 not out, as Australia made the required runs in 48.3 overs. When I reached three figures, the response from the 10,000 fellow Tasmanians at the ground literally deafened me — they just went crazy! I really appreciated their support throughout that innings.

By this point, I was Tasmanian captain once more. During the off-season, I'd been appointed to replace Dirk Wellham, the former NSW captain and Test batsman, who had been skipper for the previous three seasons. Obviously, I was pleased to resume as captain, but due to increasing commitments with the Australian Test and one-day teams, there were several seasons where I was only able to play one, two, even zero games for my home state.

The Australian team for the first Test of the summer, against India, in Brisbane, saw the return of one of my great friends in cricket, Mike Whitney, who'd missed the last three Tests in the West Indies, and also the inclusion of

Opposite: For the Australian team, the 1992 World Cup was a major disappointment.

Victoria's Paul Reiffel for the very first time. Even more significantly, the match was Allan Border's 126th Test for Australia, a new world record. Who would have thought there were still 30 more Tests to go before AB would finally call it quits?

From a personal point of view, the match went well. I scored 66 of Australia's 340 first-innings runs (we would win the Test by 10 wickets), but perhaps the highlight was my combination with Merv Hughes in India's second innings. We accounted for three of the first four wickets taken — all caught at bat-pad!

Another Victorian to make an impression on me around this time was a young leg-spinner by the name of Shane Warne, who was a team-mate of mine in the Australian XI side that played against the West Indies in Hobart. Ian Healy was captain this time, while among our opponents was a classy left-hander called Brian Lara, who had already impressed us greatly in the Caribbean, earlier in the year. On this occasion he made 83, although we dropped him four times, and 10, while Shane picked up seven wickets, including Lara in the first dig.

After Bruce Reid (six wickets in each innings), for the second season in a row, decimated an international batting order in a Test at the MCG, to give us a 2–0 lead, we headed to Sydney, which by this time in my career had become very much my favourite ground. I don't know why, but every time I walked through the SCG gates for a Test match, I felt so confident. Maybe it was the ground's

With Merv Hughes, one of the bravest cricketers I ever played with.

history, or the style of the stadium — I really don't know. It just felt like 'home', and I've scored some good hundreds for Tasmania there as well.

The wicket's not quick, but it's not an ideal batting wicket. It can turn, often slowly and sometimes a lot, and it can be slow. But there weren't too many times I missed out in Sydney.

This was the debut Test of Shane Warne. It wasn't necessarily an auspicious first match for him, in terms of his bowling, but the lad has sure come along a tad since then. The night before the Test, Warne was taken aside for a few beers with a pair of old blokes, G.R. Marsh and D.C. Boon. He

In the nets with Dean Jones.

admits that he was nervous before his first Test — who isn't? — but then his story becomes exaggerated, claiming that Marsh and I led him into inebriation. Must have been practising for his National Nine Network audition. Typical journalist! Never let the facts cloud a good story.

On the second day, when Shane came out to join me in the middle, he was still nervous. But he made 20, and helped me reach my 11th Test hundred and a record fourth Test century at the SCG. At that stage, in 12 Test innings in Sydney, I had scored 896 runs at 89.6 and in 15 innings against India, the statistics read 898 at 74.83, including four hundreds. Looking back now, I should have kept playing against India my whole career, usually at the SCG, but with a quick trip every so often to the Adelaide Oval, for variety!

Shane's bowling in this match was criticised a bit, but he was bowling against some of the best players of spin bowling in the world, on a very friendly deck. And, though he only took one wicket and conceded a truckload of runs, it shouldn't be forgotten that he only went for a bit over three an over, which is tidy for a leg-spinner. And although Ravi Shastri, who scored a superb double century, got into Shane somewhat, Warney did get him in the end.

One controversial aspect of this game, which ended in a draw, involved myself, umpire and fellow Tasmanian Steve Randell and India's cricketing legend Sunil Gavaskar. On the second day, Kapil Dev had appealed for lbw when I was on 85. But I had edged the ball into my pad, which my batting partner, Allan Border, confirmed. Randell told Kapil the same story. Unfortunately, from the comfort of the press box, Gavaskar criticised the decision in his syndicated column, which went right around the world — he reckoned the Australians were getting the benefit of close decisions, and used my case as his evidence. It read as though he was accusing the umpires of cheating, and, from what I understand, Randell and his fellow umpire Peter McConnell were later awarded significant damages in court.

No-one can argue that Sunil Gavaskar, the player, was one of the all-time, legends in world cricket. But he had disappointed me twice in my career. On both occasions, Marsh and I had arranged to talk to him about opening the batting — once in India and later in Melbourne. Obviously, there was plenty he could have taught us. The first time, at the end of our 1986 tour, we went into the Indian dressing-room and were told by a room attendant: 'No. He's too busy.' The second time, we waited at the bar of the Melbourne Hilton, but Sunny didn't turn up. I still have immense respect for him as a cricketer, though, and I know that he is a very nice guy.

The fourth Test began with Australian disaster, or perhaps we became entranced by the new Adelaide wicket: all out 145 after being sent in. Thankfully, we bounced back through McDermott's 5–76, bowling India out for 225. Then, in the second innings, Mark Taylor (100) and I (135) scored centuries, and Allan Border 91 not out, as Australia made 451. India were 0–31 overnight, but despite Azharuddin's fighting 106 on the last day, were all out for 333. A 38-run victory and 3–0 scoreline to Australia.

In something of a surprise, before the final day of the fourth Test began, it was announced to us that vice-captain Geoff Marsh had been dropped from the Australian team for the final match of the series. To say that AB was less than thrilled would be a massive understatement; first up, he refused to take the field at the start of play (he was out in the middle by the second over), then he was nowhere to be seen when we boarded our flight for Perth, venue for the fifth Test.

By this time, no-one in the team or cricket's hierarchy was in any doubt about how he felt about losing his right-hand man. AB's loyalty to his players was epitomised by his actions on this occasion. It was a difficult time for all involved; Swampy was so much a part of the team's soul.

I was quasi-captain until Allan finally arrived in Perth, and made a name for myself by giving the players a day off training (with Bob Simpson's blessing — it was his idea, but I didn't tell the boys). As well as Geoff, Mark Waugh had also been dropped, replaced by Tom Moody and Victorian opener Wayne Phillips.

The Test resulted in another Australian triumph. I managed to make a hundred in the first innings, and Jones and Moody did the same in the second,

Standing in front of the grandstand at the NTCA Ground in Launceston, in February 1992.

while Mike Whitney, with 11 wickets, was the Test's star bowler. A 4-nil series victory, coming on top of a decisive win in the World Series, was just about the perfect prelude to the upcoming World Cup, which was to be played in Australia and New Zealand. Or so, at the time, we thought.

There was one more game of personal significance before the Cup got underway — an encounter between Pakistan and Tasmania at the NTCA Ground in Launceston, which was preceded by a special dinner held on the eve of the opening of the 'David Boon Stand' at my home oval. Geoff Marsh and his wife, Michelle, flew over from Perth for the occasion. It was a tremendous evening and a tremendous honour, both the dinner and the naming of the grandstand, and another instance of D. Boon being totally humbled by other people's appreciation for my efforts for my country. And, to cap the occasion, Tasmania came out the next day and defeated Pakistan. We made 251 and bowled Pakistan out for 209.

Perhaps I should point out that Wasim Akram played, but didn't take a wicket, while Waqar Younis withdrew because of injury. And I should also mention that Tasmania's success didn't stop Pakistan going on to win the ultimate prize, the 1992 World Cup.

It's not far from the truth to say that Australia were just about nigh unbackable pre-tournament favourites for that World Cup. We were the defending champions, and up until the start of the Cup had been playing outstanding cricket in both forms of the game — Test and limited-overs. Personally, I was in great touch. After scoring hundreds in the last three Tests against India, and averaging nearly 80 in the series, I scored 107 from 125 balls in a practice match between the Australia team and NSW (who had their World Cup players, Mark Taylor, Steve Waugh and Mike Whitney in their XI). However, we only tied that game; in retrospect there might have been some ominous signs in that result.

Our first game in the Cup was in Auckland, against New Zealand. Now, while Australia gets pumped up about playing England and the West Indies, there is no doubt that the Kiwis do the same for us. And, in their own backyard, they're even tougher to beat. And here they out-thought and outplayed us, winning a game few outside the Shaky Isles thought they had any chance in.

In the afternoon, after captain Martin Crowe had scored an unbeaten 100 not out, in a total of 248, we set about chasing a target we thought was very gettable, even though Auckland tends to slow up through the day. Off-spinner Dipak Patel, though, opened the bowling for New Zealand, which was very surprising, but proved an excellent tactical move. It was rumoured that something like this might happen, but when it did Geoff Marsh and I were thrown for a while, confused as to which way to approach the situation. On a slow turner, do you take him, and risk the chance of losing wickets — not Australia's game-plan — or do you try to play him normally?

Despite the pre-match rumours, we had marched to the wicket expecting to face the much quicker bowlers, Chris Cairns and Willie Watson, so Patel's appearance was a psychological shock. But at 1–92 in the 25th over, even after Patel's initial impact, Australia were still set to challenge. Unfortunately, Dean Jones was run out at that point, although television replays suggested he might have made his ground. Not long after we were 5–125, and while Steve Waugh and I mounted something of a fightback, the momentum was lost, and with it the game. I finished up with 100, run out going for runs in the final overs. The Kiwis' winning margin at the end was 37 runs.

That first result set the tone for at least the first half of the World Cup for Australia. In Sydney, we were thrashed by South Africa and then England, with a victory over India in Brisbane in between. One win from four games was not what we had hoped for, and Australia's semi-final chances were diminishing rapidly. The overall feeling in our camp was one of frustrated disappointment. In 1987, we had been rank underdogs; perhaps because we were playing at home we were just trying too hard.

And we suffered another setback when Ian Healy tore his hamstring batting against the South Africans, which meant that 'Bacchus' Boon had to step in behind the stumps. Our offie, Peter Taylor, a superb and often underrated bowler in one-day international cricket, gave me some advice during a brief practice session we had before going out to defend our small total.

'When I'm bowling,' P.T. explained, 'I want you to cover the outside edge. In one-day cricket, the arm-ball is my big wicket-taker.'

Later on, Taylor was bowling way outside off-stump to the South African opener, Andrew Hudson, who charged down the wicket at him — there was me a mile away from the stumps covering the outside edge — but the ball turned. I was in no position to get anywhere near it, but, mercifully for me, it bowled him. I did drop Kepler Wessels, though, diving in front of first slip, trying to snare a low one. It wouldn't have carried to slip and I thought it was a magnificent effort, but when I stopped sliding, the ball fell out of the end of my glove. I was watching it all the way, thinking: 'Yes! Yes! Oh, Oh . . .

'No.'

Afterwards, Heals came up to me and said: 'Babs, great stuff! But you know, you're allowed to close your hand. It's a glove, not a paddle, mate.'

The next day, I don't think I have ever been so sore.

We actually won the game against India on a last-ball run out. Steve Waugh dropped their tailender, Javagal Srinath, in the deep, but recovered and threw the ball back to me — I was still keeping. I grabbed it on the bounce and smashed the bails off to dismiss Venkatapathy Raju as he sprinted for the third run that would have tied the game.

A victory over Sri Lanka in Adelaide gave us some respite from the critics, but then Pakistan brought us crashing down again in Perth. This meant that, even though we flogged Zimbabwe in Hobart, 6–265 to 137, with just three wins from seven matches we were fighting a losing battle with the calculator to make a semi-final berth.

In the end, the equation was simple, yet brutal — we had to beat the West Indies at the MCG and New Zealand had to defeat Pakistan in Christchurch. This time, we did our bit, and I made 100 exactly in my final World Cup innings, but earlier in the day Pakistan had won by seven wickets, which meant that they, basically on the back of a point they 'won' from a wash-out against England (which they were about to lose), finished fourth on the Cup table. And we finished fifth.

Of course, Australia should never have been in the position we got ourselves into, by only winning half our preliminary games. All in all, the '92 Cup was one of the major 'downers' of my career. Because we had won the '87 World Cup and then, in just about every Australian summer since, proved ourselves in this abbreviated form of the game, and also because we were playing in front of our own fans, we felt before the tournament that we had a big chance. We believed, too, that we were well-equipped in terms of talent and experience, but we just didn't play well enough as a team. The commitment was definitely there — despite media reports at the time to the contrary — but perhaps everyone suffered, subconsciously at least, from the pressures of playing at home, which can become, depending on the circumstances, either a spur or a bridle.

Maybe we wanted to win too much. I think we forgot that, in order to succeed, you have to enjoy what you're doing. Instead, the feeling in the camp was of intensity and seriousness, certainly so as we kept losing, and that edge of humour which pervades Australian teams that are performing well was missing.

I know, too, that I would have struggled to play in any more games in that '92 World Cup, because my knee blew up like a football after that final century against the West Indies. A week later, I was under the knife again, to repair damage to the medial ligaments of my right knee.

Fortunately, I had no more big cricket to play until August, when Australia journeyed to Sri Lanka for a three-Test tour. This was to become a very significant tour, for it contained the final Test appearance of Dean Jones — although we didn't know or imagine it at the time — and the turning point in the career of Shane Warne.

Sri Lanka, generally speaking, produces seaming wickets, totally different to anything one sees in India or Pakistan — I know Sir Richard Hadlee always declared that it was one of the best places on the planet for him to bowl. Yet, for our blond leggie, it proved, in the first Test at least, to be heavenly, although I must say that for a very long time this did not seem as if it would be the case.

When Sri Lanka declared their first innings closed, they led by 291 runs. And, even though we managed to set them 181, from a minimum 58 overs, on the last day, they appeared to be cruising at 2–127, with Aravinda de Silva in lethal touch.

But, less than 17 overs later, we had pulled off an unbelievable victory. Our spinners, Warney and 'Mo' Matthews, had taken seven of the last eight wickets between them, and we'd snuck home by 16 runs. Shane had been struggling, without a wicket in the match, but he came back to take the final three. AB had tossed him the ball and told him that he believed he could do the job, while Mo was encouraging him at every opportunity. And Warney did it!

The final two Tests were drawn, with perhaps the most significant statistic to come out of them being the extraordinary run of outs suffered by Mark Waugh, who proved that even the freakishly-talented can experience a run drought. Junior had a 'beaut'; after his first Test realised 5 and 56, he finished the series with innings of 0, 0, 0 and 0.

Junior, at times, comes under considerable criticism for his approach to cricket, in that it sometimes appears, when a huge score is in the offing, that he gives his wicket away going for another of those extraordinary shots within his repertoire.

But he does care about his cricket and about Australia's performance, even if he doesn't have the outward signs, the public passion, that marks other players. That's just Mark's character. I think if you tried to change him, perhaps even if he changed himself in a major fashion, you might destroy his inherent ability.

He is such a great striker of the ball, with so much class, that he will always get runs, despite the odd hiccup along the way. And I believe that, apart from his one-day opening role for Australia, which was so successful in 1995–96 and during the 1996 World Cup, his natural batting position in Test cricket is at No. 4.

Once on that Sri Lankan tour, when I had been dismissed for 30-odd — one of my pet hates, getting out after you've done all the hard work — I came into the dressing-room and spat it. It was Mark who tried to placate me. 'You can't get 'em every time,' he said.

I know that, and told him so, but I also repeated that lesson I'd learned in the West Indies in 1991. You can never, ever, be satisfied, even subconsciously, with yourself. You must try to get runs every day. You won't get them every time, but you have to care about your performance in each innings. Maybe Mark took a little while to realise this — maybe he didn't know it in Sri Lanka in 1992 — but I know he's aware of it now.

Mark Waugh and I have a standing bet, the amount is insignificant, but the result is important. I have bet him that he will score more Test runs than I did. And nothing would give me greater joy than to see him go way past me.

Mark Waugh with Greg Matthews in Adelaide in 1991, after Mark had scored a century on debut.

16: Clarrie

MY FATHER, CLARRIE BOON, DIED IN FEBRUARY, 1993, ONLY A FEW DAYS
AFTER THE AUSTRALIAN TEAM HAD LEFT FOR OUR SHORT TOUR OF
NEW ZEALAND.

Dad's death came as a big shock, although he had been ill with cancer for a long time. The day the Australian team departed, my mother Lesley had telephoned to say that Dad needed to go into hospital for some tests, and he wanted me to drive them there. I remember thinking that such a request was a bit strange; the night before we had said our farewells, in the same manner as every other time I had been about to depart on an overseas cricket tour. I always telephoned before a tour, or trip away, to say goodbye. 'Good luck,' Dad would say, 'Have a good time. See you when you get back — do your best.'

That morning, Dad didn't really say anything to me, which, given the fact that he had asked me to drive him to the tests, was very unusual and something which remains to this day, stuck in my mind. It's almost as though he knew he would never see me again.

When I arrived in New Zealand, I called Mum, just a little nervously, and she explained that Dad was still in hospital, having even more tests. But everything, it seemed, was all right.

However, the hidden truth was that he had a tumour on an aorta wall in his heart. When that tumour burst not long after, poor Dad died suddenly, without, thankfully, according to the doctors, feeling too much pain.

Straightaway, Pip rang the Australian media and team manager, Ian McDonald, in New Zealand. It fell to Macca to tell me, which he did while some of the guys were out training at a local Auckland gymnasium. I was rooming with Justin Langer at the time, and while I always had immense respect for Justin's cricket ability and courage, I discovered a remarkably compassionate side to the young Western Australian's character at this time; his great friendship was much appreciated during my time of personal crisis. For a while, we just sat together in our room. If I didn't want to say anything, he didn't. If I wanted to talk, he did. It was as though he'd spent years, training as a counsellor.

Opposite: My father, Clarrie Boon, in 1989.

That night, the Australian team was required at a Fourex promotional function. Of course, I didn't have to go, but, rather than sit and mope in my room, I went along, shadowed by Justin. In the end, I had quite a few beers that night, thinking about Dad and our lives together, while 'Lang' stayed with me for support — something I have never forgotten.

The next morning, I was up at 6am for a 7.30 flight back to Australia.

At the airport in Auckland, countless people were asking: 'What are you doing, aren't you supposed to be on tour?' Then, when I reached Melbourne, where I had a stop-over of some three hours, there was more of the same from the passing public: 'Didn't you go to New Zealand the other day?' I can remember not wanting to share my grief with passers-by, although I knew they were just showing concern and interest, so I just answered generally, saying I would be returning to New Zealand in a few days. By the time my plane finally departed for Launceston, I was struggling, overcome by sadness, and shed more than a few tears during the flight.

The funeral was a double-edged occasion, terrible to mark the passing of my father, but also somewhat heartening because of the huge attendance from people in Launceston and around the state. One of hardest things that I've ever done was speak at the service, on behalf of our family, to thank everyone for coming.

It wasn't until after the funeral that I realised that Dean Jones, who had missed out on the tour of New Zealand, had flown in from Melbourne to pay his respects to Clarrie and our family. I cannot begin to describe how much it meant to me to see Deano there. Similarly, my great mate, Geoff Marsh, had wanted to attend, but couldn't make the flight connections work.

Dean Jones was an enormous support to me throughout my career. When I was dropped from the Australia team in 1986–87, it was Deano who wrote to me, a letter I still possess, urging me to work hard and get back into the side. What he wanted, he explained, was for us to enjoy plenty more international cricket together.

Afterwards, back at Mum and Dad's house, I suggested to my mother that we should perhaps purchase some beer and wine for the mourners who would be coming by. 'David,' she whispered, 'you are now the man of the house. If you see fit to have a beer, do so. It's your decision.'

Which I regard as a lovely family story.

Dad was sometimes a strict man. I can remember, as a young child, being tied to a long piece of rope on a tennis court on my father's instructions because I was being a lunatic. My grandfather, who was looking after me at the time, received a phone call from the authorities, asking why this poor child was being restrained!

There were Dad's silly, little quirks. Ask him what time it was and he would answer: 'Daytime.' Or: 'Night-time.' Such responses were guaranteed to drive a child crazy. But he was just a full-on, individual who gave exactly 100 per cent all the time.

Never was this more apparent than in his relationship with his son. When I became involved with the South Esk Swimming Club at primary school, Dad became a state referee. As my cricket progressed, he became a member of the Northern Tasmanian Cricket Association committee. But his major sporting passion was football, having played with East Launceston and North Launceston in the Northern Tasmanian Football Association. Once his playing days were over, he coached in the amateurs. Then he found his niche as an administrator in Tasmanian amateur football, running the northern competition for many years, and reaching the position of Australian president for a time.

Even today, when I travel all over the country, I continually meet people who knew Clarrie through his interest in amateur football — people who come up and say hello not because of who I am, but because of Dad. I find that very satisfying.

As my cricket prowess grew, from representing Tasmania to playing Test cricket, Dad refused to claim any influence on my game, or any role in my achievements. The truth, of course, was far from that. In terms of attitude, commitment and support — the basics everyone needs — he was simply sensational. For example, Clarrie was my personal chauffeur throughout my junior years. Whether it was swimming, football or cricket — anywhere in Tasmania — Dad would get me there and back. As I got older, we had our differences of opinion, as is the norm with every father–son combination, but for the last 10 years of his life, he was one of my best mates. No matter where I was in the world, Mum and Dad would always ring on the first morning of a Test match and wish me good luck. It was a Boon tradition.

To this day, I occasionally have visions of Clarrie. Not often, but when a situation arises, similar to one that happened in the past, I can see Clarrie as clear as a bell. Take an instance during the summer after he died, when Tasmania played New Zealand in a first-class match at the NTCA Ground in Launceston. Throughout my career — playing club cricket with Launceston, or with Tasmania when the ground hosted Sheffield Shield matches — Dad used to always locate himself in the same position, under the trees on the eastern flank of this picturesque oval. I was directing the field, moving a man from square leg to deeper in the field, in front of where Dad used to sit . . . and then I saw him!

I thought I was going stir-crazy. 'Pull yourself together, David,' I said to myself. 'And get on with the game!'

I haven't seen him since at the NTCA Ground, but I still keep an eye out!

Mum and Dad watched me play a lot of cricket. They travelled to England on two tours, in 1985 and 1989, and had a ball both times. In 1989, at Lord's, Mum was sitting beside Mick Jagger from the Rolling Stones, but didn't realise who he was. Afterwards, she said to me, 'I met a lovely young man today. His hair was a bit long, but he was a lovely chap.' Then, while Jagger was visiting our dressing-room, he mentioned sitting beside a pleasant women, who was obviously a player's mother. But whose Mum she was he wasn't sure.

Like Clarrie, my mother has always been there in a support role for me, encouraging me to do my best. Her philosophy on sport is straightforward: If you can walk away, even if after you've failed, knowing that you've given it your best shot ... that's what matters. Failing, like succeeding, is just part of sport. It happens.

Mum was especially supportive in 1986–87, the season I was dropped from the Test team. She emphasised the need to work hard and get back. I found her experiences as an Australian hockey player, particularly when I was suffering a bad patch, were invaluable.

Lesley is a woman who has an enormous amount to offer, but will never force her opinion upon anyone. But if you ask her for help, she'll give you all she's got. In 1995–96, I think she was a little bit shocked when I broached the subject

With Pip, my mother Lesley and Clarrie at the dinner held to commemorate the opening of the David Boon Stand.

of my retirement from big-time cricket with her, but she soon responded. 'This is your decision. Think it through properly, and whichever way you go, I'll back you.' How could you fail to make the right choice with that sort of advice?

Back when I was still a kid, when the subject of my playing for Australia was first raised, Mum laid down the challenge: 'I'll bet you don't play for Australia before I did.' And she was right. Mum played Test hockey for Australia when she was only 18. I was 23 when first selected to play Test cricket for my country!

In the same year Dad died, Australia toured England again and I was lucky enough to enjoy some personal success. I actually scored my first Test hundred in England at Lord's, an occasion at which Dad would obviously have loved to have been present. During the post-century press interviews, there were some questions about Clarrie and the hundred, and I can recall making an innocent statement such as: 'I'm sure that he's looking down and feeling extremely proud.' The next morning, the papers had me dedicating the century to Dad, which didn't impress me, nor my mother.

Dad was alive when Georgina and Jack were born, and Georgie, being the first, was certainly her grandfather's little girl. Georgina became a glutton, her diet built around the strawberries and tomatoes Dad grew in his vegetable patch at my parents' home, down the road at Hillside Crescent. And every Sunday morning, Dad would be waiting, sitting outside on the garden furniture. 'It's about time you lot were up,' he'd growl. 'Where's my granddaughter?'

'She's still asleep, Dad.' I'd mumble.

'Oh, is the kettle on?'

When Dad died, we tried to shelter Georgina from that fact. But you can never repress a child's honesty or curiosity. One day, out of the blue, she announced: 'Come on. I want to go up and see where Pa's buried.' Then, on our way to his grave site, she ordered me to stop, to buy some flowers. And not just any flowers — she went into the florist and returned with a bunch of carnations, Dad's favourite bloom.

I miss Clarrie. And I think I always will. Not every day, but regularly, I go to visit his grave in Launceston. I think of him often, especially when there are major decisions to be made, and more than once have walked up to the cemetery, to sit, and talk to his plaque in the ground. I went there before every major tour between 1993 and 1995, and went there again before I made my final decision to retire from international cricket. I know this may sound strange, but, in essence, I was just going through my thought processes, either trying to convince myself of a certain course of action, or working out the alternatives.

And, every time, I walked away from my father's grave in peace, content with the path I was going to take.

17: The Times are A-Changin'

SEASON 1992–93, ONE WHICH INVOLVED A FULL FIVE-TEST SERIES AGAINST THE WEST INDIES, WAS THE FIRST INTERNATIONAL SUMMER, APART FROM MY DEBUT SEASON IN THE AUSTRALIAN TEAM, THAT I LOOKED AROUND THE TEST DRESSING-ROOM AND DIDN'T SEE GEOFFREY ROBERT MARSH.

I'm not going to pretend this wasn't a difficult time for me. I found my life in cricket to be different, especially on the next major tour, to England in 1993. But Geoff and I have always had similar opinions, one of which is: when you get dropped, it's because you haven't scored enough runs. I had to be realistic and get on with life — in cricket, things do change within a team.

It became a time to forge closer ties with the younger guys in the team — I had to, only Allan Border was older than me!

Once again, the summer began with an Australian XI game at Bellerive Oval, which was perhaps most significant for innings of 95 and 100 not out achieved by Steve Waugh. Stephen had not played a Test the previous season, and been left out of the tour to Sri Lanka, but, now, with Swamp seemingly out of the picture, and the relative failures of Victoria's Wayne Phillips and prolific young Queensland opener Matthew Hayden in the Australian XI game, the push was on to put the elder Waugh back into the Test batting line-up for the first Test, in Brisbane. Perhaps even at No. 3, with D. Boon going back to the top of the order.

This was the selectors' thinking, and, at least early on, it worked well for both myself and the team. We should just about have won at the Gabba, where I made 48 and 111, but the final day ended with Australia just two frustrating wickets from a precious victory. I was lucky to make that hundred, though, because in the first over of the morning, I nicked Curtly Ambrose and Carl Hooper dropped a sitter at second slip. However, I worked hard through the first session and started to find form after lunch, straight-driving Patrick Patterson for four to notch the hundred. This is one of my favourite shots, hitting the ball back past the fast bowlers — never once in my career did I think it might not really annoy them.

Opposite: Batting against Pakistan (top) and celebrating AB's Test run-scoring record (below) in '93.

And they deserved it. Only the night before, Taylor and I had to stand up and face 40 frightening minutes of West Indian pace, during which Ambrose was near lethal. I remember having to face the last over, from big Curtly, and umpire Terry Prue called a no ball! 'Jeez, Terry,' I thought, 'unless I nick one we don't need you to call no balls at this time of night!'

On that final day, the Windies top-order collapsed completely, to be 4–9, but Richie Richardson saved them by defending for nearly four hours, for 66. However, his determined innings, as well as saving the game, also ignited the first controversy of the season, as Merv Hughes and Allan Border were both put on report for dissent. The furore evolved out of three very confident lbw appeals against Richardson, that were all turned down by my fellow Tasmanian Steve Randell. Merv and AB didn't agree with the ump, and told him so. Unfortunately, AB then got himself into more hot water by refusing to appear before the International Cricket Council referee, Mr Raman Subba Row, because he thought the report was frivolous. The fine of $2000 handed down was anything but that.

We all know that umpires make mistakes, as do players. What annoys us, at times, are comments made when questions about decisions are asked. Some responses can suggest that the umpire doesn't know what he's talking about; when that happens problems can result. For example, one might enquire: 'What was that missing?', and the umpire's stock-standard is: 'Going down.' But when the ball was an outswinger, how can it be going down the leg-side?

For mine, umpires should just say: 'It's not out.' They shouldn't give an explanation. I also reckon that umpires shouldn't act as 'schoolteachers' in the way they approach the game.

Just one other small aside before I leave this first Test. Before the game, Dean Jones had been named 12th man for Australia, as the selectors preferred a young West Australian batsman called Damien Martyn, who had started the summer with multiple hundreds in the Shield. Deano, meanwhile, had become a victim of circumstances, in that Victoria had virtually no cricket scheduled — only two first-class matches, both washed out — before the opening Test. Dean Jones never played another Test for Australia.

At 4–115 on the first day of the second Test, in Melbourne, Australia were teetering, but then Allan Border and Mark Waugh bravely put on 204 runs, as we reached a more than respectable 395. Border made 110, his first ton in Australia for five years, and Junior 112, in a total which looked even better after we bowled the Windies out for just 233.

I was feeling even more confident after I was dismissed in the second dig. Seriously! Having made 46 in the first innings, I was bowled in the second by Phil Simmons for 11 — he tried to bounce me, it landed halfway down the pitch, but then just ran straight along the ground. As I walked off the ground, I, more than anyone, realised how difficult it would be to survive that pitch on the final day.

In my first innings, Ambrose had constantly struck my bottom hand, such was the bounce in the wicket. In fact, at the first drinks break, I was too scared to remove my glove, because I could see some blood leaking through. Sure enough, when Australian physiotherapist Errol Alcott gently removed the glove later, it wasn't pretty . . . just another hazard of being 'four foot-two'.

The final day of the Test belonged to Shane Warne, who took 7–52, including the key wicket of Richardson, bowled by a flipper that just about ran along the ground. The Windies, with Phil Simmons in full cry, had reached 1–143 before Warney struck. Another vital moment came just five runs later, when Brian Lara flicked a Mike Whitney delivery off his pads, and I caught it at short leg. Two hours later, the West Indies were all out for 219.

The Sydney Test a few days later was a very high-scoring draw, in which AB became only the second player in history, after Sunil Gavaskar, to score 10,000 runs in Test cricket, and Lara carved out one of the best innings I have had the privilege to witness. It was his first century in Test cricket (!!!!), and he turned it into an awesome score of 277.

There had been a lot of rain during the game, which made the ball lifeless — BUT even so, this was magic. Lara either defended, glided the logical ones down to fine leg, or hit every single forceful shot into a gap. I really don't think he hit a fieldsman with a full-blooded stroke once during his 474 minutes at the crease, and he found the fence 38 times in all. It was a great, great innings.

And then, in a moment of cruel anti-climax, 'The Prince', as we called him, was run out in a mix-up with Carl Hooper. It was a shame his innings finished like that. Perhaps the quality of that innings can be best measured by the fact that Richie Richardson, no slouch with the bat, made a superb century as well, and barely anyone can remember it!

And I scored my 5000th run in Test cricket during the game as well. Halfway to AB!

Before the fourth Test, I strained my left hamstring during the World Series finals, which meant I had to undergo a fitness test — running twos and threes — in front of Alcott and chairman of selectors Lawrie Sawle in the middle of the Adelaide Oval. I was very relieved to be declared fit; in fact, I was probably fitter than ever! Less fortunate was Damien Martyn, who collided with Simmo during a fielding drill, and damaged his eye. Consequently, another West Aussie, young Justin Langer, made his Test debut.

On day one of this crucial fixture, the West Indies batted first and were all out for 252, Merv Hughes taking 5–64. And then the real fun began. In the brief period left before stumps, Ian Bishop bowled very sharply, and Mark Taylor departed for 1 in only the second over. This brought Langer to the wicket for his first Test innings and — fourth ball — Bishop 'pinged' him on the back of the helmet, cracking the protective headgear.

'Lang' is a very gutsy little bloke. I said to him: 'Get in behind it, keep talking and watch the ball.' Not content with that, he kept gee-ing me up as well!

I did get annoyed, though, when, with Bishop running in, Langer pulled away because he was suffering blurred vision. Several of the West Indians fielding close to the wicket hopped straight into him — about being scared and weak. Which was very brave! I told Justin that the centre of the Adelaide Oval at that moment 'was no place for heroes'; if he wasn't okay, he had every right to take his time before he faced another delivery.

At stumps, Australia were 1–2. Lang and I added only one run in the 26 minutes we endured before bad light stopped play. Then, the next day, it was my turn.

Curtly Ambrose, in trying to bowl me a bouncer, struck me on the left elbow. Most of the media reports incorrectly said that I was hit by a 'rearing' delivery. In fact, I went down expecting a bumper and then tried to come up; if anything, it stayed low. Whatever, the pain was indescribable.

Errol rushed out and attempted to treat me. He asked if I could feel my little finger; I couldn't. 'Well, your arm's busted then,' was his depressing, immediate diagnosis.

The only humour in this incident came when Langer strolled up and said: 'C'mon, there's no place for heroes out here . . . '

'Shut up,' I said. 'It's only your first Test.'

This was the first, and last, time I retired hurt in a Test match.

I was taken straight to the Royal Adelaide Hospital, where X-rays revealed no break in the elbow or forearm bones. I remember a doctor coming out and saying: 'Well, David, you might as well go stand in front of a Mack truck. If that didn't break your arm, nothing will.'

To this day, though, there is still a depression in the bone of my left elbow.

As soon as Errol heard there was no break he was into me — that night he tried massage, ice, manipulation, the works.

The sweat was pouring off me; the treatment was almost as painful, but not quite, as being hit in the first place. Even so, overnight the arm seized up, although by the next morning the pain wasn't as bad as it had been the night before.

When I went out to bat again, I wore an arm-guard for the first time, but the problem was that I had no strength in my top hand and couldn't get the elbow up. When I came back in, at the fall of the fifth wicket, I knew I was going to cop it and wore one on the shoulder almost immediately. But I did manage to 'carry' my bat, for 39, as we finished with a disappointing 213.

However, by the end of the third day, after off-spinner Tim May (an incredible 5–9 on his home pitch) had reduced the visitors to all out 146, the Frank Worrell Trophy, which Australia hadn't held since 1978, was just 186 runs away.

At the start of the fourth day, January 26, Australia Day, we were very confident, but, sadly, it was not to be. I was out lbw to Ambrose for a duck (either feast or famine in Adelaide for me) in the fifth over. At 7–74, then 8–102, then 9–144, Australia's race was apparently run.

However, May, already a hero, and Craig McDermott had other ideas. Their 40-run partnership, in 88 minutes, which ended just one cruel run short of victory was nothing short of amazing. They were truly magnificent.

The mood changes in the Australian dressing-room that afternoon were amazing — darkest depression to the edge of ecstasy and back again. The decision by umpire Darrell Hair to give Billy out, caught behind by Junior Murray off Courtney Walsh was astounding, reminding me so much of a Steve Randell run-out call against Javed Miandad a few years earlier, which television replays proved correct — by a centimetre. Hair could have very easily given McDermott not out, and argued that he was giving the Australian the benefit of

'There is no place for heroes out here . . .' A gallant Justin Langer in Adelaide, 1992–93.

the doubt. Instead, he courageously made the right decision, as the ball grazed Craig's helmet and glove on its way to the keeper.

At the end of the day, the performance of our batsmen in this innings can only be regarded as a dismal failure. There can be no doubt that Australia's top six batsmen should have been able to score 186 runs on that wicket, no matter how well Ambrose, Bishop, Walsh and company were bowling. It's something I can't easily forget.

The fifth Test in Perth became the Ambrose demolition show, on a wicket which had more than a bit of juice in it. In less than three days, we were thrashed by an innings ... AB's dream of winning a series against the Windies never seemed so far away. And, to make matters worse, AB and Hughes were reported again, this time for disputing a decision by umpire Col Timmins. A 'gesture' was made from slip, after Timmins gave his opinion on an appeal, which the man in white clearly didn't appreciate. This time, both players received a severe reprimand after making their apologies to the umpires.

As an aside, that fifth Test was the one where the current Australian captain, Mark Taylor, was named 12th man. Justin Langer opened with me, and a now-recovered Damien Martyn batted at five.

Before the match began, AB received an invitation from his old mate at Channel Seven, Paddy Welsh, to go and watch the golf at the Vines Classic. AB, Tubby and I went along, and we watched — beside Welsh in his commentary position — three great players, Greg Norman, Robert Allenby and Peter Senior.

The caddies would offer their advice: 'You've got so many metres to the hole, it's a four-iron, but with this wind, do you think you should take a three and cut it into the breeze?'

Fair dinkum! I'm just happy to hit the ball! Here I was watching, awestruck, as Norman, Allenby and Senior did exactly what their caddies had suggested they do. The execution was unbelievable, a highly rewarding and enjoyable day.

Yet, AB and I carried a burden, as we knew Tubs would be 12th man. 'Should we tell him?' we asked each other. 'No, we can't.'

That night, at the team meeting, Mark finally did learn of his fate, and was very unhappy with us. 'We've been at the golf all afternoon and you didn't tell me,' he protested. 'Never hide anything from me like that. I'm big enough to take it.' He was right, of course.

After this series, we headed to New Zealand for a short tour. I missed the opening game, as I was back in Australia mourning the death of my father, and didn't rejoin the team until they had reached Nelson, for a one-dayer against the New Zealand Board's President's XI. During my innings of 75 there, I was hit on the inside of the left heel by a medium-pacer called Aaron Gale. It hurt plenty, but calmed down after a while.

However, when I woke up the next morning, I could not walk! Twenty-four hours later, though, it was as if nothing had happened.

Something similar happened in the third and final Test of the series. This time, an inside edge crashed into the ankle and by the next morning, the joint was so swollen that X-rays were ordered. The day after, everything was perfectly okay. Errol Alcott reckons that my recovery rate from injury is just different to that of other people. I'm not complaining.

The first Test of this series belonged to Allan Border, who in his 139th Test passed Sunil Gavaskar's world record of 10,122 Test runs during our only innings, and led us to a clearcut innings victory. In the second Test, a draw, I actually bowled one over at the end of this match, a maiden to their pace bowler Danny Morrison. Strangely, the umpire was deaf to my lbw appeals. I would have loved to have taken a Test wicket — I wouldn't have cared who it was!

During this match, New Zealand captain Martin Crowe was cruelly hounded by the Kiwi media about his personal life. As Martin said at the time, he didn't mind copping criticism for his batting or captaincy, but his private life should have been off limits. I felt very sorry for the Kiwi skipper, who is a tremendous person. There can't be anything pleasant about being quizzed over the most intimate details of your life.

Disappointingly, the Kiwis squared the series in the final Test, in Auckland. At the beginning of the final day, they needed another 33 runs, with five wickets in hand, and we made a 'pact' that involved everyone wearing their baggy green caps out to play — even Craig McDermott, who looks like the original train driver in his, and Merv Hughes, who hardly ever wore one. We got pumped right up and then didn't take a solitary wicket! Just a month before Australia's defence of the Ashes in England, this loss was a humbling kick in the pants for the team.

This was also John Wright's last Test for New Zealand and, although Martin Crowe might disagree, I reckon the Australian players celebrated more with 'Wrighty' than did the Kiwis — even though we'd lost the match. John was a great mate and an excellent servant of New Zealand cricket. Significantly, since his retirement, they have had a mountain of trouble finding someone to replace him.

After the Tests, we snuck home in a best-of-five one-day series, winning the final match by three runs. But, perhaps the biggest plus to come out of this tour for us was the form of Shane Warne, who, during the Test series had taken 17 wickets, the most ever by an Australian bowler in New Zealand. And he'd conceded just 1.61 runs per over to get them. By now, we all knew just how special a bowler Shane was. But we didn't think the Poms knew, and to England we were heading. Another battle for the Ashes was just around the corner.

18: England, the Third Time

IN THE MIDDLE OF THE ONE-DAY INTERNATIONALS SERIES ON
OUR 1993 TOUR OF ENGLAND, WHICH AGAIN PRECEDED THE
TEST MATCHES AND WHICH WE WON 3–0, PIP AND I SPOKE ON THE
TELEPHONE AND SHE RELATED PART OF A CONVERSATION
SHE HAD HAD WITH OUR DAUGHTER GEORGINA.
'WHERE'S DADDY?' GEORGIE HAD ASKED.
'HE'S BEEN AWAY SO LONG . . . IS HE IN HEAVEN?'
THE LIFE OF AN INTERNATIONAL CRICKETER IS NOT ALWAYS ABOUT
GLAMOROUS TOURS, EXCITING VICTORIES, BIG HUNDREDS.

The 1993 Ashes tour was perhaps a little more subdued than 1989, and different in that we were the first Australian team for many years not to hit England and be labelled 'the worst-ever touring side'. Amazing what a 4–0 result on a previous tour can do! Throughout team meetings before our adventure began, the work-rate of the '89 players was emphasised. For us to have any chance of repeating our successes in 1993, we needed to work even harder.

The major lesson Australia learned on the short tour of New Zealand in 1993, prior to returning to England, was the need for consistency in our cricket. Apart from the first Test, we hadn't played well and New Zealand had squared the series 1–1. We wanted to work hard to be a good team and not winning the Trans-Tasman Trophy back was an excellent reminder of that.

By the time we reached that one-day series, things were going okay. We were undefeated, and most of the guys appeared in encouraging touch. I was in nice form, a highlight being the twin hundreds I made against Worcestershire, while a feature had been the ongoing battle between our two young opening batsmen, Michael Slater of NSW and Queensland's Matthew Hayden, for the one available Test spot. Before the tour started, it had all but been decided that I would move back to number three. Morale was certainly high. This was the tour that saw the birth of two teams within the team — the 'Nerds' and the 'Julios'. Every time

Opposite: first Ashes Test, Old Trafford, 1993.

there was an intra-squad competition — fielding drills at practice, a ten-pin bowling tournament in Lancashire, touch football, anything, the Nerds and Julios were opposed. Which team you went into depended on your attitude towards things such as fashion, hair gel, mirrors, combs and so on. The Nerds on this trip comprised Mark Taylor, David Boon, Bob Simpson, Steve Waugh, Allan Border, Tim Zoehrer, Paul Reiffel, Merv Hughes and Ian Healy, and were led by Tim May. The vile Julios were Matthew Hayden, Michael Slater, Mark Waugh, Shane Warne, Wayne Holdsworth, Damien Martyn, Brendon Julian and Craig McDermott. Their captain was the inimitable Errol Alcott.

The Nerds wore a stylish ensemble of horrendously-patterned flowery, Hawaiian shirts and fake, eye-distorting glasses. The sleazy Julios, on the other hand, decked themselves out in jackets, white T-shirts and dark glasses.

Another feature of the tour was a fetching 'Daktari' outfit, which was worn in public, at a time and place designated by the fines committee, by a squad member responsible for an act seen as unbecoming of an Australian Test cricketer (from spitting the dummy to the absolutely unmentionable). It was a safari suit, an horrific concoction of stripes a la the ancient television series. One thing I'll never forget is Alcott having to wear the Daktari out on a Friday night — it should have cramped his style, but it didn't. We could never work that out.

For the record, D. Boon never wore the Daktari.

And we also had a 'Plucka Duck' stuffed toy along for the ride, to be carried everywhere by the last player to score zero.

Between the end of the one-dayers and the start of the Test series were two more first-class matches, against Surrey and Leicestershire, and Matthew and Michael opened the batting in both, to settle the matter of who would be padding up in the first Test, at Old Trafford. At The Oval, Hayden made 36 and 50, Slater 5 and 33, but then at Leicester the situation was resolved — Matthew made 2 and 15, Michael 91 and 50 not out.

The reason I am highlighting this battle is to underline, once again, just what a fine line exists between success and failure. Here is a perfect example of someone being in the right place at the right time and then making the most of an opportunity. Australia won the first Test easily, Slats scored 58 and 27, and then he smashed a big hundred in the second Test, at Lord's. End of story.

For poor Matt Hayden things are so, so different. While Slats' Test career has gone from strength to strength, the highly-gifted Queensland opener has played just one Test match, against South Africa at the Wanderers in Johannesburg, when he made 15 and 5, and broke his thumb. Quite possibly, he may never play for his country again, which would be a sad result for one of the country's finest players, and a tremendous bloke to boot. Unfortunately, this is one of the downsides of the strength of Australian batting in the 1990s.

If Matthew had scored runs in that final match against Leicester, or even if Slats had failed, Australia may have boasted an opening combination of Taylor and Hayden for a long, long time. But that's just another 'What if?'

On any tour, the first morning of the first Test is always the most tense. The mood of an entire series can be established in that very first session. And to some extent it was, as Taylor and Slater refused to buckle on a pitch that behaved in a manner that probably justified England captain Graham Gooch's decision to send us in. But the key moment came on day two, after we were bowled out for 289 (Taylor 124), when Shane Warne stepped up to bowl his first ball in Test cricket in England, to former England captain Mike Gatting.

I was fielding at bat-pad, so obviously I had a close-up view of 'Gatt' throughout his ordeal. The ball turned from nearly half a metre outside leg-stump and Gatt — watch the replays closely — didn't do too much wrong. But it bowled him. The look on the batsman's face was one of utter bewilderment. Mike didn't believe what had happened to him for a moment, perhaps even a tad longer.

There are three Warne wickets that I will never forget, and this, of course, is one of them. The others, incidentally, are the hat-trick ball to Devon Malcolm at the MCG in 1994–95 (when, as the catcher, I was heavily involved) and the ball which dismissed Salim Malik for a duck in Brisbane in 1995–96. This last one was part of the first spell Shane had bowled to Malik after the bribery allegations that surfaced following the 1994 tour. Warney had been pumping himself up for days beforehand.

Allan Border declared our second innings at 5–432, in which I made 93. Not out 85 at stumps on day three, I returned the next morning and faced Phil de Freitas, who delivered a ball that probably wasn't quite 'there', and I managed to hit it straight to Gatting at cover. I wasn't upset at all, and calmly walked into the dressing-room, where I was confronted by a comfortable old chair in my spot — within seconds, the bat was straight through the seat. And I left it there!

Ronny, the room attendant at Old Trafford, and a great mate of Jack Simmons, kindly and without any fuss, removed the bat and replaced the chair.

The Boon temper stayed primed for some time after, until I was approached by AB, who said: 'We all know you're busting to get your first hundred in England. It'll be better to get it at Lord's, the home of cricket, in a fortnight.'

'Maybe you're right, I replied. 'But I still wouldn't mind one, no matter where it comes.'

Perhaps captains do know something more than the average player. We eventually won the Test by 179 runs, after Merv and Shane bowled them out on the final day.

Rain affected the next two first-class matches, against Warwickshire at Edgbaston and Gloucestershire at Bristol; I missed the former, but scored 70 in the latter. And, while I was in Bristol, as I had done on my previous tours, I trekked to the marvellous antiques shops there. I know this passion probably does date me, but I have been collecting the old cigarette cards, emblazoned with famous cricketers from years gone by and, bearing all the county caps, for years. They're framed now, and adorn the walls of my home in Launceston.

The Bristol game was where the Australians played a terrible trick on Craig McDermott, who is rumoured to have a reasonable set of ears on the sides of his head. The social committee had managed to purchase a bulk order of enormous plastic ears and as Billy went back to his mark, every Australian player in the field clipped them on. Halfway through his approach, poor Billy had to stop; he was doubled over, laughing too hard!

This was also the game where the real Plucka Duck, from the National Nine Network program, *Hey, Hey, It's Saturday,* turned up with Molly Meldrum to film some segments. Merv and I did a live link-up with the host of the show, Daryl Somers, back in Melbourne, but unfortunately for my long-term career in comedy, I lost it completely and was unable to stay in my seat, as I went into hysterics at the antics of the Duck.

A famous moment. Gatting bowled by Shane Warne's first delivery in Ashes cricket.

Australia has a remarkable Test record at Lord's. We haven't lost a Test there since 1934, and just as we did on my two previous tours, we won at the home of the game again in 1993.

I was walking around the dressing-room for most of the first day, while Taylor and Slater added 260 for the first wicket. Slats was first out, for 152, then Tubs followed for 111, and at stumps we were 2–292, with Junior on 6 and myself on 11.

By stumps on day two I was 138 not out. Only two wickets had fallen all day, Mark Waugh for 99 (spoiling what would have been an unprecedented string of centuries by the first four Australian batsmen). And AB for a rapidfire 77, and we were 4–592.

One downside to the second day was the physical collapse of Craig McDermott. Our immediate fear was that he had burst his appendix. Craig had been in terrible pain at the back of the dressing-room, but no-one had realised the gravity of the situation until Steve Waugh, next batsman in, went to relieve some nerves and found Billy buckled over and in tears. The big fast bowler was rushed straight to hospital, where it was eventually discovered that staples inserted during one of two previous hernia operations had come loose and he was suffering a twisted bowel.

Not long after getting out of hospital, Craig flew home to Australia to recuperate. But following the second day's play, at around midnight, McDermott rang me from his hospital bed. I will never forget that he called to congratulate me on my achievement, despite being zonked out on anaesthetic. It was a tremendous gesture and epitomised the team's spirit.

Allan Border was right. Making my first Test hundred in England at Lord's was something extra special, It was probably the most excited I have ever been on a cricket ground, so rapt was I to finally get there! It was something I really, really wanted

I recall getting pretty tight in the eighties, and was dropped by Chris Lewis off Peter Such, trying to belt him over the top of a six-man leg-side field.

Thankfully, Lewis erred, because it's a fair drop off the balcony at Lord's . . . and I might have jumped off! After that escape I settled down and made sure I reached the hundred.

In the dressing-room, after the close of the second day, I was confronted by a man in a trench coat — it was the Rolling Stones drummer, Charlie Watts, who, I discovered, is a quietly spoken man and like his band's lead singer, Mick Jagger, a cricket nut. After a very pleasant chat, I made a rare request for me — an autograph — which he happily signed. And then he admitted that he was glad that I had asked first, because he had been wondering how he was going to ask for mine.

The next day, I finished with 164 not out, out of Australia's declared first innings of 4–632. And then, despite the fact that Mark Waugh opened the bowling with Hughes, we bowled England out for 205 and 365, to win by an innings and 62 runs. One of my favourite Test victories.

On the last day of the Test, my knee was starting to play up again and I returned to the rooms for treatment from Errol Alcott. While I was off the ground, the dressing-room was told that Her Royal Highness, the Queen, required the presence of four of her subjects from the Australian team. So Bob Simpson, team manager Des Rundle, Tim Zoehrer and myself were duly summoned, and Tim was positioned next to Prince Phillip while I was introduced to, and sat down beside, Her Majesty.

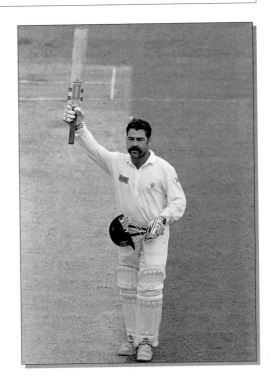

Finally, a Test century in England.

I thought, at the time, that if I was expected to make conversation, Ma'am was in for a boring few minutes. However, the Queen was, in fact, extremely knowledgeable about the game, the players and the terminology. I know one shouldn't divulge the exact nature of one's conversations with Royalty, but as we weren't discussing nuclear secrets, I will reveal that the Queen did comment that she loved coming to Lord's, that all-male domain. The members would spot a woman's head and do a massive double-take, only to realise that it was their Queen. 'Good afternoon, Ma'am.', was the usual response. That, she told me, she found very amusing.

The third Test, at Trent Bridge, was drawn, but it did include a D. Boon century. 'The elusive was now becoming a habit' was how journalist Greg Baum later described my form in *Wisden*. Then, after playing Minor Counties in a one-day game at Stone, we flew Aer Lingus to Ireland for four days of total relaxation (I had been given the game off).

Ireland, oh Ireland. Golf, the odd Guinness or two, and the chance to catch up with old friends of mine, Merv Adams and former Launceston 7LA radio announcer Dirk Anthony and his partner Michelle Matthews.

What a magnificent country! A number of the lads went to the hurling championships, which they said was one of the most barbaric games to be found. As usual, I opted to play golf. Slats and I played with a couple of local lads, who were extremely competitive — so a small wager was arranged. At about the 12th, the rain suddenly came thundering down and after duffing three straight shots, the club flew out of my hand during the fourth. 'That's it,' I wailed, 'I don't care about the bet. I'm outa here.' And I sprinted back to the clubhouse, leaving my poor caddy to haul the bag and clubs back. Okay, so I'm a 'fair weather' golfer.

Back to England, where our match at Derby was rain-affected, and then to Durham, for Ian Botham's last first-class match. I actually faced Beefy's final over in first-class cricket, which I regard, as a special privilege. There have been some tremendously gifted players in the game of cricket, but they don't come along that often, and very few of them have been as good as I.T. Botham. And there was never, ever a dull moment when he was involved — batting, bowling, or his penchant for getting his name in the papers.

How do I describe his farewell over? It included the exposure of parts of the human anatomy not usually seen on the cricket field, the pulling of faces and the mimicking of various bowlers' actions. Then he left the field of play.

By the time the day was over, Both was well into his second bottle of red. What a character and cricketer! And, because of his great love for English cricket and the game, I doubt we've heard the last of him. He desperately wants England to be successful once more, and if there is anything he can do to make that happen, he'll try to do it.

In the fourth Test, at Headingley, we once again ran up a colossal total. This time AB declared the innings closed at 4–653, after he himself had reached 200 not out. This was the highest score by an Australian captain in England since one R.B. Simpson made 311 at Old Trafford in 1964. As well, I posted my third Test century in a row, 107, and Steve Waugh finished undefeated on 157, after he and his captain had added an unbroken 332 for the fifth wicket.

I was probably in the best form of my life, and felt very, very confident. Mentally, I felt relaxed, but extremely switched on. And I believe that I had learned that hard lesson from the West Indies tour in 1991 — that if you find form, you must work hard to keep it.

By mid-afternoon on the fifth day, we had gone three-up in the series, and retained the Ashes. Victors by an innings and 148 runs. Having been the fortunate batsman to score the winning runs for Australia in 1989, I was exceptionally pleased that Border this time took the final catch.

I think it's fair to say that the celebrations afterwards were 'strenuous'. Our unofficial team song, Cold Chisel's *Khe Sanh*, something we had adopted in 1989, was played very loudly and very often. Personally, I felt sorry for the players who used the new dressing-room at the bottom end of Headingley the next day — it would have been more than an inch deep in beer and champagne. If the '89 Ashes will always live in my memory as my greatest tour, because of the feeling within the team, 1993 wasn't far behind.

Certainly, the '93 Ashes victory was special for the efforts of one player — the one and only Merv Hughes. With McDermott forced home, the workload that Hughes accepted had to be seen to be believed. Of course, he didn't do it alone; the support of Brendon Julian and Paul Reiffel was magnificent. However, after the tour was over, Hughes had to go home for major surgery himself. His ability to bowl through pain on this tour, to play injured for a long period of time, was one of the gutsiest cricket performances I have ever witnessed. In the first four Test matches, at the end of which Australia had retained the Ashes, Hughes took 25 wickets, two more than Shane Warne.

In the fifth Test, at Edgbaston, reality came crashing back into the cricketing life of one David Boon. While Mark Waugh was crafting a superb century, and brother Steve was making 59 and Ian Healy scoring a typically pugnacious 80, I was out for a duck, lbw to John Emburey. In the end, though, we needed only 120 to win, and after losing 2–12, Junior (62 not out) and myself (38 not out) hit

An Ashes tour is not all about cricket. Here I'm trying to get out of trouble, at Moorpark Golf Club.

off the runs required. This was the fifth time in five Tests that Mark and I had shared in a century partnership.

That was 4–0, a hard way for Mike Atherton, who had replaced Graham Gooch as England's captain, to start in the role. Atherton and Gooch are very different personalities. Atherton is a good fellow, who gets emotional and speaks his mind, but by telling the truth he does sometimes upset the English hierarchy. But at times, for mine, he doesn't publicly back his own players as much as he should. Sometimes, I've found that honesty should be kept for the privacy of your own dressing-room. Atherton's quite prepared to back his own judgment, and he has enjoyed some productive years as a Test batsman, so that tough personal streak can't be bad for his game.

Gooch is also a great bloke, and was a great player, who unfortunately suffered in different ways in 1989 and 1993. The former saw him stand down from the English team because of a loss of form, the latter saw him quit as captain after losing the Ashes.

Atherton won his first Test victory in the sixth Test, at The Oval. I made 13 in the first innings there, before I was caught by Gooch at bat-pad off Devon Malcolm. While I was disappointed to have failed, there was a funny story to the dismissal.

Graham hadn't fielded at short leg for years, but on this day he grabbed two catches, (Michael Slater was the other, also off Malcolm).

'I'm glad that you blokes fielded first,' he said to me afterwards. 'Because I didn't know where to stand. But your footprints were out there, so I stood exactly where you did. I didn't even have to move — you hit it straight to me!'

My final Test innings of the tour was another duck. Admittedly, I wasn't playing a shot when I was given out, lbw to their seamer, Steve Watkin, but having viewed the replays, if the delivery would have hit the stumps I will gladly bare my backside in front of Harrods in the middle of London on a Friday afternoon!

Despite the dud finish, I finished as Australia's leading run-scorer in both the Tests and all the first-class matches. But far beyond the statistics, the glorious memories remain — especially that wonderful feeling to have finally scored a Test century in England, on my third tour, and following that with two more. The Old Enemy . . . don't you just love scoring runs against them?

I know it will never change. Being part of an Ashes-winning team in England will always be the proudest moment of any Australian cricketer's career.

THE GENUINE ARTICLE

Michael Slater is a pocket dynamo. And an absolute nightmare to bat behind at No. 3!

At Lord's, in the second Test of the Ashes tour in 1993, when he made 152, I had to get up — time and time again — on the first day when he and Mark Taylor put on 260 for the first wicket. I had to walk around the inside of the dressing-room, I just couldn't sit and watch it.

It was just as disturbing in the first Test of the Ashes series in 1994–95, at the Gabba, when he slammed 176. Phil de Freitas opened the bowling and Michael hit the first two balls of the Test match for fours. The first two balls of the first Test match of an Ashes series! It takes your breath away just trying to imagine that, let alone watching it. The first shot was magnificent; the second a bit streaky, in between third slip and gully.

Considering he is an opening batsman, Michael Slater is one of the most exciting, aggressive players I have seen. And I don't believe there is any need for him to change his batting style, despite the fact that during 1995–96, he seemed to become somewhat nonplussed about his role within the Australian cricket team. This confusion came about because of, or perhaps was illustrated by, an unusual statistic — for some reason his Test average and strike-rate was far above his statistics in the one-day arena. Most batsmen's strike rates are higher in the one-day stuff, although their batting averages are lower.

There is no doubt that, as a young man, he is still finding his way in international cricket, learning how to play — a process that in fact never finishes until you retire. I just hope that he finds his level, his consistency, again, for Australian cricket would be so much worse off without him.

You see, I have a soft spot for Slats. His attitude is tremendous, while his love for what he is doing is obvious to everyone who sees him play cricket. He's a very emotional young man, clearly demonstrated by the way he kisses the crest on his Australian helmet when he makes a century. That's no publicity stunt. His famous quote in the Australian dressing-room is: 'I can feel the love in this room.' You can just imagine his team-mates taking the mickey out of him for that one. But he is the genuine article.

At times, when he's playing, Michael runs on pure adrenalin and once he gets going he's very hard to stop. When Tasmania hosted its second Test, Australia versus New Zealand, the second match of the 1993–94 series, I made a hundred, but was completely overshadowed in terms of batting pyrotechnics by Slats, who belted 168.

I kept meeting him mid-wicket, advising him: 'C'mon mate, you're going along beautifully, your job's not

Michael Slater's exuberant reaction to his first Test century might have been considered over the top by some, but, because it was sincere, I thought it was sensational.

over yet, you've got to keep going.' The usual stuff. His mouth was agreeing with me, but his eyes were looking straight through me. Having just tried to slog someone, the very next ball, he charged the medium-pacer and donged him over mid-off. By his own admission, he thinks about it, the advice offered, the situation he's in, but he just can't help himself.

Michael and his wife, Stephanie, are two wonderful, energetic people. I'm sure that they and the Boon family will stay friends forever. And I am just as sure that Michael Slater has a long future in Australian cricket.

19: Warney

SHANE WARNE IS A GENTLEMAN, ONE OF THE MOST HONEST AND GENEROUS BLOKES THAT I KNOW. ALL THE SUCCESS THAT HE HAS HAD, THE FABULOUS CONTRACTS HE HAS ATTRACTED — HE HAS EARNED AND DESERVED EVERY SINGLE ONE OF THEM.

Shane is always a team man. He's had problems with his spinning finger, copped a few blows to his feet when batting, and he'll have a whinge to the Australian physiotherapist, Errol Alcott. But once that game starts, once 11 o'clock ticks over, you would never know he had anything wrong with him. He still gets wickets and he still bowls well, trying his heart out for Australia.

In England in 1993, the benefits of confidence were illustrated perfectly after he bowled Mike Gatting with his first ball in an Ashes contest. Three or four overs later, he started to bowl his wrong-un, which previously he hadn't had enough confidence to bowl regularly. For the next 12 to 18 months, it was just wicket after wicket after wicket. He was just brilliant. But within the team environment, you would never know that he was different to the next man, because he was always thinking about the team and his team-mates.

In the past 18 months, through 1995 and 1996, Shane would be honest enough to admit that he hasn't bowled as well as he did during that golden period — but he's still taken wickets and still bowled economically. Someone looking on might say that Shane Warne was bowling normally, but we know he can bowl even better. All I can say is God help everyone when he gets it right again.

As well as being by far the best leg-spinner that I saw in my time in Test cricket, Shane also has great compassion as a human being. I will never forget when I was dropped from the Australian one-day side in 1995–96, and went back to the Sheffield Shield and played for Tasmania against Victoria at the MCG. Shane and I had spoken briefly after the Test match in Perth, when the one-day squad was announced and I wasn't included — he'd had trouble comprehending that I wouldn't be joining the rest of the team in Adelaide for the first game against the West Indies. At the Shield game, he dropped into the MCG to say g'day to his Victorian team-mates and we ran into one another. He looked at me and couldn't speak; it was almost as though he was about to cry. Then, the

Opposite: Shane Warne in Sydney, spinning through the South Africans, in 1993–94.

following day, he rang me from Adelaide, and apologised, in case I had thought him rude because he hadn't talked to me. He just couldn't believe that I wasn't going to be in the Australian team with him.

The day Shane was reported for misconduct by match referee Donald Carr, during the first Test against South Africa, in Johannesburg, in 1994, everybody missed the warning signs. You see, Shane is a predictable man, in the way that he prepares for cricket. In South Africa, there had been so much pressure on Warney to take wickets and dominate the Test, that it had built up within him. We failed to pick up how quiet he was during the morning practice, which is unlike him. Fielding at fine leg when the Test began, he was again quiet, not calling out to encourage his team-mates — which is a feature of his game.

His first few overs in that second innings were very, very tight and then he happened to get poor old Andrew Hudson out. Hudson was just in the wrong place at the wrong time. Shane exploded immediately after that dismissal, hurling a torrent of abuse at the outgoing batsman, and although no-one can ever sanction or excuse what he did or said, I have always felt that I should have apologised to Shane. As a team man, I shouldn't have missed the signs that something was wrong and should have been able to prevent what happened.

On a much lighter note, I am even willing to forgive Shane for his ties with the St Kilda Football Club, where he played Under–19 football, even though I am a long-time Carlton member, and also the fact that he has turned my son Jack into a 'Warne maniac' — Jack idolises everything about Shane.

Mentioning the Saints is another chance to highlight his compassion for other people. When St Kilda legend Trevor Barker tragically died of cancer in 1996, Shane returned from the United States early — where he was on holiday — to attend the funeral. Shane didn't fax a note of condolence, he jumped on a plane and came home.

For a bloke who was asked to leave the Australian Cricket Academy and had to pay his own way back from Darwin to Adelaide — for exposing his backside out of a hotel window — Warney's come a long way.

The other amazing thing about Shane Warne, besides the fact he's a tremendous guy with a similar amount of talent, is his diet. Shane's the absolute opposite of Merv Hughes, who will eat anything and everything (a nutritional practice to which I also adhere). Shane survives overseas tours on an intake of toast and vegemite, toasted cheese sandwiches, hot chip rolls with tomato sauce, Hawaiian pizza (without the pineapple, just ham and tomato) and his own version of spaghetti bolognaise — no mushrooms, no carrots, no onions, just meat sauce and spaghetti. Every once in a while, though, he might cut loose and have fettuccine, or even spinach fettuccine, instead of spaghetti. But he will not eat seafood and has to be starving to take on a chicken.

Warney's loathing of mushrooms is legendary. When we toured Sri Lanka in 1992, the Australian team was staying at the Colombo Hilton and Warne discovered an Italian restaurant within the complex, where he proceeded to eat his every meal, apart from the toasted cheese sandwiches he'd order once in a while from room service. One night, Shane was sitting at the table, having organised the team dinner, with Steve Waugh on one side, and me on the other.

So excited was he, that he let himself go and ordered the spinach fettuccine bolognaise — but no mushrooms, no carrots, no onions. He was in seventh heaven. I was sampling the fettuccine al fungi; basically pasta and mushroom sauce. I had a word to Stephen while Shane was chatting to someone else across the table. Steve asked to taste Warne's meal, and while doing so we slipped some mushrooms under the pasta. And then Stephen piped up: 'Warney, they've done you, they've put mushrooms in the sauce, in the bottom!'

Immediately, Shane went white, started sweating profusely and left the table to throw up. When he returned, we confessed to the trick, and the language in which we were described does not bear repeating. He was definitely not happy. But it was funny.

On another memorable occasion, Warne and Boon tackled Mark Taylor and Mark Waugh in a contest of skill and daring at the Royal Melbourne Golf Club. We came close to beating them, which was almost as good as a win, considering Tubby and Junior's abilities in this department. Warney then invited us back home for a beer at his home in nearby East Brighton.

When we arrived there, the refrigerator was opened to extract the beer, and the fridge's contents were revealed — a block of cheese, half a loaf of bread, butter, a carton of milk and a dessert bowl, covered in Glad-Wrap, full of left-over, canned spaghetti.

What more could a man desire?

20: A Century on Home Soil

MY 1993–94 SEASON BEGAN ON THE OPERATING TABLE. LESS THAN A WEEK AFTER RETURNING FROM THE ASHES TOUR OF 1993, I WAS THERE, IN MELBOURNE, FOR ANOTHER ARTHROSCOPY ON MY TROUBLESOME LEFT KNEE. THIS WAS THE FIRST SEASON WHERE MY COMMITMENTS TO THE AUSTRALIAN TEAM WERE SUCH THAT I PLAYED NO SHEFFIELD SHIELD GAMES FOR TASMANIA. NOT ONE! MY FIRST-CLASS APPEARANCES FOR MY HOME STATE WERE LIMITED TO ONE GAME, A FOUR-DAY MATCH AGAINST NEW ZEALAND IN LAUNCESTON IN NOVEMBER. AND, WHILE THAT ENCOUNTER WAS AN EXCELLENT OPPORTUNITY TO PREPARE FOR THE UPCOMING FIRST TEST, IN PERTH, I DIDN'T HAVE MUCH TIME TO CONSIDER THE KIWI ATTACK FROM THE CENTRE — OUT FOR 2 IN THE FIRST INNINGS AND 21 IN THE SECOND.

Unfortunately, my mediocre early-season form was to follow me to the WACA, where Australia batted first on a greenish wicket and Chris Cairns dismissed Michael Slater and myself with successive deliveries. I did, however, manage an unbeaten 67 in the second innings, but the game finished in a draw. This knock, the way it ran me into a bit of form, was a prelude to a special moment for me ... a Test century on home soil.

The second Test, in Hobart, was Tasmania's second ever Test match. AB won the toss, chose to bat, and at stumps we were 2–329. Michael Slater had smashed an exhilarating 168 and I was 105 not out. It was my 18th Test century and I passed 6000 Test runs in the process. And, as I did every time I wore an Australian cap in Tasmania, I really felt and appreciated the support of the spectators there.

It was a beautiful and special day, which Tasmania's tourism department couldn't have planned any better — the new ferry, the Spirit of Tasmania, was anchored in the Derwent River, directly in line with Bellerive. Seemingly every Australian television station and newspaper displayed that glorious image, either that night or the next day.

Opposite: Batting at North Sydney Oval during a one-dayer between Tasmania and NSW in 1993.

Australia finally declared at 6–544 (Boon 106, Mark Waugh 111), and New Zealand fell apart, all out for just 161 and 161, as Tim May and Shane had the time of their lives. The New Zealanders' efforts earned them an absolute caning in the media from their captain, Ken Rutherford (Martin Crowe had departed for home after the first Test, with a career-threatening knee injury), who accused his team-mates of not caring enough about their performance.

As I said when talking about Mike Atherton earlier, sometimes I think that this sort of criticism is better kept in-house. For mine, the Test result reflected how an under-strength New Zealand side had struck a professional, in-form Australian unit. And when you look at how they've fared in the seasons since that match, I just wonder if the Kiwis have never been able to recover at Test level because of the way they reacted to that loss. Certainly their display in Brisbane in the third Test suggested they hadn't coped very well in the short-term, as they were thrashed again, this time by an innings and 96 runs.

For the World Series one-day internationals in '93–94, Australia and New Zealand were joined by the South Africans, who would also play a three-Test series against Australia. And, first-up, the South Africans, back in Australia for a Test series for the first time in 30 years, prevailed by seven wickets in an emotional match at the MCG. Then, in our other clash with Kepler Wessels' team before the first Test, we evened the score by knocking them over for just 69 on a 'minefield' in Sydney, after we'd made 9–172.

The first Test, at the MCG, was wrecked by the lousy weather, but there was time for me to score 25, which pushed me past Neil Harvey's Test aggregate of 6149 Test runs and left me fourth, behind Allan Border, Greg Chappell and Sir Donald Bradman on the 'all-time' list. There was also the opportunity to witness the beginning of Australia's on-going 'love affair' with South African batsman Daryl Cullinan, which would prove to be most entertaining.

Cullinan had come to Australia with a reputation as a good player, but while we were batting he dropped four catches at second slip — while continuing to sledge our players. His mistakes were, of course, like the proverbial red rag to a bull. When South Africa batted, Cullinan finally came to the wicket. First ball, Cullinan, caught Border, bowled McDermott. From that moment on, as Warney cast his spell around him, Cullinan would be greeted with: 'Is the shower already running, Daryl?'

More than most, Cullinan suffered from Shane's flipper. 'It's going to be third ball, Daryl,' we'd tell him. 'Make sure you come forward. Oh, you're out!'

But I can assure you I was always very polite about it from bat-pad. In the end, you almost felt sorry for the bloke.

Warney was superb in the second Test, taking 12 wickets, and we required only 117 to win the match, which should have been a 'soda'. But it wasn't. We discovered that South Africa's renowned fighting spirit was very much intact and a fast-medium bowler called Fanie de Villiers was prepared to demonstrate its effectiveness under pressure.

Taylor out for 27, Slater 1. I managed just 24. We tried May as a nightwatchman . . . out for zero. Mark Waugh (4) and Border (7) were not out at stumps on the fourth day. The score was 4–63. We had been 1–51, before I was out, so you still would have backed us to get there.

I have listed all the scores to emphasise the point that the experienced batsmen should have won the match, even though the SCG wicket had been difficult from the second day. Border was out the next morning without adding to his overnight score. Mark made 11, Healy 1 and Warne 1.

Damien Martyn, batting at No. 7, had reached 6 playing the anchor to a swashbuckling McDermott. However, the Western Australian was caught trying to hit one over the top of mid-off. If he'd hit it over, we would probably have won and he would have been a hero. Instead, Australia was all out 111, losing the Test by just 5 runs. Martyn became the easy scapegoat; and hasn't played a Test match since.

Between the second and third Tests, Australia won the World Series, by defeating South Africa 2–1 in the best-of-three finals series. Then we levelled the Test series in Adelaide, in a controversial game in which the visitors became more and more disturbed with some of the umpiring decisions. And didn't the South African public let us know about it when we toured there following the completion of this series.

In fact, our departure date was just four days after the Adelaide match, so the debate about the standard of Australian umpiring was still very much a talking point. Still, this was just one aspect of what developed into a very exciting time. Even for me, a cricketer with a decade's worth of touring experience, it was all so new.

The South Africans love their cricket and, as we had already found out, their Test team was extremely competitive. And, although the air was thick with talk of violence and political turmoil (their first truly democratic elections, in which Nelson Mandela would be elected president, were still a month or two away when we arrived), while we were on tour we had not one hassle due to the political situation. Of course, like all tourists, we were warned to stay out of the city centres at night, which we did. And, on the way in from the international airport at Johannesburg, at the very start of the tour, we witnessed the aftermath of a very nasty bus accident. Sadly, people had been killed and there were others, badly injured, who were lying all over the road, an extremely sobering sight early in the morning. However, it was the only ugly episode of the entire tour.

The first game of the tour was a social occasion, against South African diamond billionaire Nicky Oppenheimer's XI and played at his own ground. Nicky and his son both played and while neither was over-endowed with talent, they made up for that with their enthusiasm and obvious love for the game. I wasn't required to play, so I was forced to recline on a leather rocking chair and enjoy the atmosphere, in what would have to be the best 'backyard' in the world — a cricket ground and a magnificent pavilion beats a barbecue and a shed every time.

It was also an honour to be introduced to Mr Mandela, whose courage and compassion were the main reasons South Africa had been welcomed back into international sport, which we were during a break in play. Another privilege came the following day, when we travelled to Soweto, to conduct a coaching clinic for some 200 black children.

Before the first Test, we played four one-day internationals (result: 3–1 to the home team) and two first-class games, the first of which was against Orange Free State at Springbok Park, Bloemfontein. Hansie Cronje, the captain of OFS, had already blitzed us in the one-dayers, and now his 'show' continued. Australia made 450 in its first innings, Mark and Steve Waugh both scoring hundreds. Then we bowled OFS out for 264, of which Hansie made 44, and declared our second innings at 6–270.

And, then, Orange Free State managed 396 in their second innings — and Cronje made 251!

Hansie is a good bloke, pretty intense about life and cricket, and an absolute fitness fanatic. He was typical of the South African players, tough and determined, and a challenge to play against, individually and as a team. Because of these characteristics, and while no-one can justify apartheid, I must say that I would have dearly loved to have played against South Africa a lot more than I did. Hansie also showed he had a sense of humour during his amazing double century. He was smashing Merv Hughes all over the park, when the big fellow, who at times can be a bit on the crass side, turned around and broke wind in Cronje's direction.

'See if you can hit that, then,' Merv snorted.

Hansie just laughed — why wouldn't he?!?! — as the Australians in the field cracked up.

The first Test was at the Wanderers, and developed into another triumph for Cronje, who scored another century as we crashed to a 197-run defeat. This was a match most Australians remember for the incidents that resulted in fines being imposed on Shane Warne and Merv Hughes. I've spoken about the Warne incident elsewhere, and the only thing I'd like to say further here is to comment briefly on the decision of the Australian Cricket Board to intervene and levy their own fine of $4000 on each player, on top of the $400 fine that had been decided upon by the match referee, Mr Donald Carr. Our tour contract had stated that all such matters should be dealt with by the tour management, and, whatever the reason behind the ACB's course of action, I know it caused a breakdown in the otherwise excellent relationship between the team and the Board.

What was particularly disappointing was that the players learned of the ACB fines through the media. When the ACB chairman Alan Crompton and chief executive officer Graham Halbish arrived later in the tour, they received a very noticeable cold shoulder from the players, especially the pair who had copped the fines. I think the ACB was guilty of an over-reaction. The matter had been dealt with by the ICC representative, whose fine may have been considered lenient by some (not, I should stress, by the team). But the pair, both great warriors for Australian cricket, had both admitted their mistake and apologised for their behaviour.

What is the point of having a world body and its representative at games, if their decisions are just ignored by other organisations? I don't condone bad behaviour by players, but this situation could have been handled so much better.

Everyone was very disappointed by our performance on that last day and AB's reaction wasn't pretty at all — but certainly justified. With his words still ringing in our ears, we travelled by bus for two hours to Sun City — what a place for a two-day break! Almost in the middle of nowhere, Sun City is a multi-complex, with hotels, casinos, restaurants and bars all within its confines.

The Australian team was obliged to stay at the Lost City, a supposed replica of an ancient civilisation. Outside the Lost City was an enormous cast iron elephant, life-sized, while inside, we were 'forced' to have a game at the Sun City golf course, where they play an annual million-dollar classic. The course had one local rule we decided to adhere rigidly to: when you hit the ball into the

In Cape Town with 'Rusty', my 'biggest' fan.

rough, your caddy goes to retrieve it because they knew how to watch out for snakes. There was also a resort golf course, which wasn't quite completed while we were there, but had little attractions like crocodile-infested moats around the par threes. And a water park which boasts beaches with artificial wave-makers and numerous rides and slides. I remember how Tubby Taylor and I cruised down together on a huge rubber tyre (perhaps not the best option for two similarly-built blokes) and almost knocked each other out in a clash of heads at the bottom.

Another ride has you finishing with a perpendicular slide of about 50 metres — you emerged from that one with your Speedos up around your ears! Talk about regressing to one's childhood.

Before the second Test at Cape Town, we played Boland at Stellenbosch, during which I heard one of the funniest lines ever uttered on a cricket field. During the home team's first innings of 155, acting captain Mark Taylor had allowed the opposition's 12th man to bat, because one of their players had become ill after the game started. But after this bloke had played and missed at Paul Reiffel for about an hour, 'Pistol' interjected with: 'You can't hit it, mate, you should have stayed 12th man.'

To which the South African replied: 'Who did you expect to come out to bat? Don Bradman?!?!'

From Stellenbosch we headed to Cape Town, where I enjoyed one of the best-ever afternoons I spent as an Australian (cricket) tourist. We went up Table Mountain by cable-car — a journey in itself hilarious because of Mark Taylor's absolute aversion to heights.

The summit revealed a restaurant–bar, which suited the Australian mood at the time, and then, during the afternoon, south of the Cape of Good Hope, you could see where the Pacific and Atlantic oceans meet — the warm current colliding with the cold current. You may not believe me, but you could actually see the line in the water. And the sunset was truly incredible. It looked as if the water had been wrapped in Glad-Wrap.

After the two first innings of the second Test, at the Newlands ground, under Table Mountain, in Cape Town, we had a lead of 74 runs. My contribution was 96, and, looking back, this dismissal annoyed me perhaps more than any other of mine that occurred in the nineties (bar, I guess, the 94 at Lord's in 1989). I was hitting the ball really well and had faced a few overs with the new ball, when de Villiers trotted in and had me caught behind, driving at a wide but luscious half-volley. Simple as that; it was a lazy shot. Now I'm retired, and South Africa is the only Test nation which I played against and didn't score a hundred.

By the time South Africa were due to bat a second time, the pitch had started to become more up and down. In these conditions, Stephen Rodger Waugh was perfect — bowling stump to stump. It was close to the best I've ever seen him bowl, and he finished with 5–28 from 22.3 overs. We needed just 92 to win and got them one down, Slater 43 not out and Boon 42 not out.

The Test series had been levelled one–all, which led to an infamous night of celebration. I say infamous because of an embarrassing moment for one D. Boon, who just tried to be too clever by half. After the odd amber and perhaps a soothing glass of red, I arrived back at the hotel and decided it would be a good idea — to give myself an extra half hour's kip in the morning — to pack everything for the early-morning bus.

Which I did, making sure to leave the few things I'd need for the morning lying neatly near my bed. To the foyer I journeyed, carrying my neatly packed bags, very chuffed with myself for my forethought and my obvious, long-time tourist's intelligence. My room was just around the corner from the lobby, luckily enough, and as I walked past one of the porter's stations an alert staff member jumped up and said: 'Mr Boon, may I help you with your bags?'

'I'm right,' I said, as I nodded to the desk. 'I've only got to take them over there.'

'Mr Boon,' he protested, 'I can't let you take them any further.' The poor bloke looked to be going to great pains to protect me from something.

It was at about this point that I stopped to examine my person, and was shocked to find myself totally naked.

Not a stitch!

I'd been so efficient in organising my attire for the morning that I had totally neglected the need for an evening outfit.

Unfortunately, the third Test, in Durban, which followed straight after the match in Cape Town, developed into a grim draw. For me, the match has few, if any, happy memories. After we had been sent in and made 269, the home team batted and batted . . . and batted some more. They made 422 in 832 minutes from 205.2 overs, which isn't racing along in anyone's language. And we then batted out the game, finishing at 4–297.

My first innings was memorable, or should I say painful, because of the nasty blow I received in the groin from their fastest bowler, Allan Donald. Without being too graphic, the ball hit me exactly side-on in the protector and moved my personal equipment across in a violent manner. Slats came down the wicket — I was struggling to stand up at this stage, let alone put on my preferred brave face — and said: 'That's hurt you, hasn't it?'

I couldn't talk, only grunt. We negotiated the few minutes until lunch and, in the dressing-room with my gear off, everything began to feel like it was returning to normal. So, with 15 minutes to go before the resumption, I started to ready myself to go back out, but when I stood up, I buckled over — the immediate sensation was of a vice being tightened around my testicles. Australia's physiotherapist, Lindsay Tregar, who stood in for Errol Alcott for this tour, came rushing over and I tried to explain my predicament. 'Trigger' summoned the doctor straightaway, but after an examination, I buckled over again. I had to go out and bat, though, and did so, reached my 50 but then, unfortunately, got out.

After I returned to the dressing-room, I kept keeling over, so the doctor took me to see a urologist at the main Durban hospital. To be honest, he was less than sympathetic. 'You'll be fine,' he said. 'You've just got a haematoma in your scrotum,' which, by this stage, was black with bruising. 'Just ice it.'

For the rest of the tour, probably once a day, I buckled over. Every time I had that feeling of the vice being applied.

Upon returning home, I keeled over in front of Pip. That was that, she packed me off to see a urologist in Launceston, Mike Monsoor, who discovered that the blood had clotted very quickly and caused a minor blockage — what should have happened in South Africa, he told me, was an immediate scan, to check that my internal workings weren't twisted. I needed three months of ultrasound and anti-inflammatories to break down the quite sizeable lump therein, and Dr Monsoor had warned that if it didn't dissipate, I would be separated from my left testicle. Thankfully, though, three months later the scan was clear and my 'set' was left intact. And in working order, because shortly thereafter, Pip was pregnant again with our third child, Elizabeth.

The only other matter of import in Durban was a rare run-in with my captain. AB had been getting uptight with the South African go-slow tactics in their innings, Jonty Rhodes was batting and I was fielding at bat-pad, off-side, to Warney. Jonty hit one and I caught it, and everyone went up, including me. But, after I thought about it, I wasn't sure that it was a fair catch. It might have bounced. The umpires had a conference, and I had to say that I wasn't positive. AB was unhappy, but in the end, everything settled down with Rhodes still at the wicket.

Enter the picture, Tim May as 12th man, bringing out the drinks. 'What do you think you're doing?' he said. 'You caught it!'

If Allan had been unhappy before, he let me know his true feelings with a real barrage. At the time, Jonty was 2 and South Africa 4–157, so it was a pretty important opportunity, especially when you consider Rhodes went on to make 78. However, at the next major break, we had time to watch a full break-down of the bat-pad chance on television. Maysie had only seen one angle, which gave the impression that I'd taken the catch. But the other six angles showed that the ball had bounced, and I'd scooped it. I didn't have to say anything. AB looked at me and hung his head, admitting that he shouldn't have doubted my call.

After the Tests, the limited-overs series was completed, with four day-night games. Australia won the first at Buffalo Park, East London, South Africa won the second at Port Elizabeth and we won the last two games on tour, at Cape Town and Bloemfontein, to level the eight-game series. Which proved to us that Australia was a much better team after dark!

It was after the last day-night match, at Springbok Park, that my long-time team-mate and friend, Dean Jones, decided to announce his own retirement. I know that Bob Simpson tried very hard to talk Deano out of it, but with no success. I also know that Dean was frustrated by not being able to win back his Test position.

That night, Australia having won the game, I was having a drink with several of the South Africans, including their all-rounder Brian McMillan. Dean was there for quite a while and I asked him if he wanted to talk to anyone about his decision. He was obviously hurting and decided to go to his room, but as he left I said that I'd come up and have a word later. Dean had been a major support to me through my career and I wanted to do something in return, as friends do. But when I did knock on his door, as I said I would, there was no answer.

Deano and I played a lot of cricket together and, for mine, he has a heart of gold. More importantly, as an Australian cricketer, he played some magnificent innings for his country, both at Test and one-day level. No-one will ever forget his guts and determination during his double century in the tied Test in Madras in 1986. In my opinion, and he'll probably come back at me about this, I believe his retirement was premature. When I made my decision to go, at the end of 1995–96, I was ready. I don't think he was ready, but was swayed by his emotions at the time. I wish he'd gone home and sat down with his wife, Jane, and family to discuss the situation.

In fact, when I read some of the things Dean has said and written since his retirement, I think they show that he regrets his decision. I truly believe that he could have played Test cricket again — he'd had a long trot on the outer and needed to keep working hard to regain his place — because there is no doubt in my mind that he was good enough to play again.

Just one final word on South Africa. I just can't believe how much the Republic has to offer — tourism, mining, the wine industry in Stellenbosch (where I fell in love with a 1986 Meerlust, so much so that I kept ordering it in restaurants and had a dozen sent home). With the exception of Johannesburg and Pretoria, all of South Africa's major cities on the coast, no wonder it reminds so many people of Australia. It is impossible not to think about the beauty and potential of this country, and all the devastation and tragedy caused by the fragile political situation, and think what might have been.

And what can be.

21: 'We've Got a Bit of a Party Going On'

THE 1994 OFF-SEASON DEVELOPED INTO A VERY TURBULENT
PERIOD IN THE HISTORY OF AUSTRALIAN CRICKET. FIRST, CAME
ALLAN BORDER'S RETIREMENT AS AUSTRALIAN CAPTAIN. AND THEN
THERE WAS THE TOUR OF SRI LANKA AND PAKISTAN, WHICH HAS
GAINED NOTORIETY BECAUSE OF THE BRIBERY ALLEGATIONS THAT
EMERGED AFTER THE TOUR'S CONCLUSION.

In mid-May, Mark Taylor, myself, Steve Waugh and Ian Healy had been summoned to the offices of the ACB. It seemed, we were told, that an announcement from Allan about his future was imminent. The media played this event up as a mass 'job interview', but I would argue that all the Board was seeking was some 'future directions' input from their senior players.

All four of us had been touted as possible captains if and when Border stood down. And when that did happen, it was, of course, Tubby who was appointed as Australia's next leader. I saw Tubby in Adelaide at a training camp not long after, and told him that he had my full support, and that I would back him in his new role to the hilt. I think he appreciated that, because I was now the most senior player in the team.

We visited Sri Lanka for a one-day tournament in August, before heading for Pakistan. That competition also involved the Pakistanis, who we played in Colombo. It would be the only game we won in that series. And, in the context of events which did occur later on — the allegations of bribery and corruption — one can look back and only wonder at what may have been the reasons for our victory. We batted first and totalled a meagre 179, but then bowled Pakistan out for 151. Wasim Akram didn't play because of a reported groin strain and we

Opposite: David Boon, natural athlete, in Sri Lanka, 1994.

dismissed Salim Malik for 22 — I can remember our players commenting on how badly he batted.

In Pakistan, I was given the rather interesting nickname of 'The Butcher'. Considering my record at the start of the tour against them, I have no idea where it came from — perhaps I looked like one?

The first Test was in Karachi, scene of our disastrous loss in 1988. This time, the state of the wicket was unknown, because it had been relaid some months before. It was, we were reassured, going to be totally different to the one we experienced in '88. There was no need to be concerned, it would be flat and turn a bit.

However, we quickly learned that at least in some ways the groundsmen don't change much. The bloke in Karachi had prepared, wait for it, two sets of nets — one allocated for Australia, the other for Pakistan. One morning we were training in 'our' nets, while the 'home team' nets were empty, because the home side was scheduled to practise in the afternoon. A few of us went into those vacant nets for some throw-downs, until the curator hustled over and proceeded to abuse us. This, he roared, was unfair and against the rules!

I tried to calm him down. 'We're not hurting anything, we're not walking on the Test wicket, it'll be okay and your presence is not required,' were my observations.

Upon which, he left the scene momentarily, but only to turn the hoses on the Pakistan nets, so that we had to depart.

Poor Mark Taylor began his new leadership role in the worst possible fashion — a pair, two ducks, in his first Test match as Australian captain. I really felt for Tub, but he demonstrated his mental strength, just one of the reasons he has become such a good captain. Some players would have sulked, but he kept supporting his players and concentrating on all the other aspects of the captaincy.

Despite our captain's dismissal, after batting first we reached a respectable 337. Then, lo and behold in Karachi, we bowled Pakistan out for 256. Saeed Anwar, a very nice guy and extremely aggressive player, top-scored with 85 in quick time, while Jo Angel and Shane Warne each took three wickets, Glenn McGrath and Tim May two apiece.

In our second innings, we were bowled out for 232, of which I contributed 114 not out — my first century against Pakistan. Mark Waugh managed 61, but six Australian batsmen were out for either 1 or 0. The major problem occurred when Mark was dismissed near the end of the third day, after he and I had put on 152 for the third wicket. Pakistan's two super quicks, Wasim Akram and Waqar Younis, were just starting to hit their straps, and we suffered for a decision (which nine times out of 10 would have been the right one) not to use a nightwatchman. Michael Bevan, in his first Test match, and Steve Waugh both fell for ducks, to Wasim, before the close, and we finished the day at 5–181. Bevan (82) and Waugh (73) had been our top scorers in the first dig.

For a large part of Pakistan's second innings, Australia were absolutely set for victory. The target was 314, and at stumps on day four, we had them 3–155, with nightwatchman Akram Raza on 1 and Saeed Anwar 67. Fifth ball of the final day, Warney trapped Raza lbw with the flipper and we were away. Saeed attempted to drive Angel and the big fellow took a magnificent catch. Wasim Akram then charged Warne, but the skied shot came down in the bowlers' hands. 6–179. Five runs later, when Warne trapped Basit Ali in front, things were looking fine.

When the ninth wicket fell, 56 runs were still required. Unfortunately, we hadn't counted on a brave partnership between one of Pakistan's batting heroes from the 1992 World Cup, Inzamam-Ul-Haq — who came in at eight! — and their leggie, Mushtaq Ahmed, who in matches against Australia prior to this had barely hit the ball off the square. Inzamam would finish 58 not out and Mushtaq was unbeaten on 20 when the winning 'runs' were scored.

The last pair actually won the match from four leg-byes, a ball which was technically a stumping chance. Warney bowled to a charging Inzamam . . . and after it pitched the ball ran along the ground, flicked the bottom of his pad, and beat the bat, the stumps, the keeper, everything. Heals, typically, took the entire responsibility for the loss upon his shoulders, which he shouldn't have done. But he's a perfectionist who works so hard at his game.

Afterwards, the dressing-room was silent, much like it had been in Adelaide when we missed winning the Frank Worrell Trophy by two runs in 1992–93.

Despite the disappointment, though, there were two humorous incidents to recall from the match, one involving the neutral umpire, England's famous Harold 'Dickie' Bird. At Karachi, there were manual sightscreens and their attendants were less than switched on to the task at hand. As the game progressed, Harold became more and more frustrated, until he finally screamed in that inimitable voice of his: 'Is there any chance of moving that bleeding screen?'

After which, he shortened his plea to just: 'Scr-eeeeeee-n!' And the middle syllable grew longer, the more frustrated he became.

And, having scored my first-ever century against Pakistan, I was forced to honour a bet — and have an earring inserted. For years, Geoff Marsh and I had ummed and ahhed about such a decoration. On a couple of occasions, we'd almost gone through with it. Fellow Pakistani tourist, Justin Langer, knew of this situation and made the bet that if I scored a hundred against Pakistan, I would be wearing an earring afterwards. Having virtually never scored a run against Pakistan, it looked like a reasonably safe wager. But there I was, with Australian physiotherapist Errol Alcott and Langer, dragged away to an earring shop. Errol was even kind enough to take his gear with him, and sterilised the necessary equipment.

I had no choice but to send word back to Australia, and soon after my daughter Georgina sent me a fax which read: 'Dad, who do you think you are? A pirate on the Seven Seas looking for treasure?'

And later on, after I returned, my son Jack became fascinated with the earring, saying in memorable fashion one day, 'When I grow up, I'm going to get my ear pissed, just like my Dad.'

In Rawalpindi, for the second Test, Tubby banished the demons of his first-Test pair with a gallant 69. There was no need, before the Test, to talk to Mark about relaxing or anything like that. He put up the bravest front; we knew that he was killing himself inside, but his exterior was one of positive enthusiasm. Mind you, we were very concerned when he nicked one on nought and was just about walking when it dropped short of the slips cordon!

Chasing our 9 (declared) for 521, Pakistan were reduced to 260, with Craig McDermott taking four wickets and Damien Fleming the same on his Test debut. But, after following on, the home team were saved by their captain, Salim Malik, who made 237 and played very, very well.

This was the Test where Fleming made history with his hat-trick. He had Aamir Malik caught by Bevan and Inzamam-Ul-Haq lbw with consecutive balls. The first ball of Flem's 24th over is one I will never forget — I was at mid-off, McDermott at mid-on. Flem was talking to Billy, asking for advice. He decided to bowl his best outswinger. And then, at the top of his run, he uttered the immortal words: 'Salim Malik, you are about to become a part of history.'

Salim Malik, caught Healy, bowled Fleming — the perfect outswinger.

Australia then headed off around the country for six one-day games in six different cities, as part of a triangular series involving Pakistan and South Africa. In our first three games, we beat South Africa in Lahore, Pakistan in Multan and South Africa in Faisalabad. And then to Peshawar, where we discovered the potential danger of an excited Pakistani crowd. Thank goodness we were only playing South Africa, who batted first and made 6–251. While we were fielding, the crowd — largely made up of university students who had been given the day off — kept up a constant barrage of missiles.

At one point, I was at mid-on when, suddenly, the favoured 'weapon' — firecrackers in a paper bag, weighted down with stones for good distance — landed at my feet and exploded on impact. Thankfully, I emerged unscathed from the smoke, although I had been peppered with rock fragments, and completely lost it with the umpires. The students, it was explained to me, were only having 'fun'.

When I left for Pakistan in 1994 I didn't have an earring. By the time I returned, I did.

But it wasn't funny when Warney was hit with a big padlock, or when Slats copped a blow from a large rock.

Peshawar was, in many ways, an extremely crazy place. The day before, the Australian team had had the experience of firing AK–47 machine guns into the deserted depths of the Khyber Pass. I remember that, in the local markets, there were weapons shops everywhere, and the streets were filled with young men carrying guns. And it was here that Errol asked our team liaison officer if it was possible to buy any rugs.

'Yes,' was the reply, 'you can get just about anything for 100 rupees a kilo.'

That was rugs, mate, not drugs!

If that wasn't enough the Peshawar Pearl Continental, where we were staying, was hit by an earthquake early the next morning. The epicentre, we were told later, was a long way away, but it was still very disturbing. I was already half-awake when the tremor hit, at 5.55am, because my roomie, Gavin Robertson, the NSW off-spinner who had played several seasons with Tasmania, had received an early-morning phone call from his wife. All of a sudden, my bed was shaking!

Now, I must admit that I wasn't too worried at this moment, and rolled over to go back to sleep. But then Gavin started shouting down the phone: 'I've got to go, it's just like Newcastle! I've got to go!' This, I thought, might be serious.

Robertson had experienced the Newcastle earthquake and was going into overdrive. Taking his lead, I began to panic: 'What do we do?!' I shrieked.

'We have to get under the beds.'

'We can't get under the beds, there's only two inches of room underneath them!'

'We've got to get into a doorway then!'

But then, as suddenly as it began, it was over. By this stage a lamp had fallen off a table and the pictures in the hotel room were all askew. Looking out the window, there were waves in the swimming pool; later on, downstairs, we noticed large cracks in the walls of the hotel lobby.

As soon as we could, the Australian team packed their bags and left Peshawar.

And this all happened before we went to Gujranwala, where it poured the night before the game against Pakistan. The next morning, there was a mini-riot because 20,000 people were locked out after a fake ticket scam. The problem was the crush of people outside collapsed a gate and several spectators were injured, most because of their over-eagerness to get into the ground. The wicket was extremely wet, but we played a 20-over exhibition to keep everyone happy.

We eventually won the final of that one-day series, defeating Pakistan, but the third and final Test, in Lahore, ended in a draw, which gave the home team the series.

Of course, the biggest story of the tour was still to emerge, and didn't do so until months later, when bribery allegations against Salim Malik were raised by three Australian players — Shane Warne, Tim May and Mark Waugh.

For many years it has been known that there are large gambling syndicates based in Bombay who liked to wager on the cricket. We knew also that when we toured Sri Lanka in 1992, Dean Jones had been asked to join such a syndicate. He wasn't offered a bribe, just a substantial amount of money to provide information about teams, wicket conditions and what he thought the result might be — before a game started. Deano, being an intelligent man, spoke to Allan Border and myself about the offer. His gut feeling was that, despite the cash involved, he should decline. We agreed, and that's what he did.

As to our 1994 Pakistan tour, I would go to court quite happily and confirm the contents of a conversation between myself and Salim Malik which occurred at the end of the first Test. I remember vividly, at the presentation ceremony, the Pakistani captain approached me and asked me what I was doing that night.

'What is there to do in Pakistan — nothing,' I replied.

'We've got a bit of a party going on. Do you smoke?' was his rejoinder.

I told him that I enjoyed the occasional Benson & Hedges, but I think I was being offered something else. I thanked him for the invitation to the party, but declined. 'You can still come. We can talk about all sorts of things,' the Pakistan skipper said.

After the tour, it was revealed that, allegedly, Warne and May had been offered considerable amounts — $US50,000 — to play poorly and Mark Waugh was asked to do the same in a one-day game. The beauty of the last offer was that Junior scored a hundred after knocking the offer back.

I believe Shane, Tim and Mark — what possible reason could any of them have for inventing the allegations? Why would they say anything if there was no offer of a bribe?

I know that it created huge pressure on all three players in the summer of '95–96, when the matter became public property. Warney was enormously upset, Maysie similarly, and while Mark didn't appear so on the surface, that's his character. In the end, the ACB backed their players to the hilt, which was tremendous.

The greatest pity is that, from where I stand, Pakistani cricket — until this matter is resolved properly — remains under suspicion. For example, does one immediately doubt the validity of all injuries before important games?

I think the ICC was quite weak in their handling of the entire situation. The ICC was asked to intervene, but didn't. They should have done. I'm sure they could have brought the players together at a neutral venue and investigated the matter thoroughly — for the benefit of all four players involved and the game of cricket itself. Expecting the three Australians to return to Pakistan to face a non-independent panel was just ludicrous.

It was never going to happen.

22: Target Practice

MY FIRST EXPERIENCE IN THE FIELDING POSITION OF BAT-PAD
OCCURRED AFTER ALMOST BEING CASTRATED
AT THE ADELAIDE OVAL IN DECEMBER 1985.
I WAS FIELDING IN SLIPS WHEN MARTIN CROWE, NEW ZEALAND'S
PREMIER BATSMAN, EDGED THE BALL IN MY DIRECTION.

Unfortunately, I missed the catch and the ball nicked the bottom of my scrotum. I have been struck some fearful blows facing pacemen all over the world, but this pain was searing in its intensity, made perhaps more acute because I couldn't let on that I was in agony — the ball had gone for four!

That same summer, Australia also played India in Adelaide (everything in my career, be it positive or negative appeared to happen with more drama in either the city of churches or Brisbane). Having been expelled from the slip cordon, I was sent to field in close — 'target practice' if you like — and managed to catch their wicketkeeper, Syed Kirmani, off Bruce Reid.

And that was that. As Allan Border observed: 'Right you're it. I can't hide you anywhere else.' That was a match of great significance. I scored my first Test century and, in the second innings, Geoff Marsh and I opened up together for the first time.

Not long after he was appointed coach, in early 1986, I approached Bob Simpson about establishing a long-term livelihood at short leg. Before that time, the spot was generally regarded as a spot for the junior pro — as I said, target practice. I asked Simmo if there were any fielding drills by which I could hone my skills in close, to make bat-pad a wicket-taking position.

And so it began. Every day, he and I would do 15 minutes extra — at training, on match days, off days, continually working to build up my reflexes, to increase my anticipation. Simmo definitely helped me a great deal in this area. There was never a problem about doing the extra training, to persevere with a drill until I got it right.

Opposite: Devon Malcolm, caught Boon, 0. Shane Warne (centre) has just taken a Test hat-trick.

Kim Barnett, caught Boon bowled Merv Hughes, at Lord's in 1989.

Now, it would be unfair to expect every cricketer to aspire to field at bat-pad. In fact, I would describe myself as a lunatic for wanting to stay there, make it mine and, in the end, enjoy fielding there. I'd have loved to have been the West Indies' Gus Logie, who was a wonderfully athletic fieldsman, anyway. He had that armoury of fast-bowling team-mates banging the ball into the ribs of opposing batsmen — eventually, they had to pop one up. I did, though, have Merv Hughes . . . I caught more than my quota of easy ones from him.

From a slightly humorous angle, bat-pad is an excellent vantage point. First and foremost, you don't have to do as much running as other fieldsmen. Just practise your diving skills, fall over, lie down and watch someone else chase the ball to the boundary.

More technically, it's a position in which no-one should be scared, if you follow the basic rules — stay low and watch the batsmen's feet. Mark Waugh, who often fields in close on the off-side, follows the theory of watching the ball. I can't do that at bat-pad, but by focusing on the feet and the player's front pad, I usually gave myself a good indication of what sort of shot the batsman was contemplating.

My satisfaction came from knowing that all my hard work had paid off and I had taken a catch that, generally, would not have otherwise been caught. For any bowling team, it's such a bonus to take an unexpected catch. Such an occasion can lift a side out of the doldrums, or turn a problem period for your team into a major disaster for the opposition.

Having fielded in the position for most of my Test career, there are several catches which stand out:

ALLAN LAMB, caught off Terry Alderman at Headingley in the second innings of the opening Ashes Test of 1989. The ball went high and quite quickly to my right. Technically, this was a good one.

DESMOND HAYNES, on the same Ashes tour, when Australia played Middlesex at Lord's. Again the catch came off Alderman, and was low and to the right.

MOHAMMAD AZHARUDDIN, off Craig McDermott at the SCG in 1991–92. I stood slightly deeper than usual, having discussed a theory with Allan Border. 'Azhar' wasn't really a bat-pad player, not many subcontinent cricketers are, because they tend to play the ball very efficiently through that area. So I gave myself a metre and Azharuddin, who is a tremendous fellow, was dumbfounded by what he saw as his misfortune.

SANJAY MANJREKAR, in the first Test of that series, in Brisbane, off Merv Hughes, when he took the first four wickets to fall and I caught three of them at bat-pad. Technically, this was the best, because of what I did in moving to the ball and positioning my hands, rather than making a reflex take — Manjrekar hit the ball off his hip and I took it in both hands.

BRIAN LARA, off Steve Waugh in the second Test against the West Indies, in Antigua, in 1995. No, I wasn't fielding at bat-pad, but in the 'box', an extremely straight, short mid-on, to the left-hander. Stephen planned that dismissal. His theory was that on a slow wicket, a bowler of his medium pace could frustrate Lara by bowling wide outside off-stump to a packed off-side field. 'With a bit of luck,' said Steve, 'Lara will try to whoop one over the top.'

It took only two overs before 'The Prince' went for it and yours truly snared one that I shouldn't have even got near. I would have preferred that he'd hit the ball at me rather than high and to my left, but you can't expect everything to be handed to you on a platter.

And there's another catch I'll never forget, but I'll get to that one in a moment.

Bat-pad is now becoming more of a specialist position. It's like first slip or second slip. You can take wickets at bat-pad and you can save a lot of runs through a day and more throughout an entire match. Plus, you can sledge opposition players to pieces from underneath the helmet and rarely, if ever, get picked up by umpires.

The negative, of course, is that you face the possibility of being cleaned up. But if you follow the basic rules, such moments are, thankfully, few and far between. Mind you, there is a distinct difference to being cleaned up and being hit — the latter happens 10 times a day. Wear shin pads if you like, I didn't because I found I couldn't run in them, but be prepared to wear the ball on your back and legs (both of which are preferable to your head).

In 1989, I copped two of the worst blows I received at bat-pad in the same week. The first came against Nottinghamshire at Nottingham, when Derek Randall was at the wicket. Marvellous bloke, Derek, but he jumps all over the crease at the best of times. On this occasion, Carl Rackemann bounced him and he pulled the ball . . . and it hit me right in the front of my helmet grille. I was dazed for quite some time.

About a week later, Australia played the fifth Test against England at Trent Bridge and Robin Smith was facing our leggie, Trevor Hohns. Now, Robin is another wonderful fellow, but when he hits the ball, it tends to stay hit. And my helmet was still recovering from the Randall strike. I had borrowed Rackemann's helmet, which had side pieces and a low grille at the front . . .

I just saw Smith's shot in time to turn my head side-on — and the entire helmet shattered. Pieces went flying everywhere and so did Smithy. He was really quite distraught, fearing I had been seriously hurt. However, I reassured him, and must confess that I didn't feel too bad immediately afterwards.

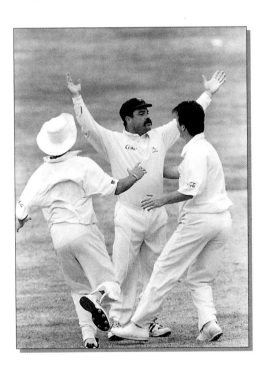

One of my favourites. Brian Lara, caught at short mid-on, off Steve Waugh's bowling, in 1995.

Australian physio Errol Alcott wasn't there at the time, so I was attended to by a woman named Sheila, the Nottingham physio. She asked me how I felt and I complained of feeling an ache high on the right-hand side of my head. When I opened my mouth to demonstrate, my entire jaw clicked back into place!

Sheila advised me to go off the ground, which was wise, because 10 minutes later, I was feeling very, very ordinary.

At the end of the day's play, into the dressing-room, marched Dean Jones. 'How are you, Babs?' was his query.

'I'm okay now, thank you, Dean,' my reply.

'That's good,' said Jones. 'I think this must be yours,' he

continued, passing me a fragment of helmet plastic, 'I found it outside the boundary rope.'

Deano had stepped out exactly 100 paces to the wicket after discovering the debris, but that's just the sort of perfectionist he is.

When Australia toured Pakistan in 1988, Javed Miandad hit me during their second innings of the third Test match, in Lahore. One of the finer points to watch for at bat-pad is the batsman who can pull the ball off the front foot, because, normally, as soon as a player moves forward, you do, too. I did all this, but it didn't help: fortunately, the ball from Javed missed my head; unfortunately, it cannoned into my neck.

Rather than quieten me down, on this occasion the pain fired me up. AB tried to send me off, but I was in a 'no, I'm perfectly all right!' mood. However, about 10 minutes later, Allan again advised me to leave the field, pointing out that one side of my neck had swollen to twice the size of its counterpart. In the dressing room, Errol made me apply an ice pack for a period of time, but I was able to go out and field again. And then, the next morning, 'Hooter', caring physiotherapist that he is, was extremely worried about me, in terms of suffering concussion, but, honestly, I felt no great pain. That's what you get for having a bull neck.

Other than being smacked in the shins, the back and backside with the ball, you can take a lot of good catches and have a good time at bat-pad.

Opposition batsmen will try to talk to you. It's only natural, you're under the helmet concentrating, everyone else on the field is trying to kill them. But there weren't many to whom I'd talk back. You might agree with their observation about the weather or concur with their judgment of the situation: 'Yes, you are correct. Merv Hughes is trying to kill you. My best advice is for you to leave the area as soon as possible.'

But cricket does have its genuine humorists.

Playing against South Africa in the first Test of the 1994 tour, at the Wanderers in Johannesburg, Jonty Rhodes was batting and having the odd slice of luck along the way. Normally, I wouldn't have said anything, but as Jonty is widely-known as a religious young man, I couldn't resist.

'I'm going to have to start going to church,' I told him. 'It must be working for you because I've never seen anyone bat like this before.'

He just smiled at me. You can't upset Jonty, anyway, and he went on to make 69. Then, in Australia's second innings, I scored 83. During that knock, I went to hook a ball and top-edged it back over the keeper's head for four. As I patted down the wicket, Jonty ran past and called out: 'I see you made the right decision and went to church this morning!'

I'll pay that comeback.

The hat-trick.
Victim No. 1 —
Phil de Freitas, lbw.

Victim No. 2 —
Darren Gough,
caught Ian Healy.

Victim No. 3 —
Devon Malcolm,
caught Boon.

By the beginning of the 1994–95 season, I was just about sick of fielding in close. I'd gone through a period where very few catches had come my way, in fact, it almost seemed as if I *was* being used for target practice on occasions. But then, one day in late December, 1994, my 34th birthday to be precise, a special something happened that more than made up for all the hard times.

It was the final morning of the second Ashes Test, in Melbourne. Australia was already one-up in the series, having won easily in Brisbane after Mark Waugh and Michael Slater had hit brilliant centuries and Shane Warne had taken 8–71 in the Englishmen's second innings. At the MCG, we thought that England would fight to the bitter end, to at least try to drag the result out, and for a while it seemed that might occur. For a while . . .

Then Warney decided that he was going to take a hat-trick. First, he trapped Phil de Freitas lbw. Next delivery, Darren Gough edged one through to Healy.

Warney went back to his mark, and began talking to Damien Fleming, who was fielding at mid-off and had been the last Australian to take a hat-trick — very recently too, in the second Test of our '94 tour of Pakistan. 'What am I going to bowl?' Shane kept imploring his Victorian team-mate. 'What am I going to bowl?'

Flem started by offering reasonable advice, but Shane kept asking the same question, so in the end he simply said: 'Just bowl anything!'

Shane decided on the top-spinner.

The wicket was turning, and Devon Malcolm, the English No. 10 waiting for the hat-trick ball, wasn't very likely to hit something that spun too far. Shane bowled, Malcolm prodded at it, the ball bounced on him a bit . . . and the edge ballooned up in the air.

I had to make a bit of ground, but I made it, with one finger hanging on underneath. I must admit, I did 'erupt' off the turf, both arms pumping the air in absolute elation. And I reckon Shane ran the fastest he's ever run to congratulate a team-mate on taking a catch off his bowling.

The umpire at the bowler's end was Steve Randell, my fellow Tasmanian, who'd made the lbw decision against de Freitas and raised the finger on Gough. But he didn't get a clear view of my effort and had to look to West Indian Steve Bucknor, the square leg umpire, for confirmation. Last man in, Phil Tufnell, then annoyed us for a little while, but we ended up winning the match by 295 runs. England had capitulated in less than a session!

The 1994–95 Ashes series had been preceded by some sad news — Merv Hughes would not be able renew his great rivalry with the Old Enemy. So much an important part of the 1989 and 1993 tours of England, especially the latter when he became Australia's strike bowler after Craig McDermott was incapacitated, the big fellow had himself been slowed by injury. So, despite taking 4–51 for the Australian XI against England at Bellerive Oval in the lead-up to the first Test, Hughes was overlooked for Fleming, who had been so impressive on debut in Pakistan during the winter.

I desperately wanted to find my top form against England. Despite my hundred in Pakistan, I had not been happy with my overall return from that tour. But, sometimes when you want something too much, you can over-compensate and become too tight. Having scored just three runs, after Slater and Taylor had started the series by adding 99, I went to leave one from Darren Gough and got an inside edge. Bowled. And didn't the Gough boy enjoy this, his first wicket in Ashes cricket! Good luck to him. This was the beginning of an enjoyable contest between us that would last most of the summer.

By the conclusion of the third Test, the Ashes had been retained. In Melbourne, I had scored my first Test century on the ground in the second innings, but that achievement, inevitably, had been overwhelmed by Shane's hat-trick. Well, overwhelmed everywhere but in the Boon household! The Test in Sydney then ended in a draw, leaving us with a 2–0 lead, with two to play.

That Sydney Test had a curious finish. Needing all of 449 to win, for a while on the last day it seemed we might even pull off an amazing victory. Slater (103) and Taylor (111) added 208 for the first wicket, but then, the combination of rain

Shane Warne (centre) was also a hero in Brisbane, where he took 8-71 in England's second innings. Surrounding him here are (from left) Michael Slater, Mark Taylor, Ian Healy and myself.

An on-drive in Melbourne during my innings of 131, my first Test century at the MCG.

and an Australian batting collapse left us with no alternative but to bat out time. Which Tim May and Shane Warne did. But there was confusion at the end, when, after what we thought was the last over had been completed and we had commenced our celebrations, the umpires decided there was, in fact, still one more over to go. So Shane defended for six more balls, and then we started partying once more. Shane admitted later that he thought about trying to slog Graham Gooch for six off the last ball, but didn't, even though it didn't matter whether he got out or not.

It's the only time in my career that I've hugged a number of my team-mates twice in the space of five minutes, for exactly the same achievement!

The fourth and fifth Tests were shared — England winning in Adelaide, Australia in Perth. Perhaps the highlight from our point of view was the impressive debut of South Australian batsman Greg Blewett, who scored a century in both games. This was the dream start for anyone's Test career, but one thoroughly deserved by an extremely talented player and an excellent bloke, whose company I have enjoyed many times since he first burst onto the international stage. Unfortunately, though, Pip — whose judgment is usually excellent — has developed a soft spot for both Greg and Justin Langer. Somehow, they've conned her into thinking they are both lovely, young gentlemen.

The summer of '94–95 also featured a rectangular, as opposed to triangular, World Series one-day competition, with Australia, England, Zimbabwe and Australia A doing battle. And, as things turned out, it was the two local teams who met in the finals (victory going, thankfully, to the senior side). Interestingly, media interest heightened whenever Australia played Australia A. Perhaps it was the novelty, perhaps, though, it was more than that.

I am an Australia A advocate — I reckon such a concept is a sensational idea, as it gives young players around the country an opportunity to play at international level, without having to wait to reach the real Australian team. I see no problem at all, so long as there is a genuine distinction drawn between the Australian one-day team and Australia A.

Of course, the sponsorship dollar is everything, and in reality the advent of Australia A resulted from a need to cover for any shortfall caused by the largely unknown Zimbabwe being the third international team in the World Series. However, rather than concentrate on any perceived slurs towards Australia's visitors, let's hone in on the positives, the largest of which was the fact that the Australia A concept gave the Australian public the chance to witness — either live or on television — the depth of the game in this country. There are some tremendously talented players in the Sheffield Shield and Mercantile Mutual Cup each season, but unless you're a real cricket fan, you might never know who they are. Australia A gave some of these cricketers an opportunity to demonstrate their gifts, against England, Zimbabwe and Australia, and press for higher honours. Blewett and Ricky Ponting, to name just two, were both products of Australia A.

A feature of the World Series finals was my bowling. Seriously! I even managed a wicket, bowling what I like to call 'nudies' (they've got nothing on them!). As a tactical move, slow bowling on a sluggish wicket that's keeping low can be very effective, because you either cost nothing, or force the batsman to go over the top and perhaps even be dismissed.

It was in the second final, in Melbourne, that Mark Taylor called on my assistance, as a way of halting the A's onslaught . . .

I bowled five overs for 13, and the wicket of Phil Emery, the NSW wicketkeeper, who will have nightmares about the dismissal for the rest of his life. I've spoken to him about it since. Basically, he can't believe it — neither can I! — and just says: 'Shut up. I don't want to hear about it again!' But, of course, he's never going to hear the end of it.

In fact, to the end of the 1995–96 Australian season, I'd taken 10 first-class wickets, and I am very proud of every single one of them. However, I won't bore you with a ball-by-ball description of each and every one of them. It might embarrass those who have been outwitted by my guile.

Perhaps in my second life, I will come back as a fast bowler, to torment batsmen by using all the tricks that those mentally-challenged pacemen have taught me during my career!

By the end of the Australian season, despite my wicket and my century in Melbourne, I was again under media pressure, having scored a mere 43 runs in the final three Tests. But I was still feeling positive, even if, in the lead-up to our forthcoming West Indies tour, a touch of run-getting consistency would have been appreciated. The only media report which truly angered me was one that claimed that I was overweight and unfit. While I will never be a sylph, at that stage of my career I was kilograms under the weight required by the Australian Cricket Board.

Before the West Indies tour, Australia headed across the Tasman for a one-day series with the home side and South Africa, to commemorate the centenary of New Zealand cricket. Sadly for the Kiwis, we ruined New Zealand's birthday party, thrashing them in the final at Eden Park. Ricky Ponting and I were at the wicket when the winning runs were scored — it was great to be touring again with another Tasmanian, especially one as talented as Ricky, so obviously a key component of Australia's long-term future.

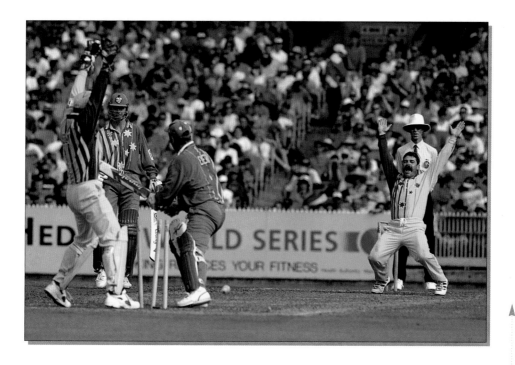

A memorable moment in Australian cricket history. Australia A wicketkeeper Phil Emery, bowled Boon, 10, in the second final of the 1994–95 World Series.

A TRUE 'SWAMPIE'

I haven't played that much cricket with Ricky Ponting. When he made his debut for Tasmania, as a 17-year-old, and began carving his niche in the cricket world, for most of the time I was away from the state team playing for Australia. However, I have known Ponting for a long time, virtually from the moment he burst onto the Northern Tasmanian Cricket Association scene by scoring centuries in the 'Under–13 week' series they conduct annually.

Ricky toured the West Indies with the Australian team that won the Frank Worrell Trophy in 1995 and, although he didn't play a Test on that trip, he was very much a part of our success. On that tour, Ponting learned a lot, while I was very happy to have a fellow Tasmanian along, even though I joked with him afterwards about how rough it was that he'd been part of the team which beat the West Indies . . . at his first attempt. By 1995, of course, I'd had half-a-dozen goes at them!

Ricky did, though, have some setbacks on that tour. I remember how he was set to play for Australia in the first-class match against the West Indies Cricket Board XI at Basseterre on the island of St Kitts, but became ill. This cost him the chance he had of making a big score and forcing his way into the team for the third Test in Trinidad. As a consequence, he became frustrated, because all Ricky wants to do is play cricket, but we had a long chat — about how important it was for him to learn,

and how important the tour experience was for his future.

I believe it was good for him that I was there, as someone who could understand his feelings and frustrations and as someone who knew him. We have always got on well and I feel honoured to have helped him in any way. And privileged that I was still playing when Ricky made his Test debut, scoring 96 in his first innings, against Sri Lanka at the WACA Ground in Perth. He had always impressed me with his natural talent and capabilities, but what struck me — and no doubt the rest of Australia — was the maturity that has come to him so quickly, at 21 years of age. Ricky stated after my retirement from international cricket that he was disappointed that he didn't get to play much Test cricket with me. However, I feel very lucky that I was able to continue long enough to participate in three Test matches with him.

There are so many stories about his natural ability. Rod Marsh, the director of the Australian Cricket Academy, couldn't sing his praises enough — and that doesn't happen too often with Bacchus. Ricky's talent and temperament are so immense that I am willing to put him under pressure by stating that I believe he will play cricket for Australia for a long, long time and — I have no doubts about this — that he will score more Test runs than I have.

When you think of Ricky Ponting, you think of a down-to-earth bloke, a true 'Swampie' from the North Launceston Football Club, where he and I both played football. Ricky, or 'Punter' as he is known, loves the greyhounds, the dogs. It's not something that I can understand, but you know that when Ricky's at home, and it's a Thursday night, he'll be at White City watching the 'dishlickers' sprint about.

Something else I don't get, in this day and age, is why Ricky is still without a driver's licence. But, in typical impish fashion, he has told Tasmanian all-rounder Shaun Young and myself — we're three Launceston lads who play Sheffield Shield cricket for our state — that when we stop playing, he'll get his licence, because at that point he'll no longer be able to get a ride with us!

Personally, I would like to see Ricky Ponting bat at No. 6 for Australia for a little while longer. I know he has aspirations to bat much higher for his country. But I'm biased, and want the best for him, which is at six, where he will have the experience of batting with Steve Waugh and Ian Healy on either side of him. Ricky's career has long way to run yet!

The only thing Ricky Ponting fears on a cricket field is facing my bowling. The thought of losing his wicket to me obviously has him petrified, and was well illustrated when I bowled to Ricky when he was playing for Australia A in 1994–95.

In Brisbane, I conned Mark Taylor into letting me bowl to him: 'When he comes in,' I explained, 'he'll be that scared of getting out, we might not go for many runs for a few overs.'

And so it proved. I sent down five overs for 13 runs, which isn't too shabby in a one-day situation and I almost had Ricky caught at short cover. Throughout, I kept verballing him: 'Don't get out, Pont, I won't ever let you forget it!

'And neither will you!'

I reckon living in Tasmania will help Ponting. Everybody knows of him and a much higher percentage of the population — more than a Test cricketer in Melbourne or Sydney —know him personally.

As they do with me, in Launceston, people will say 'hello' in the street, maybe stop for a quick chat and keep on moving. Tasmanians will always say 'G'day!', and show their support, whether he's in form or out of it. What a contrast to Melbourne and Sydney, where the mere process of saying hello becomes a far greater production.

I know that, as his career progresses, Ricky will be compared to me. It's inevitable, because there's not too many home-grown Tasmanian Test cricketers, but I think he will handle the scrutiny, because he has the strength not to let it bother him.

But I shouldn't be his benchmark. Ricky should worry about what Ricky Ponting is doing and not how critics compare him to an old man of the past.

Keeping score of how many runs someone has made in so many matches compared to someone else is meaningless. The real value of a cricketer is what is done on the day, what is required on the day, and in the circumstances on that day.

23: Champions of the World

IN MY OPINION, THE MOST SIGNIFICANT MOMENT OF OUR TOUR OF THE CARIBBEAN IN 1995 CAME AT A SPECIAL MEETING, HELD IN ST LUCIA, WHEN COACH BOB SIMPSON PRESENTED OUR OWN, COLLATED ANSWERS TO SEVERAL KEY QUESTIONS, ASKED A FEW DAYS BEFORE. WE WERE STILL BEMOANING OUR 4–1 LOSS OF THE ONE-DAY INTERNATIONAL SERIES, WHICH TOOK PLACE BEFORE THE TEST MATCHES BEGAN.

Question 1: Why haven't we been playing as well as we can? Answers: Batting — no forward thinking, the cardinal sin of too many wickets being lost together, inconsistency, not being tough enough, not building partnerships, not capitalising on good starts. Bottom line: basics are not being adhered to, and we're not batting as a team.

Bowling — not accurate enough, bowling to both sides of the wicket, poor concentration, lack of communication between team-mates, lack of aggression, little enjoyment.

Fielding — lack of communication, aggression and confidence, not enough enjoyment.

Question 2: What can you do to improve performance?

Answers: Pull together, more confidence, train with more focus, communicate more, lift intensity, more pressure at practice. And very important: enjoy the challenge of the series. Assist others, stop the 'whinge'.

Question 3: What sacrifices are you prepared to make?

Answers: Rest more, put cricket first, spend more time with team-mates, spend more free time training, assist team-mates.

This was a big meeting and, to be honest, a few blokes disagreed on some matters — some thought they had been putting in and, simply, that things hadn't been going our way. But while that may or may not have been right, things hadn't been working. We had to look ahead, and search for ways to improve our performances.

Opposite: This is the look of a man on the verge of playing his 100th Test for Australia.

The guys, especially the senior men, were very open and candid with their opinions. It was re-iterated just how important this tour was, and the carrot was dangled — seven weeks of cricket, followed by rest and recreation in Bermuda. We had enjoyed a superb end-of-tour trip in 1991. How good would such an experience be if we won?

The major difference between Australia's most recent tours of the West Indies, in 1995 and 1991, was attitude. On both tours, the Test series was promoted as a world championship of cricket, but the Australian touring party of 1995 was definitely more relaxed about the whole situation.

Even when we lost Damien Fleming and then Craig McDermott to injury before the first Test, we failed to lose our resolve. Strangely, and with no disrespect to those two guys, who were the first picked and obviously earmarked for specific jobs, even their loss became a positive. Those who stayed and those who came as replacements knew that we had our backs against the wall. Two of our three front-line pace bowlers were out injured, so everyone else had to step up a notch, and cover for their departure.

From the day we'd arrived in the Caribbean, the psychological war had begun. Not from the media, just the public. 'We're gonna give you licks, man!' they would yell at us. 'Curtly's gonna kill you!'

At Acra Beach, down the road from the Rockley Resort in Barbados, the Australian team would train and then play paddle ball with the locals on the water's edge. West Indians play this game every day, and invariably beat us resoundingly. 'Just like our players will do to you!', was their post-match call. Shane Warne, Mark Waugh and Ponting went to the races in Barbados and were told: 'Brian Lara is the best batsman in the world. And on Mars, too.'

Warney asked the guy behind that legendary quote what he thought of Junior. 'Very, very pretty player,' was the reply.

And David Boon? 'Big man. Most stubborn batsman in the world.' I liked the sound of that!

The early days of the tour were relatively stress-free. For the young guys, though, there were lessons to be learned, such as the cost of phone calls. Don't ring home, rather, get your loved ones to ring you. Poor Ricky Ponting spent about six weeks of his daily expenses in two phone calls — one to his mum, the other to his girlfriend!

Mark Taylor discovered, on a boat trip around the beautiful St Vincent, that throwing Craig McDermott's favourite hat overboard is not a clever thing to do. Craig soon had Tubby in after it, while the boat continued on at the rate of knots! Of course, I went to grab my skipper, but I just missed. And we all learned, time and again, that flying between the islands is never easy. The trip from St Vincent to Trinidad and then down to Guyana was perhaps the most interesting.

We knew in advance that our gear wouldn't be able to fit on the same plane, but it seemed no-one had told the airline that if there's only 50 seats on the plane there's no point selling 53 tickets. So the last three in the line — Ian Healy, Shane Warne and Mike Walsh, the Australian tour party's scorer — were left behind, to catch the next flight. At least, we laughed to each other, there was now someone to accompany all our gear.

The original plan was for the trio to rejoin us in Trinidad, but (surprise, surprise!!) something went wrong, and we headed on to Guyana without them. They, we learned later, had to spend six hours wasting time in a Trinidad gate lounge.

I was down to room with Warney in Guyana. I think it's fair to say that when he finally arrived, the Warnster did deserve, and need, the small beer or two Dr Boon prescribed to quell the steam gushing from his ears. However, the saga wasn't over, because our gear was nowhere to be found. No suitcases or cricket equipment had come with our missing team-mates. By the time they did turn up, the following day, we'd just about written them off as vanished.

From Guyana, we travelled to St Lucia, scene of that all-important team get-together, and then onto Bridgetown, Barbados, for the first Test. The fact that we were playing only four Tests on this tour, instead of the customary five (so fragile was the Guyana economy that the West Indian cricket authorities simply couldn't afford to stage a Test there), meant that it was imperative we started the series well. Before the game, we thought that, perhaps — but only perhaps — the West Indies bowling attack lacked its usual depth. In 1991, Australia had faced Curtly Ambrose, Courtney Walsh, Malcolm Marshall and Patrick Patterson. This time, the first two pacemen were still there, but their back-up came from the two Benjamins, Kenneth and Winston, and Carl Hooper's off-spin. And when Australia knocked the West Indies over for 195 on the first day, the criticism in the local media was severe, which we saw as another indication that there was some unrest within the home camp.

The most controversial moment of the opening day — and the tour — came when the Prince, Brian Lara, was caught by Steve Waugh in the gully, off Brendon Julian, for 60. I can remember this incident very, very clearly. When the umpire's finger was raised, I am positive Lara accepted that Stephen had caught it and that the umpires had given him out. However, at some point between the middle of the ground and the dressing-room, he apparently changed his mind. And, in the next few minutes, the crowds, via television replays and radio commentary, learned that there was some dispute as to the validity of the catch and began to give Steve a verbal caning. But I can say this. I was fielding in front of square leg at the time, in line with Stephen in the gully. There's me, Lara and Steve, pretty much in a perfect line. And, for mine, there is no doubt that he caught it.

I'll swear that I had a clear sight of the ball, all the way from bat to hand, and that it didn't hit the ground at any time. I've never seen a replay and, at the time of the dismissal, neither did the umpires. Most importantly, the fieldsman believed the ball came out of his hand and bounced off his wrist — not the ground — and back into his hand. And I will back Stephen Rodger every day of the week.

In this innings, the Windies lost their last seven wickets for 65, establishing a trend that prevailed throughout the series. In the past, Australian teams had often had the West Indies on the ropes, but failed to knock over the lower-order batsmen. To try to put a stop to this, Glenn McGrath became our weapon. 'Pigeon,' we would say to him, 'when you go out to bat, it'll be bouncer, bouncer and yorker — and you're out of there. When you go out there to bowl, just give it to them! Give it to the tail!'

Glenn did this magnificently, and we discovered that the West Indian lower-order didn't like it at all.

Australia made 346, and then we knocked the West Indies out, for 189. Thirty-nine runs later, the match was over in three days, completing Australia's first-ever victory at Bridgetown. And afterwards, of course, there was chaos within and outside of the dressing-room, as the Australians in Barbados sang and danced with joy. Unfortunately, though, Simmo was missing, hospitalised on day two with a blood clot in his calf. Steve Waugh, Ian Healy, Justin Langer and myself went to visit him after the victory and found the old bloke to be extremely happy with our efforts.

At team meetings before the second Test, we kept emphasising that the West Indies had been down before and come back. Barbados, however marvellous, was just the beginning. The West Indians should never be underestimated. In the past, their pride had always dug them out of some cavernous holes, and we expected them to come fighting back in

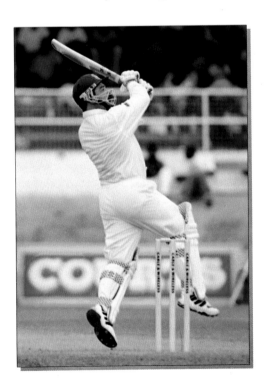

A shot from my 100th Test, in Trinidad.

fiery fashion. But we also knew we could dish it out in return. One of our key aims was not to allow the West Indians to over-run us, as had happened in previous series.

The Test ended in a draw, after rain had played a part. I scored 21 and 67 in the match and, while I was annoyed at getting out in the first innings after making a start, I did have the consolation of going past the 7000 Test runs milestone, and past Sir Donald Bradman's total of runs scored for Australia. But again, let's quickly put that in perspective — The Don scored 6996 runs in just 52 Tests; I was playing my 99th match! Sir Donald averaged just under one hundred every time at bat; when I passed 7000, I was moving along at a tick over 44.

The third Test, then, was my 100th Test — a memorable event, but unfortunately a game we lost to the West Indies.

We went into the game with a fair degree of confidence, but what we couldn't predict was the wicket's condition. Traditionally a turner, the curator had been hampered by torrential rain — much like the storms which washed us out in '91 — and the wicket was grassy. Even worse, whereas in most circumstances you would delay the start if the wicket was wet in patches, this one began on time — and the whole strip was soaked!

It was probably the worst track I ever played a Test match on. It bounced and seamed everywhere, and I was out in the middle in the second over, after Michael Slater had been dismissed for his first Test duck.

As I walked out, all the West Indians applauded, even Courtney Walsh who was bowling, which was a very moving experience. Then . . . the very first ball. I let it go, because it was well outside off-stump — and it almost bowled me, leg-stump.

I ended up getting 18. Ambrose aimed a delivery at leg-stump, I went forward , but the ball was an excellent leg-cutter and the resultant nick went to Richardson in the slip cordon. Even after watching the replays, I didn't think I'd done much wrong, which is one of the only times I have ever thought that. Generally, I reckon a batsman makes some sort of error to assist in his dismissal.

Australia were all out 128, with Steve Waugh remaining 63 not out. He took the West Indies on — anything loose, he swung at. It was stirring stuff to watch. And, of course, at one point Stephen and Curtly had their infamous run-in.

It was strange how the presence of grass on the wicket had caused a miraculous cure to the big man's much-publicised shoulder problems. Curtly was back to the pace, line and length of past series.

However, he was frustrated when 'Tugga' hit him over slips for four on a couple of occasions, and, after a fiery riser nearly took Steve's head off, Curtly followed through to stand about a metre away from the batsman, and applied his impressive stare.

Steve Waugh isn't a man to back away from a challenge and asked Curtly something along the lines of: 'What are you looking at?'

Which riled Ambrose immensely. We actually thought for a second that Curtly was about to deck him, but Richie Richardson, as any good captain would, dragged his player out of it. While the confrontation received a lot of coverage, in the context of the game, it was understandable. On a shocking wicket, Steve was fighting for his country, in a match where victory would mean an unassailable lead in the series; in contrast, Ambrose was trying to square the ledger for the West Indies. Two hardened competitors . . . and the situation boiled over. End of story.

To stress the unsuitability of the wicket, Australia bowled the West Indies out for 136 — a lead of only 8. Their top score was Jimmy Adams' 42; McGrath took 6–47. But any hope of an Australian revival was quenched when we were again knocked over, this time for a paltry 105. Soon after, the West Indies were celebrating a nine-wicket victory. And, certainly, they deserved to party, they'd handled the dreadful pitch much better than we had.

During this match, there was an example of the good relationship that exists between Australia's cricket and golf fraternities — Queenslanders Wayne Grady, the 1990 USPGA champion, and Ian Baker-Finch, the 1991 British Open winner, came down from their US base, in Miami, to watch the Test in Trinidad. We appreciated that although 'IBF' hadn't been playing with his former consistency, he still managed to find time to come and support his country, while Grady had been a supporter and friend for years. It gives one a great lift to know that other sports people possess just as keen an interest in your performance as you do in theirs.

Wayne's generosity towards me has been extraordinary. I remember how, before the 1990–91 Ashes against England, he organised to play a game with me and Ray Phillips, the former Australian wicketkeeper, in Brisbane. However, Wayne didn't arrive, but I found out later that his daughter had been ill. Then, on the last day of the Gabba Test, he walked into the dressing-room and gave me a box — containing a customised set of Mizuno irons, one through sand wedge. The only thing wrong with them is that they are far too good for me.

While he was in Trinidad, I asked him for the name of the Australian representative of Cobra, so that I could order a stiff-shafted driver. Wayne told me not to worry about it, despite my protests. Shortly thereafter, Pip phoned to tell me a set of woods, one, three and five had arrived on our doorstep. Wayne Grady is just one of life's gentlemen. Consequently, as this was my 100th Test, I really appreciated his presence and arranged for a bat to be signed by both teams, and added a special inscription to Wayne for his long-time support and friendship.

In the lead-up to the series-deciding fourth Test, I was wrestling with my own personal demons of series past. Memories of the 1991 tour and the Australian summer of 1992–93, series I believed we could win, came flooding back. I kept it within myself, but the thought of being railroaded again was extremely painful. The mood of the team, though, was positive. Without being too cliched, I kept thinking back to one of my schoolboy heroes, Joe Frazier, and his 'Thriller in Manila' with Muhammad Ali. That's what this was going to be like.

On the first day, Richie Richardson answered his critics with a century. This was an innings of hard work, not unlike the one I would put together against Sri Lanka in Melbourne in 1995–96. There was no doubt that Richardson was under pressure. If the West Indies lost the Test and the series, he would cop a fair proportion of the blame, but he responded magnificently. The innings total, though, was only 265.

Australia replied with 531, an innings completely dominated by the Waughs, whose fourth-wicket partnership of 231 really set up Australia's opportunity to finally win the trophy we craved so much. Mark made 126, and played as we know Mark Waugh can play, while Stephen was the last man out, for exactly 200. His was a knock that reminded me in many ways of Dean Jones' incredible effort in Madras in 1986. At Sabina Park in Kingston, Steve Waugh faced very different trials to those Deano suffered — but, similarly, they involved both physical and mental pressure. Stephen's effort was something special, an innings I will never forget, especially in the context of how he had been criticised in the past for his methods of playing fast bowling.

By stumps on the third day, with Australia holding a first-innings lead of 266 and the West Indies 3–63 (and Lara and Richardson both out), we felt that only rain on the rest day and two final days of the Test could deny us. Fortunately, the sun kept shining, and the West Indies were all out for 213. When last man in, Kenneth Benjamin, was dismissed, caught Taylor, bowled Warne, Sabina Park — or at least the Australian contingent therein, went completely ballistic.

The music started, *Khe Sanh* pumping. Needless to say, *Under the Southern Cross*, was sung several times. One considerate moment came when an Australian supporter, a Tasmanian, handed me two cans of Boags beer through the dressing-room window — he had carried them around the world, especially for me and Ricky Ponting. We put them on ice and shortly afterwards enjoyed the local elixir of Launceston.

Unfortunately, the only West Indian to accept our open invitation to join us for a drink was Jimmy Adams. I understand that the Frank Worrell Trophy had been lost, but I still believe that you should head in for a beer, show your face, win, lose or draw. But the post-match comments by Richie Richardson, that we were 'the weakest Australian team I have ever played against', I will defend.

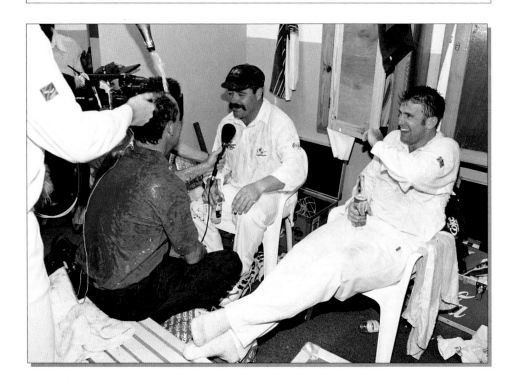

Being interviewed by former Test batsman David Hookes in the Sabina Park dressing-room.

I think that his words may have become twisted because of the line of questioning being put to him. Under that pressure, I believe what he was making reference to was the Australian bowling attack, which had lost McDermott and Fleming before a ball was bowled in the Test series. A lot of people won't believe that, but that's what I think Richie meant to say.

The great irony of all this is that it was the Australian bowlers who were the real heroes of our victory. Undermanned on paper, they were willing to stick to the game plan for the four Tests, and came out on top in the end.

The post-victory party back at the Pegasus was memorable, but not outlandish. The emotional relief was similar to the World Cup win in 1987, the euphoria and adrenalin rush meant that we were pretty much exhausted even before we were overcome by alcohol. Mind you, I was rooming with Tim May, who had been a tireless 12th man — he definitely made up for a few of the fellows who were overcome by weariness.

And then it was off to Bermuda, for 10 amazing days which did involve a few social games of cricket, but the emphasis was on relaxation. Several of the wives and girlfriends were there and, by the end of it, I was feeling very jealous of my team-mates, because Pip couldn't join me. She has been involved with so many memorable occasions in cricket, but with Elizabeth having just been born and Georgina and Jack at school, it just wasn't possible.

After returning home to Australia, the NSW Government organised a ticker-tape parade in Sydney, which started on the steps of the Town Hall and finished in Martin Place — there was an estimated 150,000 people lining George Street to cheer us. The support was unbelievable. It was amazing to walk through thousands and thousands of people to get to the stage in Martin Place. When you look across such a gathering of people, you realise just what it means to them and how much they care about their Test cricket team.

There were mothers with small babies, right through to people in their 80s and 90s. It was a truly humbling experience, equal to the buzz of the parade we enjoyed after winning back the Ashes in 1989.

Which is saying something.

I thought again back to the dressing-room in Kingston, to the scene immediately after our fantastic victory. Champagne was flying everywhere. The young blokes — Slater, Blewett, Ponting and Langer (draped in an Australian flag) — were having the time of their lives. Steve Waugh would stay in his whites all night, even down to his spiked cricket boots.

I was just sitting back, taking it all in. My mind was a strange mix of joy and relief at our success, and also the memories of the pain and disappointment of previous series against the West Indies, and against other countries in my early days as an Australian Test cricketer, in the mid–1980s. They were hard times. Yet, here was a group of extremely gifted Australian cricketers passing the Frank Worrell Trophy around their dressing-room, having finally beaten the Windies in the Caribbean. It struck me: I had been part of the resurgence of Australian cricket, to the point, I reflected, where we could be regarded as perhaps the best cricket team in the world.

My only disappointment, which belies my age and experience, was that I felt exceptionally sad that Allan Border was not an on-field part of this incredible, long-awaited success. But AB was at Sabina Park, commentating for a television network (and, I reckon, on the field in spirit), and it was a special moment when he walked into the dressing-room — his excitement and pride at our achievement was as fierce as anyone's.

When he saw me, I reckon he knew exactly what I was thinking.

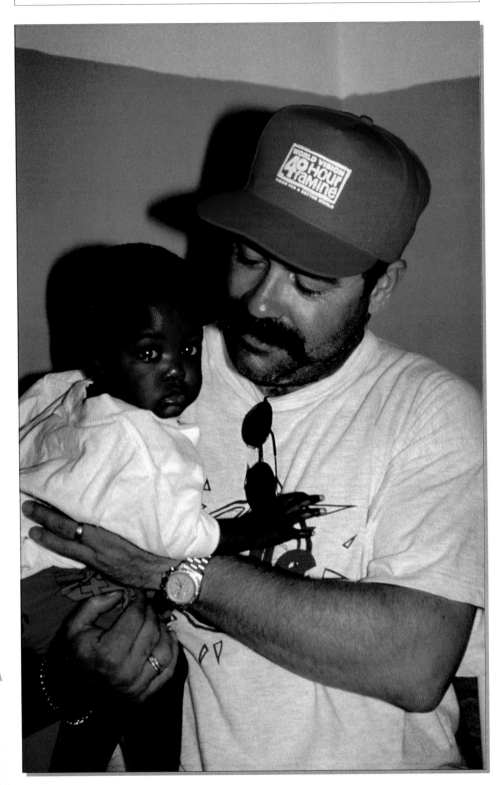

24: Mozambique

AFTER I RETIRED FROM INTERNATIONAL CRICKET, IN LATE JANUARY, 1996,
WORLD VISION INVITED ME TO ACCOMPANY A TEAM ON A FIELD TRIP TO
MOZAMBIQUE — TO VIEW THEIR PROJECTS AND CONTRIBUTE TO THE
PRODUCTION OF A MINI-DOCUMENTARY ABOUT THE PLIGHT OF THAT COUNTRY,
WHICH HAS SUFFERED TERRIBLY FROM NEARLY TWO DECADES OF CIVIL WAR.

I have been involved with World Vision and their promotion in Tasmania of the '40-Hour Famine' for the past six years, and, when cricket commitments permitted, had participated in the 40-Hour Famine on a few occasions myself. In other years, I have been involved with media promotion of this major fund-raiser, before and after the event.

And, 1996, I started sponsoring a child in Vietnam. I knew, though, that it would not just be the child I supported who would benefit from the $30 a month I intended to donate, but the entire village. You get to help many children, not just one, by investing in a World Vision project. The Boon family sponsors Viet Tung Nguyen, who lives in the Hoa Binh province in Vietnam. He was born on January 1, 1983, and is in grade three at primary school. His favourite game, he tells us, is marbles. It's very difficult for Georgina and Jack to understand how marbles can be his favourite game — but he has nothing else.

To describe Mozambique, a country on the East coast of southern Africa, bordering South Africa, as an eye-opener would be an understatement. As a Test cricketer, I had travelled the world, or at least places where cricket is played, but for most of the time, my team-mates and I were protected. We may see terrible hardship, but usually from a distance, and never as a 'hands-on' experience. I had seen poverty and third world conditions on the streets of India, including a revealing drive over the bridge at Calcutta to see the infamous Black Hole, where American actor Patrick Swayze made the film *City of Joy*. But Mozambique in 1996 was something again, even if the country was three years into their rebuilding phase. For 17 years, civil war, funded largely by interests within South Africa and Zimbabwe, raged. The majority of the population fled to the neighbouring countries of Malawi and Zimbabwe, where they existed in huge refugee camps. Just about all of Mozambique's wildlife — with the exception of snakes, crocodiles and hippopotami — was destroyed.

Opposite: Seeing the suffering in Mozambique was one of the most moving experiences of my life.

I flew to Africa with Ray Walker, from World Vision's head office. In Harare, the capital of Zimbabwe, we met up with Scott Kelleher, a World Vision photo-journalist based in Nairobi, who had worked all over the African continent, particularly at Vision projects in Sierra Leone and Rwanda. The documentary team also boasted Adam Shand and Mick Purdy, the latter an ex-National Nine Network cameraman, both Australians based in Harare.

The stories Scott and Mick told of what they had seen and experienced in Rwanda were, for me, almost incomprehensible. In Mozambique, the process of re-educating the people in the basics of farming was underway, but, after years of war, almost two generations had missed out on that knowledge, which had previously been passed down through families. And the country was in the midst of drought; the soil, it was explained to me, was badly depleted.

World Vision was introducing different seed varieties for maize and sweet potato, which they hoped would produce crops quickly. There was also a major water well program, to battle disease. The objective is to bring the country and the people to a level where they can begin to look after themselves.

What struck me almost immediately was that Mozambique's general population possessed absolutely nothing. World Vision had introduced 'food for work' programs and children were fed one meal a day if they went to school — there was a 100 per cent attendance rate. Yet, the kids were so happy all the time. I suppose, not having anything, not realising what we take for granted, was a blessing.

I remembered, with more than a tinge of guilt, an everyday incident which had occurred in the Boon family just before I went to Africa. Pip had gone to the milk bar and bought the children some ice creams — she got the right one for Jack but the wrong one for Georgina. Like any other Australian eight-year-old, Georgie was very unhappy and told the world. Kids are kids. But when I had the chance to see Mozambique, her tears just stuck in my mind — how ridiculous is it to complain about the type of ice cream you're eating?

The children in Mozambique don't know what ice cream is, let alone that there are different flavours and types. We have all seen the advertisements for World Vision and other international aid organisations, pictures of diseased and starving children. But to meet these kids face-to-face, malnourished children who were literally reduced to skin and bone, or children bloated from internal gases, their bodies breaking down from vitamin and mineral deficiencies, their hair orange — that is completely different. The remorse and sadness I felt when I saw these children was devastating. The first time I saw them, I cried.

We were in a city called Mutarara, where we visited orphanages and hospital camps run by different religious and welfare groups. When a child is severely malnourished, the nurses feed them milk through pipettes, because that's all their systems can accommodate. The second, third and fourth stages of their rehabilitation involve more substantial food intakes. There has been a clear attempt to centralise aid facilities in Mozambique, which, of course, has many advantages. But to reach the health centre in Mutarara, a mother needing to bring her sick child to be treated may have to endure a 20 kilometre walk from their village, even 100 kilometres in extreme cases. There are no alternatives. Until the country reaches subsistence, the children remain gravely at risk.

We saw one child, who was just skin and bones, and on her third visit to the feeding centre. The doctors told us she'd deteriorated to that condition three times in the past 18 months.

In Mozambique's hospitals, we watched doctors from all over the world trying to perform major and minor operations, vaccinating against disease and healing with extremely limited equipment and supplies. Once again, I walked away with the dawning realisation of how lucky we are in Australia. Never again will I complain about services we take for granted. It is so difficult to comprehend the level of hardship and deprivation. But to see the work of World Vision and other organisations was very heartening. I came away believing there is a long-term solution to the problems in Mozambique.

In Tete, one of Mozambique's major cities, we stayed at the World Vision facility — which we nicknamed the 'Tete Hilton'. It was just an ordinary house, with three bedrooms. World Vision workers lived downstairs. I was told how, when the Portuguese pulled out in the mid–1970s, concrete was poured down the water mains and sewers, which, inevitably, created a truckload of problems. There is a continuing problem with tuberculosis, while, as it is in many African countries, AIDS is rife. We drank only bottled water, while the local water system was available for an hour in the morning and two hours at night — and it was cold showers only. The streets are pot-holed, there was rubble everywhere. Things that had been destroyed during the civil war were still lying around, relics from an angry past.

We learned not to throw away our soft drink cans — the people used the empties to fashion cups, or toys for their children. Before we set out for the fields, we packed not just these drinks but also rolls for lunch. They were filled with an extremely garlicky, chewy type of meat; after eating them you could have set your breath alight. But, when we took a lunch break, we had to drive away a discreet distance so that we weren't eating and drinking in front of the children. In Tete, the weather was extremely hot — coming into winter, the thermometer still topped 40 degrees. However, by the end of the day, everyone was exhausted, not so much from the heat but from trying to comprehend everything — emotionally, it was very draining.

Interestingly, the way to reach the people of Mozambique is through the country's women — all World Vision's educational classes are for women.

Because of their culture, the men in Mozambique are the 'chiefs', the women and children the workers. For their agriculture projects, World Vision concentrate on tutoring the women, as they do the majority of the work in the fields. In the villages, the aid organisations target the head woman, because she can get things done. According to the local culture, this isn't 'men's work'.

Mozambique is a country with what we in Australia would consider to be strange customs. On the Zambezi River, there are enormous problems with crocodiles, which attack people who are washing clothes on the river's banks, and carry them away and eat them. However, the people won't kill these reptiles, because they believe the spirits of their ancestors live on through them.

And it is not just crocodiles you have to look out for. It was in Mutarara that I came face-to-face with a cobra, an experience I am not looking forward to repeating. We were walking along a path and this huge snake crawled out of the undergrowth and sat up and looked at us! It was about three metres long, and, while more than half its body was waving around in the air, its head was flared. I thought I was scared then, but when I jumped back into the four-wheel-drive and a huge grasshopper flew into my lap and started banging around from window to window ... that's when I really lost it! After that, every time we walked through a maize field, I was looking under every bush and behind every tree, because I suffer from an absolute fear of snakes.

An angry residual of the civil war are the thousands and thousands of land mines and anti-personnel mines that litter Mozambique's landscape. The authorities have managed to clear the roads and the airports, but the fields remain extremely dangerous. We were told to stick to the tracks. I had no problem with that instruction, although it made me think — here is a part of the world where you can't even go off for a wander without running the risk of having your leg blown off.

I spent eight days in Mozambique with the World Vision team. Most days we began at about six in the morning, travelling in the four-wheel-drives and finishing in the late afternoon. After dark, we were advised not to travel around, because the country still has a bit of a problem with bandits. Certainly, the crims have some advantages, for at night it was pitch black, there wasn't a street light in sight. In Kuelimane, 10 kilometres inland from the mouth of the Zambezi, we visited a 'feeding centre', which was some 80-odd kilometres away. This was the most bone-shattering journey — it took three and a half hours to get there. When we came home on the second day, I congratulated our driver for his consistency — he had not missed one pot hole, there or back. He just laughed. So, eventually, did I.

In Kuelimane, we made a commercial for World Vision, coaching children who couldn't speak English to say: 'Thank you, Australia.' The television advertisement was designed to remind people in Australia to send in the money they had pledged to the 40-Hour Famine. Our mini-documentary was produced for the Nine Network's program, *A Current Affair*.

World Vision in Mozambique is not just in the business of distributing aid. The organisation has programs by which a family can borrow a duck or a cow for a period of time — after the animal reproduces, it can be returned or replaced. A sort of credit system. I saw also that donations from overseas to the various aid groups in Africa DO get there. This is, of course, a major concern to most people in Australia. Of course, any organisation has administrative costs and advertising costs, but I can assure you this money is having an impact.

Working with the children of Mozambique was tremendous. They have nothing, are probably never going to have anything, but they're happy. In a sense, just like kids anywhere. When we were filming or taking photographs, the majority of the children were keen to become involved — they puffed their chests out, straightened their shoulders, checked that their hair was in place. We were, though, also very wary of invading their personal space. The World Vision crew told the story of Gary Ablett, the Australian football superstar from Geelong, who, on a similar trip, walked into a school with a video camera on his shoulder, recording. When the children saw the red light flashing on the camera, they evacuated the room — they thought it was a weapon.

When I left Mozambique, I realised that the people desperately need more assistance, but also that their plight isn't irreversible. If World Vision can raise the country to subsistence level, they will be able to scale down their level of aid and move on to another country which is trying to cope with an emergency situation. From what I saw, their objective in Mozambique is far from impossible. But not easy.

When we flew out of Kuelimane, to return home, we were lucky enough to have a local World Vision officer accompany us to the airport. We made it through customs and immigration all right, in the process handing over our passports. We paid the departure tax and everything was stamped correctly. But then came the catch — to get the passports back, we had to pay a cash bonus!

I came home to Launceston, spent half of Mother's Day with my family and then started the World Vision promotion for the 40-Hour Famine in Sydney. We did radio and newspaper interviews and called on a number of schools, talking to the children about my experiences in Mozambique. This was the best time to do the promotion, while my memories were still fresh. And I kept thinking: 'Where was I two days ago?' Emotionally, I was very charged, able to speak from the heart about the fact the we had 'everything' in Australia, while the people of Mozambique had virtually nothing. Only now do I really appreciate what we have in Australia and just how lucky we are.

25: One Last Look Back

I CANNOT ESCAPE THE STATISTICAL FACTS ABOUT MY CAREER — THEY ARE THERE IN BLACK AND WHITE, THE TOTAL OF MATCHES AND RUNS. AND, FOR A PERIOD OF TIME, MY STATISTICS WILL STAND, SECOND BEHIND ALLAN BORDER. EVENTUALLY, THOUGH, I WILL BE SURPASSED, BECAUSE THERE ARE SOME EXCEPTIONALLY TALENTED CRICKETERS PLAYING FOR AUSTRALIA (HOWEVER, I'M NOT SO SURE ABOUT AB'S RECORD. SOMEONE'S GOING TO HAVE TO PLAY FOR A LONG, LONG TIME AND BE ABLE TO REALLY PLAY THE GAME TO KNOCK HIM OFF!).

I could never, ever have dreamed that I would finish my international cricket career having achieved what I have. Deep down, I know that I managed some good innings and must have been able to play a bit. But to compare myself with Doug Walters, Neil Harvey or Greg Chappell — the great champions of past eras who finished their careers with similar statistical records to mine — is extremely difficult. For me, it is just about impossible. After all, Walters and Chappell were my childhood heroes and I feel guilty even thinking about putting myself near their level. Statistics paint different pictures depending on their interpretation. But can you remember how Walters and Chappell played? I do, and I never played like either of them.

What does more than embarrass me, in fact, makes me quite irate, are comparisons of any kind between my career and that of Sir Donald Bradman. The Don scored 6996 runs at an average of 99.94 in just 52 Tests. I played 107 Tests, more than twice his career total, and only made 446 more runs!

I should never even be mentioned in the same breath as Bradman.

However, I will never forget having dinner with Sir Donald at Government House in Adelaide, while I was vice-captain of Australia, back in 1986–87. We talked about cricket of different eras and he stated that there could be little or no comparison. The players of his time, for example, had to deal with the vagaries of uncovered pitches, while today we play on covered wickets. I recall he reckoned that, with a few different field placings, what we in the modern era call

Opposite: With Ricky Ponting, batting for Tasmania against NSW in Sydney, October 1995.

'normal' cricket, he called 'bodyline'. And he explained how the game had changed and improved in many aspects, especially bowling, fitness and fielding.

'But, David,' he said, with a very wry smile, 'I'm quite confident that I could still average 60.'

I just feel very privileged to have been able to enjoy dinner, with my wife, Pip, in the company of Sir Donald and Lady Bradman.

Memories such as this remind me just how good cricket has been to me. Right through, I was just doing what I loved doing, what I had immense pride in doing. I loved playing cricket for Australia, the blokes I played with and the cricketers I played against . . .

I believe my main strength in cricket was that I was extremely single-minded. Once I was focussed, it was all that and nothing else. I might not have had loads of 'natural gifts', but I did have some talent for the game, otherwise I wouldn't have been able to play at Test level for so long. The way I see it, there are very few pure 'naturals' — over a generation, you could probably count them on one hand. And maybe not use that many fingers. Everybody else has to work hard.

When Geoff Marsh and I came together as an opening pair, one of our practice philosophies was having extra hits, after everyone else in the net had batted. This was especially important when things weren't going so well for one or the other of us. It became a ritual. I was a creature of habit, preparing to play Test cricket for Australia. However, for many people, my routines would have been quite boring. We would train or play, and have a couple of beers in the rooms afterwards; then it was back to the hotel, for a meal and perhaps a couple more beers. But only very rarely was I out of bed after 10.30pm on a Test match night.

This was not the philosophy of a puritan. Although cricketers are not athletes preparing for an Olympic 100 metres final (and the game has always had a social aspect), over the years of my career it became a necessity for players' fitness and attitudes to alter considerably. It was personally valuable, as my career progressed, to observe the approaches of the younger blokes as they came into the team. They knew the way to the gym, they went on those extra road runs. I had to keep up with them, as best I could, or I wouldn't have been able to keep playing.

I will always remember Australia's media manager Ian McDonald's comment on one particular night during the first Test against Pakistan in Brisbane in 1995–96. This was my last international in Brisbane, the scene of my Test debut 12 seasons before. I hadn't done much during the day, so I headed for the Brisbane Bears' gym with the Australian physiotherapist, Errol Alcott. Meanwhile, Australia's captain Mark Taylor ran laps of the Gabba. Not one beer was drunk in the Australian dressing-room at the end of the day. And Macca, who'd been with the Australian team for just about all my career, could not believe it.

I'm not suggesting such sobriety is a regular occurrence. Perhaps it was just a one-off. However, it is an indication of the change in attitude that has occurred at the top of Australian cricket in the past decade.

I can look back and say that I have enjoyed every single minute of my international career — from the hard times from which I had to extricate myself to the challenges and successes that came my way. Most of all, I enjoyed being part of the resurgence of Australian cricket. When I made my Test debut, Australian cricket was a long way down the sport's totem pole. Now we are at the top.

There are so many treasured memories. Sure, I also had disappointments, when I didn't achieve what I wanted or didn't perform to the standards I had set myself, but I hope that, overall, people saw me as someone who took immense pride in representing Australia and achieving what he did.

Retiring from international cricket was such a difficult decision — the realisation that what I had done for so long was going to end was very hard to swallow. Even if I was 80 years old the decision wouldn't have been any easier. People ask me the question: 'Are you happy with your retirement?' And my answer is always: 'No, I'm not.'

And they envisage all sorts of dire scenarios.

But there was no malicious sub-plot. I wasn't the victim of any dastardly cricket politics. Not at all. In fact, I am very content with the decision that I made and confident it was the correct one for D. Boon. But that doesn't mean I have to be happy about it!

Come the summer of 1996–97, and the seasons to come, I will go downstairs to my cricket museum in Launceston and no doubt feel a little sad, among all the great memories and experiences cricket has provided me. I will look at the inscription Allan Border wrote to me in his book, *Beyond Ten Thousand,* and feel extremely emotional.

Not long after I retired, Pip commented to Greg Chappell that she thought we would now be able to spend more time together.

'No,' Greg replied, 'David will be involved in cricket for the rest of his life. And he will think about his career and retirement for years.'

And I hope I do.

EPILOGUE

THROUGH HIS CAREER, DAVID BOON EARNED THE ADMIRATION AND
FRIENDSHIP OF A GREAT MANY PEOPLE FROM ALL SECTIONS OF THE
CRICKET COMMUNITY. HERE IS A COLLECTION OF TRIBUTES, WRITTEN BY
A RANGE OF PEOPLE WHO HAVE ALL CLOSELY FOLLOWED BOON'S CAREER,
AS COLLEAGUES, COMMENTATORS OR CRICKET ADMINISTRATORS.
TOGETHER, THEY CAPTURE JUST HOW SIGNIFICANT HAS BEEN THE IMPACT
OF BOON ON AUSTRALIAN CRICKET, AND ON THE GAME THROUGHOUT
THE WORLD.

RICHIE BENAUD

Old Trafford is an unusual cricket ground. The pitch square is in such a position that the sun can be a problem. Some cricketers are inclined to say that it is a difficult ground for catching, others that they love the atmosphere. I remember it because it was, for me, part of four of the most spectacular happenings of my career as a player and as a commentator.

The first was in 1956, when Australia was thrashed by England and that great off-spinner Jim Laker took 19 wickets in the match and Tony Lock took just one bowling left-arm spin. Five years later, when Australia retained the Ashes in England, it all hinged on the Old Trafford Test and England was giving us such a hammering on the final afternoon. Then Wally Grout caught Ted Dexter at the wicket off me and we finished up winning the match and retaining that little urn.

Contrasting matches. Contrasting despair and pleasure, too, with the second game, in 1961, making up for some of the disappointments five years earlier. That was the playing side. As a commentator over the past 33 years, I have some particularly special moments to remember from when I have been behind the microphone. One of these was Shane Warne's first ball in a Test in England when he bowled Mike Gatting at Old Trafford.

The finest memory I have as a commentator, though, was four years before that day, when David Boon swept a four to deep square-leg and the Ashes were regained by Australia, in England, for the first time in 55 years. A single boundary doesn't sound much in the context of Anglo-Australian Test cricket, but it was all that was needed and it was a superb victory.

I saw David's debut at the Gabba against the West Indies in 1984–85, after he'd made his name in the Prime Minister's match. I then watched him play all his subsequent cricket in Australia and England, through to his retirement match against Sri Lanka in Adelaide in 1996.

There will be plenty of work to do in the future with Tasmania and in other areas, and the Sheffield Shield beckons in alluring fashion. That match in Adelaide, where David announced his retirement, was an interesting week.

In the hurly-burly of international cricket these days, it is quite possible to lose sight of the quality of players you have been watching over an 11-year period. At the farewell

Opposite: Two special moments — winning the Frank Worrell Trophy in Jamaica in 1995 (top) and dressing-room celebrations in Adelaide after my final Test match (bottom).

function, at a restaurant in Adelaide, Channel Nine showed a five-minute videoclip of Boon's batting in his Test career and, naturally enough, there was an emphasis on the good parts. His half-century on debut, his first Test century in Adelaide, his 164 not out at Lord's in 1993, and one of his greatest efforts, the hundred he made against the West Indies at Kingston, Jamaica, in 1991.

The video was so good that I then made it my business to have a look at some more footage, which just underlined what a good player he had been. Not just as a batsman, but as a team man, and not just as a team man, but as one who made the team what it was. He had an immense influence on Australian cricket in the time he played, because it was the period when the West Indian team were top of the world and Australia were fighting to get on even terms with them.

Statistics don't always tell the story, but in David's case they do. They provide a perfect picture of what he did for Australia, often in the most adverse circumstances. He deserves all the good things that will happen to him in retirement from international cricket.

ALLAN BORDER

I first met David Boon in his initial season of cricket, 1978–79, when he was something of a child prodigy at the tender age of 17. What was immediately evident was the maturity he displayed, even at so young an age. It wasn't that you looked at Boonie and thought: 'Oh, this kid is definitely going to go on to bigger and better things,' but his bulldog spirit was readily apparent.

When Boon was playing cricket for Australia, it was the bulldog in him that came to the fore, the gritty determination he had not to throw his wicket away. In the field, he didn't say much fielding at bat–pad. In fact, we used to tap him on the helmet sometimes to see if he was still awake.

Fielding at bat–pad is another part of the Boon legend. Early in his career, we experimented with David, as we did with most of the team, in and out of the slips. However, in the latter half of my captaincy, he found his niche at short-leg and, because he had no fear, took many memorable catches in that position.

Throughout my tenure as Australian captain, Boon gave me total support, for the period he was vice-captain and afterwards. Off the field, he was a good man to have a beer with and I took great delight in our off-the-ground friendship.

Within any team, from club to Test level, there will always be underlying currents of opinion and quite natural differences of thought and personality. This is especially so when the team isn't playing well, as was unfortunately Australia's lot in my early years as captain. It was in those situations that David was invaluable and right in his element playing the devil's advocate. Throughout his career, Australian cricketers have fed off his natural strength.

Babs is pretty quiet, but he will yak it up over a few beers, enjoying the fruits of the team's labours. After a Test win, he was certainly in his element. Of course, in the second half of my captaincy, there were more and more opportunities to enjoy Australia's success.

Boonie had the crucial job of leading the team anthem, *Under the Southern Cross*, after our victories; it was those five or 10 minutes after coming off the ground that he made his own. Generally doused in celebratory beer, sometimes suitably dressed in jockstrap and baggy green, Boonie would jump up on the nearest table and set the ball rolling for the victory celebrations. It will be interesting to see how the Australian boys cope from now on.

As I have said before, Boon was a confidant for me, both on and off the field, particularly during the tough times of the 1980s. I refer to him as my 'Rock of Gibraltar' and perhaps people will gain some understanding of how much he meant to me from that comparison. It was very hard for me to bear the load of the Australian captaincy at times; Babs was always there to bounce ideas off, even to calm me down when the pressure was about to blow.

As a player, David took great pride in being in the engine room of the team's batting, the top three. If you've got a solid engine room, it takes a lot of pressure off and allows the more flamboyant players further down the order to play their natural game. For most of his career, you just expected Boon to perform with the bat; he rarely let Australia down.

When you think of the attacks Australia had to face during his career, especially the West Indies in full flight, I can't think of too many people I'd rather have had out there in the middle.

There was a day in Jamaica in 1991 when the West Indies were throwing everything at us. Most of the boys succumbed, except for Boon. In the middle of a great century, not out, he copped a rising ball from Patrick Patterson right on the chin. Babsie just shook his head, walked towards our physio, who bandaged him up, and simply walked back to the crease to resume the battle. At lunch, he calmly sat through four or five stitches — no anaesthetic, of course!

It was a great sight to see him waddle to the crease for Australia.

I think that cricket history will judge David Boon in a far brighter light than has already been cast upon him. The lack of accolades during his international career came not through neglect, it is just that he was such a quiet achiever. For the majority of his career, Boon wasn't spectacular or pretty; he just went about the job required of him in his own inimitable fashion.

Both Boon and I, along with a few others, experienced the frustrations of the mid–1980s and the subsequent rebuilding of Australian cricket. A few of the younger blokes in the current Australian team haven't suffered too many disappointments during their Test careers; it was David Boon who provided the voice of experience tempered by hardship. I think he has left an excellent legacy for the young players to follow.

Having said all that, it's still difficult to find exactly the right words with which to describe the 'Keg on Legs', David Clarence Boon. Let's face it, I love the guy!

IAN CHAPPELL

For a period of three years, David Boon was consistently Australia's best batsman, yet he was often ignored when it came to awards. No doubt, Boon was unperturbed, believing his greatest reward was to lead the Australian team song, *Under the Southern Cross*, after each victory.

It's typical of Boon that on the rare occasions he was animated and stringing a few words together, it was behind closed doors with his team-mates. Out in the middle, his reaction was always the same, whether he was hit a full-blooded blow to the shins at bat-pad or had just scored a hundred. He did raise the bat when he passed a hundred, but he didn't lift a finger when he was hit a painful blow.

Ask David about his amazing consistency during that period and he'll mumble into his 'mo' about being lucky, or of how he always recalled 1986–87 when he couldn't make a run. It was in the middle of that horror stretch that his mother told him: 'David, we've got three tapes at home to remind us that you can bat.'

David's mother was referring to the Test centuries he had scored to that point. It was the best advice he could have received, and it wasn't long before a flood of Test centuries flowed from her son's bat. In the end, the whole world was aware that 'Boon can bat'.

Boon's batting was simple, in keeping with his approach to life. He was quickly into position, stopping the good balls with a straight bat and dealing ruthlessly with the loose ones. In his early days, he was much stronger through the on-side than the off. However, with typical Boon determination, he worked hard on improving his off-side driving. Boon's image was that of a silent hard-working type, rather like a wharfie in a navy-blue singlet who rounds off his productive day with a dozen bitterly cold beers and half as many words. Despite his portly figure and the hint of being a late maturer, David was a natural who first came to notice as a talented 16-year-old when he was selected in the Australian under–19 side. He was also a natural team man.

David is a man of few words, but he chooses them wisely and he contributed a lot in the team environment. He was a tower of strength to Allan Border and it was his ex-skipper who anointed Boon as the man to lead the singing after each Australian victory, having originally inherited the job himself when Rod Marsh retired. Marsh would have approved of Boon's appointment to such an esteemed position in the Australian team. The two have more in common than just a bristling moustache, both of them enjoying more than just the odd beer or two.

In recognition of Boon's ability as a 'stayer', the Australian team dubbed him the 'Keg on Legs'. Those short, but strong, legs took a pounding because of his almost permanent residency at bat–pad. However, Boon shrugged off those minor inconveniences to finish second only to Border on the Australian run-scorers list.

Nevertheless, it's doubtful whether his profile will ever match his record, although I suspect that will be the least of Boon's worries. If you could drag it out of him, Boon would explain that he had no cause for complaint. After all, he led the team in singing the victory song and his team-mates spoke of him as a great batsman and a terrific team man.

Most of all, however, David Boon will be remembered as a player who was always a credit to the baggy green cap.

IAN HEALY

When I first met David Boon, I wasn't sure what to make of him — because I just wasn't sure what he was making of me.

On my first Australian tour, to Pakistan in 1988, I was not the most assured character, having been chosen on the strength of six, first-class matches. Battling with personal form and the inevitable inferiority complex which comes from being a rookie abroad, my self-esteem was further sapped when I noticed Boon, with that famous stone Buddha expression of his, staring at me bleakly from under the shade of a green helmet at short-leg.

'There's another one who hates me,' I thought. It took me weeks, perhaps months, to work out that Boonie didn't hate me. It was just his way. His stare was all part of the toughening-up process which was good for me, even though I didn't realise it at the time.

Boon's toughness is the stuff of legends, although I am pleased to report there is a softer side to the man. It was first apparent to his Australian team-mates in the novel setting of the men's toilets in a restaurant in Manchester on the 1993 Ashes tour.

David, as usual, was minding his own business and staring at the wall in front of him when a fellow of similar height with tight, black hair came in and stood at the urinal beside him. Boon didn't even have to look sideways to sense that it was Tim May. The fact that Boon didn't acknowledge May's presence enhanced the effect of a small practical joke, as he dropped down his right hand to tickle May's private parts. It was quite a laugh ... particularly since the person standing next to him wasn't May. He wasn't even Australian. In fact, David didn't even know him. He looked vaguely similar to May and had a similar-coloured shirt, but that was as far as the resemblance went. Boon was horrified — the man of stone went to water and emerged from the toilet pale-faced.

Boonie is a strong man and a tough individual to get on top of. I rate this quality very highly in cricketers because it is the one trait I have tried to hone in my own game. He was a heavy-duty Test batsman who used to tune his walkman to heavy metal music when he wasn't instigating wrestling matches on the team bus. This was one of his favourite pastimes and he was always hard to beat. He had the strength of a sumo wrestler, something which his body suggests he might have been in another lifetime.

IAN McDONALD (Australian team manager)

Under the Southern Cross he stands . . . as solid as a rock.

Things won't be the same without David Boon in the Australian team. He's a hard act to follow. Throughout his 107-Test career, he typified the fighting spirit of Australian cricket. He occupied the crease, bristling with determination; refusing to show any sign of emotion even when rattled in the ribcage by a West Indian speedster.

However, in the years I've known him as a player and a friend — I was there when he made his Test debut in the second Test against the West Indies at Brisbane in 1984, and when he said farewell in the final Test against Sri Lanka at Adelaide in 1996 — I've come to realise that, within that tough exterior, there really is heaps of emotion. Mixed emotions, admittedly, some fiery, others of a caring, sentimental nature.

Like the time at the Gabba when he had just been dismissed in a decision that obviously displeased him. As he strode from the ground, he kept glancing over his shoulder at the umpire and muttering to himself as he walked. He was walking directly towards the television cameras stationed on the roof of the dressing-room. Watching the television monitors in the rooms, it was pretty obvious he was muttering the most famous four-letter word quite emphatically.

Into the dressing-room David stormed and, as he hurled his bat and gloves at his coffin, the phone on the wall rang. I answered it and a lady asked: 'Can I speak to David Boon, please?' After I explained that we don't take dressing-room calls during a match, she said: 'It's his mother.'

I looked across at her fuming son and said: 'David, your mum wants to talk to you.' I'd have to say the mood swing was quite dramatic, and the conversation ended with him saying: 'Sorry, Mum.'

The moral of the story is you shouldn't dispute decisions in public and you very definitely shouldn't 'mouth off' the four-letter word in front of television cameras . . . especially when your Mum is sitting at home in Launceston watching! Come to think of it, in all the years I watched him play after that, I don't think he ever opened his lips when walking off after being dismissed.

Yet this same tough man, who had a pact with his mate and opening partner Geoff Marsh not to show any emotion when being intimidated by the West Indies pace battery, was so choked with emotion when he decided to retire, and when he played his last Test, he couldn't bring himself to talk about it too much. Instead, he wrote all his friends notes thanking them for their support throughout his career.

Really, he didn't have to thank anyone. We all owe him huge thanks for the tremendous contribution he made in restoring fight and pride to the Australian team as the side fought its way out of the cricket wilderness and up the ladder of world cricket during the Allan Border era.

When Border retired in 1994, Boon was the only member of the team who had played under any other Australian captain. His first Test in Brisbane was the Test in which Kim Hughes caused a sensation by resigning from the captaincy.

Boonie's achievements as a player are well-documented and will be mentioned elsewhere in this book, but it is important to emphasise that his 7422 runs at an average of 43.66 took him to second on the list of all-time Australian run-getters. This impressive statistic means, in any era, he ranks as one of Australia's truly great players. A top score of

200, 21 Test centuries, 32 half-centuries and his legendary fielding at short-leg, with 99 catches over his career, indicate he was a key player in the Australian team.

For me, it was a sad day when he walked from the Adelaide Oval and it was fitting that he received such a tremendous ovation from the crowd. I'll miss his mateship, for he was always available for a beer and a chat at the end of the day. He was the type of team man that makes a manager's life easy — honest, determined in a crisis and with a sense of humour that his tough exterior often hid.

David was the 'old hand' in the team and whenever young, new players came into the Australian team environment, I would put one of the new boys with him as a room-mate. When they got older, they would plead for protection from his snoring.

It was apt that young Tasmanian Ricky Ponting made his debut in the first Test against Sri Lanka in Perth with Boon still in the side. Boonie would have felt great sympathy for him when he was unlucky to be given out lbw for 96, four short of a century on debut. In the next Test at Melbourne, Ponting was in the side when Boon scored 110, his 21st and last Test century. For Ricky, it is all ahead of him, for David, it is now all memories.

He knows the heights of a Test 200, the glory of an Ashes win and the ultimate triumph: a series win over the West Indies on the 1995 tour of the Caribbean. He also knows the lows of being dropped from the team when he was vice-captain. Throughout it all, the man never changed, never got carried away with fame, was always the dependable bloke who typified what it was like to wear the 'baggy green' with pride and determination.

That's why he became famous for leading the team's rendition of *Under the Southern Cross* in victory celebrations. For those of us privileged enough to be present at the final rendition in Adelaide, it was a performance that will long be remembered — he did it three times!

Thanks for your time on the scene, David Boon. Your contribution to Australian and Tasmanian cricket will never be forgotten.

GEOFF MARSH

David Boon was the gutsiest cricketer with whom I ever played. He wasn't the most gifted, but he was definitely the toughest, both physically and mentally.

There is no doubt that for about five years there he had as good a claim as anybody to being the best batsman in the world. That was in the era after Viv Richards and before Brian Lara. He was one of a handful of great players — perhaps Desmond Haynes and Martin Crowe were up there with him.

The thing about Babs is that he wasn't selfish. He certainly made me a one-day cricketer. I remember after we made a pact that we would open for Australia together, the only way it could work out was if he took the risks and played shots while I knocked the ball around and rotated the strike. There were times when we would be behind the run-rate and I'd go down the pitch and tell him to pull his finger out and get the score moving. Sometimes he did, other times he would get out trying. But never once did he complain. We had made a deal that that was how we'd play and he stuck by it. Now, when you look at our one-day averages, mine is around 40 and his is 33-odd. I don't know how many times he got out trying to take the pressure off me.

I don't think there's any question that Boon and Allan Border set a new benchmark for what is required from Australian batsmen, both mentally and professionally. It's well known that they both like a beer, but they were always ready to play.

They never copped excuses and I think that has rubbed off on the batsmen who have come in around them. Certainly, Steve Waugh is very much from the same mould these days. Boon and Border helped give Australia's batting a tougher edge, which coincided with our climb up the international standings. I can remember when Boonie and I were opening together as Australian cricket was trying to rebuild. We would organise our own net bowlers and go down and have an hour of batting each before the team arrived, when we would bat again. That's one of the secrets of David Boon's longevity. He loved representing Australia as much as any player has ever done and he never took anything for granted. He was always prepared to work to stay there. Boon, however, was a real creature of habit. He would have dinner at about the same time, have a few beers after that at the bar, then go to his room at about 10.30pm.

It was always the same. I know he has a reputation as someone who likes to enjoy himself and get stuck into the beer, but that wasn't the case. He was very much a professional above all else.

Obviously, as an Australian selector in 1995–96, I didn't like to think about David coming to the end of his career. You certainly feel for any player struggling for form, but the bottom line was that when David chose to retire, he got out of the game in fantastic style. When he made his decision, he was very positive about it — and retired in the way of the greats before him — Rod Marsh, Dennis Lillee and Greg Chappell.

I suppose the best way to sum up our relationship when we were in the Australian team together was that we really enjoyed it when we went out to bat together. It was over a beer, in the famous Charlie's Bar at the Adelaide Hilton, that we vowed together to win the opening spots in the national team and hold them for a very long time.

He was almost the perfect partner to bat with and we both understood how to support the other when one wasn't going too well. I used to do most of the talking in the middle of the wicket — he used to do his talking with his bat. Our partnership came to an end when Mark Taylor came into the team. But the fact was, rather than being disappointed, we both welcomed Tubby into the engine room.

David went back to No. 3; it suited the team balance and he had started his career there and went on to enjoy even more success batting there again for Australia.

There is no doubt that David Boon will be missed within the team environment. He never said much, but, when he did, people listened carefully. David would go in at No. 3 for his country and do his job, taking the shine off the ball for the middle order and scoring runs. You have to have courage to do that and no-one had more than him.

ROD MARSH

It wasn't difficult to tell that David Boon was going to play for Australia. We from Western Australia reckoned we knew about four years before he actually pulled on that beloved baggy green cap.

You see, the benchmark of a batsman back in the early 1980s was how well he fared against the best of all fast bowlers, one D. K. Lillee. Of course, Lillee had a few handy team-mates during that time, like Terry Alderman and Bruce Yardley, to name just two. It got down to the fact that if you could succeed against a full-strength Western Australian attack, you could get runs in Test cricket.

I don't recall David making a century against Lillee and the lads, but I vividly remember him making 99 at Devonport. It was a fantastic innings and he thoroughly deserved a century. He might well have reached three figures, if not for a raucous appeal by bowler Bruce Yardley and bat–pad fieldsman Graeme Wood.

The appeal was the result of one of those 'bat and pad all together and the ball squeezes out' situations. It was a nice take by Wood, but umpire Steve Randell really should have given the young Tasmanian the benefit of the doubt. I honestly thought that it was just too questionable and don't remember appealing (which, of course, doesn't mean that I didn't shout!).

However, things have a habit of evening themselves out over the years and I'm sure Steve Randell has given David not out on a few occasions when perhaps the fielding side were more justified in their appeal. Still, an innings of 99 was more than enough to make us realise that we had a future Australian batsman in our midst.

He went about his work as though he was always in control. There were no unnecessary foot movements, no flourishes of the bat and no real anxiety. David Boon batted basically the same way in every innings for Australia. He was so often the foundation around which a winning Test-match score was accumulated. Initially, I didn't think much of his batting against spin bowling, and I remember thinking that perhaps this was going to be his Achilles heel in Test-match cricket. However, I have to say, the more he played the spinners, the better he batted against them.

NEVILLE OLIVER (ABC commentator)

I first met David Boon when he was about five years old. I was involved with amateur football in Launceston and his father Clarrie was the secretary of the league. I used to go into Clarrie's newsagency and this pugnacious little fellow used to come into the shop, which was about 150 metres down the road from Charles Street Primary School.

You usually remember children as either friendly or shy, but my recollection of David was as a fiercely determined little bloke — whether that was determination to get a packet of chewing gum or whatever. I don't think I've ever had to reassess that first impression; it underpinned his cricket success, that fierce determination.

I suspect there have been players as good as David, but they were inevitably much lesser players because they didn't have that determination to succeed. I think David's taken that characteristic into whatever he's done; he's determined to succeed in his marketing position with the Trust Bank; he was determined to succeed in cricket, he was a good footballer and he was a good swimmer.

Whatever he did, he just wanted to be good at it. Maybe that didn't mean the absolute best — I mean, he's not going to be the world's best golfer — but he's determined to be as good as he can possibly be. There's a richness in that, that not a lot have got. It's not an overwhelming determination, it's an internal thing; he doesn't wear it as a suit coat, it's just there. You're aware of it when you talk to him, but he doesn't hit you over the head with it.

He's not as reticent as he once was, but he remains a shy person. Sometimes that shyness in his early days was seen as being aloof. However, when you put that shyness together with that determination you get a fairly special individual. His personality was largely misread by a lot of people early on. If you are a famous figure, regardless of whether you are shy, you're almost expected to be extroverted as well. People want to be able to see you off the ground as they see you on the ground, expressing yourself.

I think he found that difficult, although perhaps less difficult as the years have gone by. It's inconceivable to me that the 22-year-old David Boon could have gone on a television program and sang — I use the word 'sang' in the widest and loosest possible sense — as he did on *The Late Show*.

Yet, he's still a very private person. As I said, that was mistaken as aloofness, which is a quality he doesn't possess, he's the most personable of people. I can remember in 1989 when I toured England for the first time with the ABC. David said that he trusted me and he would make sure that the team understood that — and I'd be accepted on that basis, virtually on his trust.

When he was young, you couldn't even peek over the fence. Now the fences are a lot lower, you can see a lot more of David — obviously fame from cricket, fame worldwide in the cricketing sense, has moulded his character.

As a cricketer, he has to be regarded as a great player. You only get the longevity that he and players who have played that amount of Test cricket get because you're bloody good. You don't get it because somebody likes you, you get it because you're good. There's a very valid argument that for the period from 1989 to 1995, isolating figures from that time, he was by far and away the best batsman in the world. And I don't make that comment lightly.

History will judge him very well. I judge him very well now. In 50 years time, however, people will talk about David Boon in just the same way that they talk about Neil Harvey and Victor Trumper now. I'm not making comparisons, but I am saying that the game brings along wonderful players and the wonderful players are remembered forever.

He is a great player and some people always thought he was going to be, even despite the hiccup in 1986–87, because the majority of good players go through those patches. It's the determination factor which again comes out — David's dropping from the Australian Test team was only going to be a temporary situation.

Lesser players would have been gone forever, but with him and the huge determination that he has, you realised that it was a temporary aberration. He was going to come back. Not only did he come back, he came back at the top of the scale.

Prior to 1987, David Boon was a mid- to bottom-range Test cricketer with an average of just in the thirties. From then on, he became the player who played strictly within the comfortable limitations of his ability. Gone was a lot of the flair, but also gone were the shots that used to get him into trouble. Very occasionally in the later years, in a one-day innings, he'd remind you of the 18-year-old who hit everything into the boundary fence.

You realised that what he'd been able to do was gather his talents and funnel them into a corridor that was suited for him to become a very good Test cricketer. That says a lot about the bloke and it also says a lot about all these very good players: the fierce determination, the eradication of the shots that got them into trouble.

The West Indies don't talk about many players because they don't want those players to understand how they perceive the opposition. However, if you read what the West Indian cricketers say about David Boon — Curtly Ambrose, Richie Richardson, Courtney Walsh — they say his was a wicket prized. I don't think you can have a higher accolade than that. Sunil Gavaskar who, of the modern-day players, was one of the real greats, he rated David Boon the best batsman in the world for quite a few years.

I still remember the first Test I ever called. Australia was playing against India and Boon opened with Geoff Marsh and made a hundred. In the early days, because of the family friendship and because he was a Tasmanian, which was a bit of a badge to carry — a Tasmanian had to be about twice as good as anyone else or else he was a Tasmanian and not an Australian — basically every ball he played my heart was in my mouth. I was only relaxed when he was at the non-striker's end!

However, as he became a better player — when he'd made half a dozen Test centuries, when he'd made eight and then a dozen Test centuries — I was aware that he was batting and I enjoyed what he was doing. I was disappointed when he got out, but basically there was no concern.

When David first started playing Sheffield Shield cricket, he used to make some of the best 20s, 30s and 40s you could ever hope to see. He made his first Shield hundred at the old TCA Ground playing against Victoria and it was a majestic annihilation. He and Brian Davison got stuck in and just pasted them. At that stage, David was batting with Davo and trying to bat like Davo — Davo was a demolition expert. I think that David thought that was the way to go — he was an almighty hitter of the ball and knew no fear.

I remember going around to the dressing-rooms after that innings — of course, now we're talking about the youngster Boon — and he said: 'I couldn't handle that, I'd be too nervous.' So here he was, he'd just announced himself in the middle of the TCA with a brilliant hundred, but it was almost like mining for diamonds trying to get 50 words out of him in an interview.

I just think that because Tasmania was new to Sheffield Shield and he was a kid with a lot of promise, the expectations of every Tasmanian were squarely on his shoulders. I don't think Ricky Ponting will feel anything even vaguely approaching that because of David, and I think that's a marvellous thing. David was a focus for public opinion. He bore the weight of expectation from a tiny island state and although it wasn't a cross for him to bear, it was still an added dimension of pressure that a lot of people would have found unacceptable. As a result of David's achievements, there's an acceptance now. You don't have to open doors or prove anything now, apart from your ability. But David has always belonged to Tasmania and Tasmanians.

There's also the side to sporting fame that not many of the public understand, the fact that your privacy is utterly destroyed. People see it as their right, and maybe it is, to come up to you in a restaurant when you're having a quiet meal with your wife and get an autograph, or talk to you about an innings in Manchester or what it was like in the West Indies. There is an enormous sacrifice of one's self, all in the name of success. I think David has always handled that part of the business very well.

However, I did have one rule with David: when he'd failed or when he was hot after success, I didn't talk to him. He terrified me! You would see him stroll towards you at The Westbury Hotel, two days after he was out for 94 at Lord's and I could always find a very good excuse to turn and head back the other way as though I'd forgotten something. I'm sure he probably would have wanted a chat, but you've got to realise that these people require a bit of space; he was a bit like that.

He set some goals for himself, everybody does that. I don't know that he ever wrote them down on a piece of paper, but they were there. To make a hundred in England was obviously one of them. He toured England in 1985 and hadn't had the best of times against the English spinners. He then proceeded to teach himself how to play spin. He went back in 1989 and batted very well, but still couldn't get a hundred. For Australian cricketers, a hundred at Lord's would be close to the top of the list of ambitions.

There he was, on the verge, with his father and mother there. There are lots of reasons why he should have made a century, but the cricketing gods aren't always kind. He was out to the worst shot he ever played and I say that without reservation — and he wasn't terribly happy about that dismissal.

In 1993, however, he just started to peel off hundreds in Test cricket and they just couldn't get him out, much like Steve Waugh four years earlier. That tour rolled so well for him. I'm pleased now to be able to look back on that tour of 1993. I'm just so happy that the great judges of cricket are in England — they don't think Doug Walters was a good player because he didn't make a Test hundred there, which is a flawed judgment — as the English press and the English public saw Boon at his very best. There's not a cricket nation in the world now that can't say of him: 'He was a good player. He was a great player.'

He made a real tough hundred in Jamaica, I mean a real tough hundred, they gave him the lot. The West Indies people said afterwards: 'Gee, that Boon, he's special.'

They love him in India, maybe because he's about the right size!

Cricketers can be respected and even deeply respected, but it doesn't necessarily mean that they're loved. With David, however — whether it was in England, Australia, South Africa, India, the West Indies or New Zealand — he was a player that they loved. (I don't know if they loved him in Pakistan, because I never went there with him, but I went just about everywhere else.)

I'm not sure that David Boon was finished as a Test player, that's what worried me on his retirement from international cricket and still does. However, there was a time in the last summer that it seemed to me that the eyes weren't quite as good, the feet weren't quite as good. I think with that, there was some self-doubt starting to grow.

During his final season of international cricket, I went out with him for a quiet meal in a restaurant in Perth and we talked about a lot of things: when he was kid; what it was like to make runs; what it is like to analyse failure and how much you enjoy success. I got the feeling that he was really going into decision mode about how long he could continue. I truly believe that he made the best possible decision because he set his own agenda.

I think it would have been abysmal for Australian cricket to have tapped him on the shoulder after the central role he played in rebuilding the team. He'd been there for all of it — the World Cup in 1987, the Ashes victory in 1989, the victory in the West Indies in 1995. As we restored our cricket stocks, he and Allan Border, and I suppose Geoff Marsh, had been there through the lot of it. I think to make the decision himself to retire was the way to go because I believe people were getting ready to tap him on the shoulder.

He made a hundred in Melbourne in the Test against Sri Lanka. He'd batted better in his Test career and he had probably batted worse. But if ever you wanted to see Boon at his most resolute, that was it.

I'm sure he'd remember prettier innings, he'd remember innings that he'd enjoyed more. However, I reckon the satisfaction he got that day out of saying 'Well, cop that,' would be very high on his list of achievements. Because he was not only a bit out of form, he was a lot out of form.

His last innings, during his retirement Test in Adelaide, was very special to me. It was not just because he was retiring, but also because in that 40-odd that he made, he played just about every signature shot — the flick off the toes, the straight drive, the cut. It was a good way to remember him.

I was disappointed that he decided to retire, I could see every good reason why he should, but I was still disappointed. As he walked off, like every Australian cricket lover, I was sad to see him go. I was bloody sad when he invited me to his farewell party that night. The next day I felt like I'd been hit by a train. But it was terrific, a very emotional night.

I don't think David Boon has ever understood his position, his standing, in cricket. As David climbed up the list of Australian run-scorers, it embarrassed him. Sir Donald Bradman retired in 1948 and it took another 35 years for someone to pass him — first Greg Chappell and then Allan Border went hurtling past.

The blokes that David was passing: The likes of Greg Chappell, who he'd watched on television as a young boy. The early blokes who went past Bradman had to read about him in books. With David, he watched all his heroes as a kid; he aspired to be like them and 15 years later he was going past them in the record books.

It's happening more and more as records continue to tumble and it will keep doing so, but you can understand David's feelings about it. He's never rated himself with them, yet they certainly rate him. Ian and Greg Chappell and Doug Walters rate him, and I must say their judgment is better than David's in this particular case.

DENIS ROGERS (ACB chairman, TCA chairman)

In general terms, David Boon is one of the few Tasmanian icons. In relation to cricket, you could be more specific, but he was larger than cricket.

Cricket allowed David Boon to be larger than life. It also allowed people to gain insights into his personality and strong character. That those personal characteristics manifested themselves in the way in which he often fought for his state, and later on, his country, exemplified the very nature of the man. Even in his retirement, which I was privileged to be a part of in Adelaide, he stood out above the rest — he'd earned his icon status and advanced into the category of legend. That reputation, as the years roll on, will be further enhanced. To be at the Adelaide Oval and listen to thousands of people chant 'Boonie!' — one could feel the emotion outpouring from those people — you couldn't help be anything but impressed.

David Boon revealed himself by his authentic dignity and grace. There was no showmanship in it, not an ounce of insincerity. That's why thousands upon thousands of people clapped and cheered, thanking him, and why hundreds of thousands of people watching on television could relate to the man — it was typical of the way in which he lived his life and played his cricket and cherished his role as an Australian Test cricketer.

From a Tasmanian point of view, he is undoubtedly our greatest-ever player. His personal recognition factor in terms of the Tasmanian public is second to none. He has not only done us proud in the context of cricket, he has also done us proud in the context of being Tasmanian. He deserves all of the acknowledgment that people have poured on him, and continue to pour on him. They know that wherever life takes David, he will continue to repay them.

My experience of David is that the more he encounters support, the more it encourages him to return that recognition. He has had the benefit of a supportive family — I know he's a proud husband and a proud father. That in itself has allowed the public to see that there is a very human side to these great players and that they, too, have to cope with the tasks set before us all as husbands, wives and parents. It appears to me that David has done that well.

David has pioneered so many things — he came from a state which was in its infancy in the Sheffield Shield; Tasmania were still trying to cope with its disadvantages and understand what it meant to be in the first-class cricket arena. There is no doubt at all that, along with other people, David played a major role in helping Tasmania to come to terms with just how important it was to be competing in this competition and also how demanding.

Now that pioneering work is done, it will make the task a little easier for the people that follow him. While it won't make the task of being selected to play for Australia any easier at an individual level — it will help to know that they are following in the footsteps of not only a great Tasmanian player, but also most certainly a great post-World War II Australian player.

David isn't just respected in Australia, but around the entire cricket world. When I was at the 1996 World Cup, one of things that I found very useful, was to tell people that I was a Tasmanian, not simply an Australian. The immediate response was: 'Boonie'. This simple fact was a passport to all sorts of other interesting things. He's very much revered on the subcontinent.

At an Australian level, I think his influence will linger on for some time, the team knew that the little bloke would always be there fighting for his country, not giving the opposition an even-money chance. That influence will be heard in the expression, 'We need to do a Boonie.' In other words: 'We need to tough it out.' He was a tough man and highly respected by opposition players.

Now that David Boon is back playing for Tasmania, I'm hoping that he and his family can continue in the game for a long time. Personally, he's always been an inspiration for me, knowing that we had such a great player available for Tasmania from time to time when his Australian commitments allowed. Now, however, if he can find his way clear to play for a number of years, his strength of character will definitely rub off on other players — and it will rub off on administrators.

In the longer term, I hope David will play a major role in not just Tasmanian, but also Australian cricket. He is equipped to play a senior administrative role at both state and national levels. David certainly has the credentials and I think there needs to be a healthy mix of ex-players and administrators running the game. There's nothing better than asking the opinion of someone who has been out in the middle and done all the hard things.

JACK SIMMONS

It has been a long time since I first set eyes on David Boon. He would have been around 10 or 11 years old when I took up my appointment as coach to the Northern Tasmanian Cricket Association. But even then, in terms of cricket ability, he was head and shoulders above anyone his own age, or even anyone a couple of years older.

David was keen to play, but also keen to learn. At the time, many top judges felt he had to be even better than he was, and tougher, to achieve the ultimate, to wear that baggy green Australian cap. In my view, though, he had the ability, the desire, and needed only a fair roll of the dice to reach this goal. And there was another reason why I knew he would get to the top . . . the support from his family. His dad, Clarrie, and mum, Lesley, had the same faith that I had. Probably even more.

So this quiet, unassuming youngster continued along the long, long road, overturning all the hurdles that came along — including some that youngsters in the mainland states did not need to climb. And when the chance to represent his country finally came, at the Gabba against the great West Indies, I don't think there was anyone more proud than the Simmons family. Tears came to my eyes when Clarrie rang to tell me of David's selection.

Since then, apart from the odd hiccup, David has continued in his own silent way, never criticising or making controversial statements, never failing to praise his own team-mates, and always showing that proud desire for the job he has loved to do.

Family support has always been an important part of the Boon armoury. Now, Pip and the children continue in exactly the same manner as did his parents. David has been a very fortunate man in this department. How can anyone have a wife who moves the family house on her own, three times, while her husband is on tour with the Australian team? Pip has been a saint, especially when coping with the responsibility of looking after the children while the building of their new house was taking all those months. But those sacrifices were a part of why David Boon became only the second Australian, next to the great Allan Border, to play in over 100 Test matches. He knew everything back home was in good hands.

When David rang me in South Africa (I was watching England succumb in the Cape Town Test) to tell me he was going to retire, I knew how difficult that decision was. However, I'm sure it was the correct one, and now he can set his stall out and share his vast experience with the young players of Tasmania. They, like the Australian team-mates he played with, will know what high standards he sets. They will learn also of the commitment he gives, on the field and off, and how his attitude and toughness remains the same after 107 Tests as it was after his first.

I sincerely hope, in his testimonial year, that not only Tasmania but all Australia will salute a great cricketer, but, more importantly, a bloody good person and a very, very special friend.

DAVID BOON'S
FIRST-CLASS CAREER

STATISTICS BY IAN RUSSELL
(all stats correct as at September 1, 1996)

1. DAVID BOON IN FIRST-CLASS CRICKET

Debut December 15-18, 1978 v Queensland, Brisbane, scoring 22 (batting No. 6).

Season	Mat	Inn	NO	Runs	High	100	50	Av	Ct	Ovt†	Runs	Wkts	Best
1978-79	2	3	–	34	22	–	–	11.33	2	–			
1979-80	7	13	1	404	90	–	3	33.67	3	6	37	1	1-19
1980-81	7	13	–	518	114	1	3	39.84	6	–			
1981-82	7	13	2	473	88	–	3	43.00	4	3	18	–	–
1982-83	12	18	1	682	115	2	3	40.12	8	–			
1983 (Zimb.)	2	3	–	274	148	2	–	91.33	3	–			
1983-84	11	19	–	667	227	1	4	35.11	8	–			
1984-85	10	18	2	664	147	3	2	41.50	8	3	12	1	1-12
1985 (Eng.)	15	20	5	832	206	3	3	55.47	13	6	33	–	–
1985-86	9	17	1	818	196	3	3	51.13	3	0.4	2	–	–
1986 (N.Z.)	4	7	1	302	109	1	2	50.33	2	–			
1986 (India)	6	8	1	476	122	1	3	68.00	4	2	5	–	–
1986-87	13	26	–	821	172	3	1	31.58	8	37.1	124	1	1-18
1987-88	12	21	2	1287	184*	5	6	67.74	13	13.4	45	2	1-20
1988 (Pak.)	5	8	–	258	76	–	2	32.25	11	–			
1988-89	13	23	2	939	149	2	6	44.71	13	7	26	–	–
1989 (Eng.)	17	28	5	1306	151	3	8	56.78	21	1	–	–	–
1989-90	8	14	2	657	200	3	1	54.75	6	–			
1990 (N.Z.)	1	2	–	12	12	–	–	6.00	–	–			
1990-91	9	17	2	809	121	2	4	53.93	10	–			
1991 (W.Ind.)	10	14	1	456	109*	2	2	35.08	6	–			
1991-92	10	16	2	819	135	4	1	58.50	11	–			
1992 (Sri L.)	5	9	–	235	68	–	2	26.11	3	3	4	–	–
1992-93	8	15	2	635	111	1	4	48.85	7	16	57	1	1-56
1993 (N.Z.)	3	4	–	125	53	–	1	31.25	3	1	–	–	–
1993 (Eng.)	14	23	4	1437	164*	9	2	75.63	10	–			
1993-94	7	11	1	441	106	1	3	44.10	4	1	1	–	–
1994 (S. Afr.)	6	11	1	392	96	–	3	39.20	6	–			
1994 (Pak.)	4	6	2	250	114*	2	–	62.50	5	3	9	–	–
1994-95	7	13	–	334	131	1	1	25.69	3	6.4	16	1	1-16
1995 (W. Ind.)	6	8	–	190	67	–	1	23.75	4	–			
1995-96	15	25	–	1134	152	4	5	45.30	13	21.3	78	2	1-0
Total	**265**	**446**	**40**	**18681**	**227**	**59**	**82**	**46.01**	**221**	**131.4**	**467**	**9**	**1-0**

* = not out   † indicates all overs are 6-ball   career bowling average = 51.88

FIRST-CLASS BATTING (BY COUNTRY)

Country	Mat	Inn	NO	Runs	High	100	50	Av
Total in Australia	167	295	20	12136	227	36	53	44.13
in Zimbabwe	2	3	–	274	148	2	–	91.33
in England	46	71	14	3575	206	15	13	62.72
in New Zealand	8	13	1	439	109	1	3	36.58
in India	6	8	1	476	122	1	3	68.00
in Pakistan	9	14	2	508	114 *	2	2	42.33
in West Indies	16	22	1	646	109 *	2	3	30.76
in Sri Lanka	5	9	–	235	68	–	2	26.11
in South Africa	6	11	1	392	96	–	3	39.20
Total outside Australia	98	151	20	6545	206	23	29	49.96

FIRST-CLASS HUNDREDS

1980–81
114 Tasmania v Victoria — Hobart (TCA)

1982–83
115 Tasmania v Queensland — Brisbane
109 Tasmania v South Australia — Adelaide

1983
109 Young Australia v Zimbabwe — Harare
148 Young Australia v Zimbabwe — Harare

1983–84
227 Tasmania v Victoria — Melbourne

1984–85
138 Tasmania v New South Wales — Launceston
104 Tasmania v Victoria — Carlton
147 Tasmania v Western Australia — Hobart (TCA)

1985
119 Australians v Sussex — Hove
138 Australians v Essex — Chelmsford
206* Australians v Northants — Northampton

1985–86
196 Tasmania v New South Wales — Hobart (TCA)
123 Australia v India (1st) — Adelaide
131 Australia v India (3rd) — Sydney
1986 (in New Zealand)
109 Australians v Central Districts — New Plymoth

1986 (in India)
122 Australia v India (1st) — Madras

1986–87
117 Tasmania v Queensland — Brisbane
103 Australia v England (3rd) — Adelaide
172 Tasmania v Queensland — Launceston

1987–88
143 Australia v New Zealand (1st) — Brisbane
101* Tasmania v New Zealand — Devonport
184* Australia v England — Sydney
108 Tasmania v Queensland (First Innings) — Launceston
143 Tasmania v Queensland (Second Innings) — Launceston

1988–89
149 Australia v West Indies (4th) — Sydney
132 Tasmania v New South Wales — Sydney

1989
151 Australians v Essex — Chelmsford
103 Australians v Hampshire — Southampton
102* Australians v Nottinghamshire — Nottingham

1989–90
200 Australia v New Zealand — Perth
100 Tasmania v Queensland — Hobart (Bell.)
133* Tasmania v Sri Lankans — Devonport

1990–91
108 Australian XI v England XI — Hobart (Bell.)
121 Australia v England (4th) — Adelaide

FIRST-CLASS HUNDREDS (CONTINUED)

1991

105	Australians v Jamaica	Kingston
109*	Australia v West Indies (4th)	Kingston

1991-92

130	Tasmania v South Australia	Adelaide
129*	Australia v India (3rd)	Sydney
135	Australia v India (4th)	Adelaide
107	Australia v India (5th)	Perth

1992-93

111	Australia v West Indies (1st)	Brisbane

1993

108	Australians v Worcestershire (First Innings)	Worcester
106	Australians v Worcestershire (Second Innings)	Worcester
123	Australians v Leicestershire	Leicester
164*	Australia v England (2nd)	Lord's

1993 *(continued)*

146	Australians v Hampshire	Southampton
101	Australia v England (3rd)	Nottingham
112	Australians v Durham	Durham Uni.
107	Australia v England (4th)	Leeds
120	Australians v Glamorgan	Neath

1993-94

106	Australia v New Zealand (2nd)	Hobart (Bell.)

1994 (in Pakistan)

101	Australians v President's XI	Rawalpindi
114*	Australia v Pakistan (1st)	Karachi

1994-95

131	Australia v England (2nd)	Melbourne

1995-96

110	Australia v Sri Lanka (2nd)	Melbourne
108	Tasmania v Victoria	Hobart (Bell.)
152	Tasmania v Western Australia	Perth
117	Tasmania v South Australia	Adelaide

* = not out

WHERE CENTURIES WERE SCORED

Country/State	Centuries	City/Grounds
in Tasmania	13	Hobart, Bellerive 4; Launceston 4; Hobart, TCA 3; Devonport 2.
elsewhere in Australia	23	Adelaide 7, Sydney 5, Brisbane 4, Melbourne 3, Perth 3, Carlton 1.
in England	15	Chelmsford 2, Southampton 2, Nottingham 2, Worcester 2, Hove 1, Northampton 1, Leicester 1, Lord's 1, Durham University 1, Neath 1, Leeds 1.
in Zimbabwe	2	Harare 2.
in New Zealand	1	New Plymoth.
in India	1	Madras.
in Pakistan	2	Rawalpindi 1, Karachi 1.
in West Indies	2	Kingston 2.

FOR WHOM CENTURIES WERE SCORED

for Tasmania Sheffield Shield	18 centuries	in 88 matches
for Tasmania in other matches	2 centuries	in 16 matches
for Australian XI in Australia	1 century	in 3 matches
for Australia in Australia	15 centuries	in 60 Tests
for Young Australia	2 centuries	in 2 matches
for Australians on tour	15 centuries	in 49 matches
for Australia overseas	6 centuries	in 47 Tests

2. DAVID BOON IN TEST CRICKET

Test debut November 23–26, 1984 v West Indies, Brisbane, scoring 11 and 51 (batting No. 6).

Year	Opponent	Tests	Inn	NO	Runs	High	100	50	Av	Ct
1984–85	West Indies	3	5	–	132	51	–	1	26.40	2
1985	England	4	7	–	124	61	–	1	17.71	4
1985–86	New Zealand	3	6	–	175	81	–	2	29.17	1
1985–86	India	3	6	1	323	131	2	–	64.60	1
1986	New Zealand	3	5	1	176	70	–	2	44.00	2
1986	India	3	5	–	325	122	1	1	65.00	1
1986–87	England	4	8	–	144	103	1	–	18.00	1
1987–88	New Zealand	3	5	–	237	143	1	1	147.40	6
1987–88	England	1	2	1	196	184*	1	–	196.00	–
1987–88	Sri Lanka	1	1	–	64	64	–	1	64.00	–
1988	Pakistan	3	6	–	117	43	–	–	19.50	10
1988–89	West Indies	5	10	1	397	149	1	2	44.11	9
1989	England	6	11	3	442	94	–	3	55.25	9
1989–90	New Zealand	1	1	–	200	200	1	–	200.00	1
1989–90	Sri Lanka	2	4	–	67	41	–	–	16.75	1
1989–90	Pakistan	2	4	–	55	29	–	–	13.75	1
1990	New Zealand	1	2	–	12	12	–	–	6.00	–
1990–91	England	5	9	2	530	121	1	3	75.71	4
1991	West Indies	5	9	1	266	109*	1	1	33.25	1
1991–92	India	5	9	2	556	135	3	1	79.43	8
1992	Sri Lanka	3	6	–	161	68	–	1	26.83	3
1992–93	West Indies	5	10	2	490	111	1	3	61.25	5
1993	New Zealand	3	4	–	125	53	–	1	31.25	3
1993	England	6	10	2	555	164*	3	1	69.38	5
1993–94	New Zealand	3	4	1	262	106	1	2	87.33	3
1993–94	South Africa	3	5	–	156	50	–	1	31.20	1
1994	South Africa	3	6	1	277	96	–	2	55.40	3
1994	Pakistan	3	5	2	149	114*	1	–	49.67	3
1994–95	England	5	10	–	246	131	1	–	24.60	2
1995	West Indies	4	6	–	152	67	–	1	25.33	4
1995–96	Pakistan	3	5	–	110	54	–	1	22.00	3
1995–96	Sri Lanka	3	4	–	201	110	1	–	50.25	2
Total		**107**	**190**	**20**	**7422**	**200**	**21**	**32**	**43.66**	**99**

Notes 1. In Test cricket, Boon bowled 6 overs, conceding 14 runs and taking no wickets.
2. 'Double' seasons e.g. 1984–85, indicate in Australia; 'Single' seasons, e.g. 1985, indicate overseas.

TEST BATTING AND FIELDING (BY OPPONENT)

Country	Tests	Inn	NO	Runs	High	100	50	Av	Ct
West Indies	22	40	4	1437	149	3	8	39.92	21
England	31	57	8	2237	184*	7	8	45.65	25
New Zealand	17	27	2	1187	200	3	8	47.48	16
India	11	20	3	1204	135	6	2	70.82	10
Sri Lanka	9	15	–	493	110	1	2	32.87	6
Pakistan	11	20	2	431	114*	1	1	23.94	17
South Africa	6	11	1	433	96	–	3	43.30	4

TEST BATTING AND FIELDING BY VENUE (IN AUSTRALIA)

City	Tests	Inn	NO	Runs	High	100	50	Av	Ct
Brisbane	12	20	–	750	143	2	4	37.50	12
Adelaide	12	23	3	920	135	4	2	46.00	10
Sydney	11	21	3	1127	184*	4	4	62.61	7
Perth	11	19	2	846	200	2	6	49.76	7
Melbourne	11	20	2	717	131	2	2	39.83	14
Hobart (Bell.)	3	5	–	181	106	1	–	36.20	1
Total	**60**	**108**	**10**	**4541**	**200**	**15**	**18**	**46.34**	**51**

TEST BATTING AND FIELDING BY COUNTRY (OVERSEAS)

Country	Tests	Inn	NO	Runs	High	100	50	Av	Ct
in England	16	28	5	1121	164*	3	5	48.74	18
in New Zealand	7	11	1	313	70	–	3	31.30	5
in India	3	5	–	325	122	1	1	65.00	1
in Pakistan	6	11	2	266	114*	1	–	29.56	13
in West Indies	9	15	1	418	109*	1	2	29.86	5
in Sri Lanka	3	6	–	161	68	–	1	26.83	3
in South Africa	3	6	1	277	96	–	2	55.40	3
Total	**47**	**82**	**10**	**2881**	**164***	**6**	**14**	**40.01**	**48**

TEST BATTING BY BATTING POSITION

Position	Inn	NO	Runs	High	100	50	Av
1	29	1	968	131	3	4	34.57
2	34	4	1646	200	5	6	54.87
3	111	14	4412	164*	13	20	45.48
4	5	1	201	94*	–	1	50.25
5	5	–	56	22	–	–	11.20
6	5	–	127	51	–	1	25.40
7	1	–	12	12	–	–	12.00
Opening	63	5	2614	200	8	10	45.07
Not Opening	127	15	4808	164*	13	22	42.93

HUNDRED PARTNERSHIPS

With/wicket	1st	2nd	3rd	4th	5th	6th	Total
M.E. Waugh	–	–	10	–	1	–	11
M.A. Taylor	1	7	–	–	–	–	8
A.R. Border	–	–	4	3	–	1	8
G.R. Marsh	5	–	1	–	–	–	6
M.J. Slater	–	2	–	–	–	–	2
W.B. Phillips	–	1	–	–	–	–	1
T.M. Moody	–	1	–	–	–	–	1
S.R. Waugh	–	1	–	–	–	–	1
M.G. Bevan	–	–	–	1	–	–	1
G.M. Ritchie	–	–	–	1	–	–	1
Total	**6**	**12**	**15**	**5**	**1**	**1**	**40**

HIGHEST PARTNERSHIPS

235	2nd wicket with	M.J. Slater	v	New Zealand	Hobart	1993-94
221	2nd wicket with	M.A. Taylor	v	India	Adelaide	1991-92
217	1st wicket with	G.R. Marsh	v	India	Sydney	1985-86
187	3rd wicket with	G.R. Marsh	v	England	Melbourne	1990-91
175	3rd wicket with	M.E. Waugh	v	England	Lord's	1993

HOW DISMISSED

Caught in the Field	Bowled	Caught Behind	Leg Before Wicket	Run Out	Caught & Bowled	Stumped	Total
74	32	27	25	8	3	1	170

WHICH BOWLERS GOT HIS WICKET MOST TIMES

10	M.D. Marshall	(West Indies)	6	P.A.J. deFreitas	(England)
9	R.J. Hadlee	(New Zealand)	5	Kapil Dev	(India)
8	C.E.L. Ambrose	(West Indies)	5	Mushtaq Ahmed	(Pakistan)
7	C.A. Walsh	(West Indies)	5	D.E. Malcolm	(England)

AUSTRALIANS SCORING OVER 5000 TEST RUNS

Runs	Player	Tests	Inn	NO	High	100	50	Av
11174	A.R. Border	156	265	44	205	27	63	50.56
7422	**D.C. Boon**	**107**	**190**	**20**	**200**	**21**	**32**	**43.66**
7110	G.S. Chappell	87	151	19	247*	24	31	53.86
6996	D.G. Bradman	52	80	10	334	29	13	99.94
6149	R.N. Harvey	79	137	10	205	21	24	48.42
5502	M.A. Taylor	72	129	9	219	14	33	45.85
5357	K.D. Walters	74	125	14	250	15	33	48.26
5345	I.M. Chappell	75	136	10	196	14	26	42.42
5234	W.M. Lawry	67	123	12	210	13	27	47.15
5002	S.R. Waugh	81	125	26	200	11	28	50.53

AUSTRALIANS TAKING OVER 95 TEST CATCHES (EXCLUDING WICKETKEEPERS)

156	A.R. Border	110	R.B. Simpson	105	M.A. Taylor
122	G.S. Chappell	105	I.M. Chappell	**99**	**D.C. Boon**

3. DAVID BOON IN INTERSTATE ONE-DAY CRICKET

Debut December 10, 1978 v Queensland, Brisbane, scoring 18* (batting No. 9).
(Gillette Cup 1978-79, McDonald's Cup 1979-80 — 1987-88, F.A.I. Cup 1988-89 — 1991-92, Mercantile Mutual Cup 1992-93 — 1995-96.)

Mat	Inn	NO	Runs	High	100	50	Av	Ct	Overs	Runs	Wkts
39	37	4	1317	94	–	13	39.91	14	4	38	–

Highest score 94 v Queensland, Brisbane 1983-84.

4. DAVID BOON IN INTERNATIONAL ONE-DAY CRICKET

Debut 12 February, 1984 v West Indies, Melbourne, scoring 39 (batting No. 3).

Year	Venue	Comp	Mat	Inn	NO	Runs	High	100	50	Ct	Av
1983–84	Aust	WSC	1	1	–	39	39	–	–	–	39.00
1984–85	Aust	WSC	8	7	–	194	55	–	1	3	27.71
1985	Eng	Texaco	3	3	–	70	45	–	–	–	23.33
1985–86	Aust	WSC	12	11	–	418	83	–	4	2	38.00
1986	NZ	Rothmans	4	4	–	101	47	–	–	2	25.25
1986	UAE	Australasian	1	1	–	44	44	–	–	–	44.00
1986	India	Charminar	6	6	–	205	111	1	–	2	34.17
1986–87	Aust	Perth Challenge	2	2	–	3	2	–	–	–	1.50
1987	UAE	Sharjah Cup	3	3	–	206	73	–	3	–	68.33
1987	Ind + Pak	World Cup	8	8	–	447	93	–	5	2	55.88
1987–88	Aust	WSC	10	10	–	393	122	–	–	–	33.00
1988	Aust	Bicentennial	1	1	–	33	33	–	–	–	33.00
1988	Pak		1	1	–	38	38	–	–	–	38.00
1988–89	Aust	WSC	11	11	–	264	71	–	1	4	24.00
1989	Eng	Texaco	3	3	–	52	28	–	–	2	17.33
1989	India	Nehru	5	5	–	69	49	–	–	4	13.80
1989–90	Aust	WSC	3	3	1	99	49*	–	–	–	49.50
1990	NZ	Rothmans	5	5	1	131	67	–	1	2	32.75
1990	UAE	Australasian	4	3	2	159	92*	–	1	–	159.00
1990–91	Aust	WSC	10	10	2	188	42	–	–	1	23.50
1991	W Ind		3	3	–	48	34	–	–	1	16.00
1991–92	Aust	WSC	10	9	2	432	102*	1	4	2	61.71
1992	NZ + Aust	World Cup	8	8	1	368	100	2	–	–	52.57
1992	Sri L		3	3	1	104	69*	–	1	1	52.00
1992–93	Aust	WSC	10	10	–	224	64	–	2	–	22.40
1993	NZ		4	4	–	99	55	–	1	1	24.75
1993	Eng	Texaco	3	3	–	96	73	–	1	1	32.00
1993–94	Aust	World Series	11	11	1	381	67	–	4	1	38.10
1994	S Afr		7	7	–	249	76	–	2	1	35.57
1994	UAE	Australasian	2	2	–	89	68	–	1	1	44.50
1994	Sri L	Singer	2	2	–	59	40	–	–	1	29.50
1994	Pak	Wills	5	5	1	195	82*	–	1	1	48.75
1994–95	Aust	World Series	4	4	2	196	98*	–	2	1	98.00
1995	NZ	Centenary	4	4	1	101	44	–	–	1	33.67
1995	W Ind		4	4	1	170	85*	–	1	2	56.67
Total			**181**	**177**	**16**	**5964**	**122**	**5**	**37**	**45**	**37.04**

Notes 1. In one-day international cricket, Boon bowled 13.4 overs, conceding 86 runs without taking a wicket.

2. Matches v 'Australia A' in 1994–95 were not official one-day internationals and are therefore excluded from this table.

3. Boon's 815 runs at 54.33 in 16 World Cup matches is the most by any Australian in World Cup history.

4. He was man of the match in Australia's victorious World Cup Final v England at Calcutta in 1987, scoring 75.

5. Only two Australians have scored more runs in one-day internationals.
They are A.R. Border, 273 matches, 6524 runs at 30.63
D.M. Jones, 164 matches, 6068 runs at 44.62

Hundreds in International One-day Cricket

111	v	India	Jaipur	1986†
122	v	Sri Lanka	Adelaide	1987–88
102*	v	India	Hobart	1991–92
100	v	New Zealand	Auckland	1992
100	v	West Indies	Melbourne	1992

† As part of world record first-wicket partnership (212) with G.R. Marsh.

Photo Credits

Australian Picture Library/All Sport: Front cover, back cover (all pics), pages 2, 19, 51, 65, 99, 104, 107, 114, 118, 134, 135, 139, 157, 160, 179, 190, 193, 213, 224, 234, 250 (both).

Patrick Eagar: Pages 8, 61, 63, 76, 87, 91, 95, 121, 123, 130, 143, 158, 182, 186, 188, 216, 218, 222 (all pics), 225.

Sport the Library: Pages 14, 16, 22, 30, 42, 54, 58, 81, 127, 146, 227.

Ray Titus: Pages 28, 220, 231, 238.

The Australian: Page 46.

Mark Ray: Pages 53, 85, 128, 161.

Clifford White: Pages 78, 112, 174 (top), 194, 198, 246.

Nikhil Bhattacharya: Page 90.

Graham Morris: Pages 122, 124, 126.

Gregg Porteous: Pages 140, 147.

Launceston Examiner: Page 150.

Trent Parke: Page 155.

A. MARK THOMAS, David Boon's co-author, was born at The Entrance, NSW, in 1959. He spent the first five years of his life in New York, New York, with his family, before returning to Melbourne, Victoria, where he completed his primary and secondary education. Mark attended Monash University, Victoria, graduating with a Bachelor of Arts degree in English and American Literature, and American History. He also read law at the University of Tasmania, Hobart. Mark worked with *The Examiner* newspaper in Launceston from 1984 to 1994, joining as a general journalist and finishing as sports editor. He joined WIN Television, Hobart, in 1994, where he is currently a journalist/presenter. He lives in Hobart with his wife, Kathryn, and son, Benjamin.